CW00523912

Cambridge Studies in Social Anthropology

General Editor: Jack Goody

41

ECOLOGY AND EXCHANGE IN THE ANDES

Ecology and exchange in the Andes

Edited by
DAVID LEHMANN

CAMBRIDGE UNIVERSITY PRESS

Cambridge
London   New York   New Rochelle
Melbourne   Sydney

Published by the Press Syndicate of the University of Cambridge
The Pitt Building, Trumpington Street, Cambridge CB2 1RP
32 East 57th Street, New York, NY 10022, USA
296 Beaconsfield Parade, Middle Park, Melbourne 3206, Australia

First published 1982

Printed in Great Britain at the University Press, Cambridge

British Library Cataloguing in Publication Data

Ecology and exchange in the Andes. –
(Cambridge studies in social anthropology; 41)
1. Peasantry – Andes (South America) – Economic conditions
I. Lehmann. David
330.98   HD 1531
ISBN 0 521 23950 8

TP

Contents

Contributors

Barbara Bradby is a Lecturer in Sociology at Trinity College, Dublin.

Adolfo Figueroa is Professor of Economics at the Pontificia Universidad Católica de Lima.

Antoinette Fioravanti-Molinié is Attaché de Recherche in the Centre National de Recherche Scientifique.

Olivia Harris is a Lecturer in Social Anthropology at Goldsmiths' College, London.

David Lehmann is Assistant Director of Development Studies at Cambridge University.

Tristan Platt is a British social anthropologist living and working in Bolivia. He is at present engaged on a research project in collaboration with the Instituto de Estudios Peruanos.

Rodrigo Sánchez is Director of the Instituto de Estudios Andinos, Huancayo, Peru.

Fiona Wilson works for the International Work Group for Indigenous Affairs and is a guest researcher at the Development Research Centre in Copenhagen.

Acknowledgements

This book has its origin in seminars held at the Centre of Latin American Studies in Cambridge in 1977, and at a small meeting attended by most of the contributors in 1978. Acknowledgement is due to the Ministry of Overseas Development (as it then was) for contributing to the costs of that meeting, and to the Director of the Centre of Latin American Studies, Dr David Brading, for his support of the project. Above all, thanks are due to Miss Helen Wilson for her efficient and accurate typing of an often complicated manuscript, and to Sue Allen-Mills of Cambridge University Press for her patience and encouragement.

We are grateful to M. Isak Chiva and the journal *Etudes Rurales*, for permission to publish a translation of the paper by Antoinette Molinié, which appears here in a very slightly modified form from the version published in *Etudes Rurales*, no. 57.

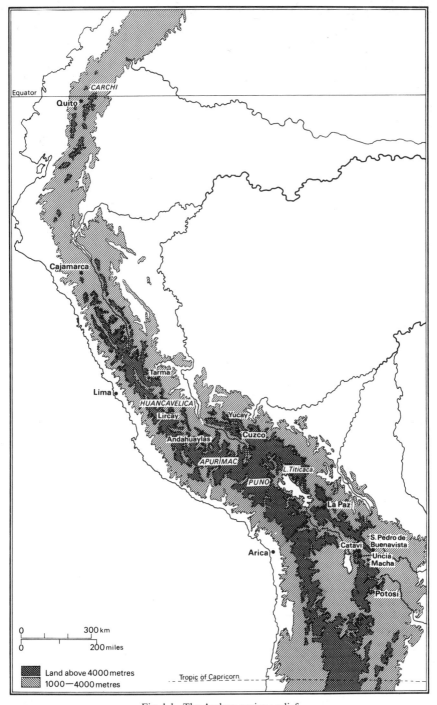

Fig. 1.1. The Andean region: relief

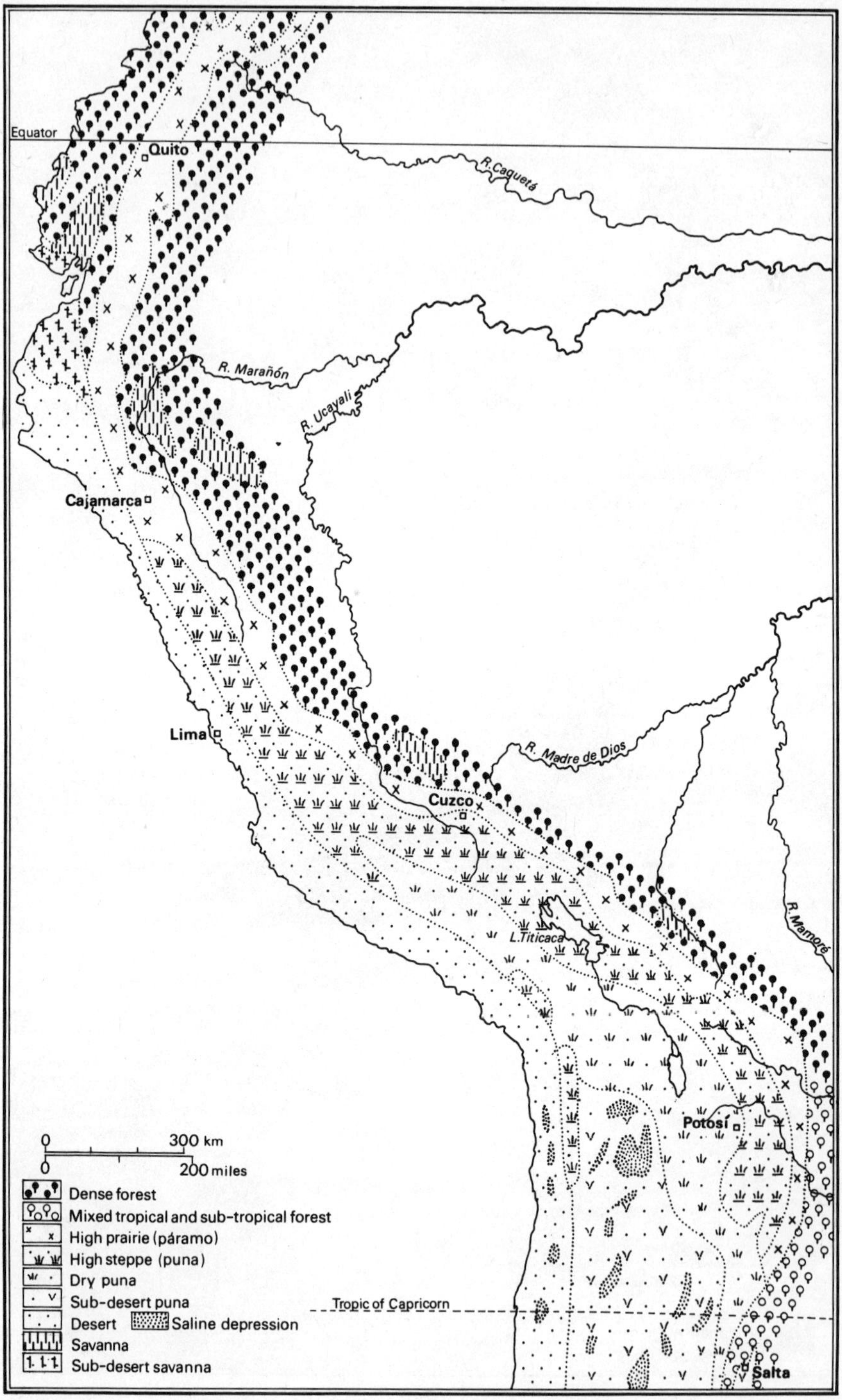

Equator
Quito
R. Caquetá
R. Marañón
R. Ucayali
Cajamarca
Lima
R. Madre de Dios
Cuzco
L. Titicaca
R. Mamoré
Potosí
Tropic of Capricorn
Salta
0
300 km
0
200 miles
Dense forest
Mixed tropical and sub-tropical forest
High prairie (páramo)
High steppe (puna)
Dry puna
Sub-desert puna
Desert
Saline depression
Savanna
Sub-desert savanna

Fig. 1.2. The Andean region showing ecological levels (after Troll 1968)

1

Introduction: Andean societies and the theory of peasant economy

DAVID LEHMANN

1. Capitalist unity and peasant diversity

The common theme of this book can be condensed into one question: in what ways has the impact of market penetration and capitalist development on peasant economy and *haciendas* in Andean countries been shaped by a heritage of political culture and the characteristics of ecology and climate?

The relationship between capitalism and peasant economies has been the object of much abstract theoretical discussion based on case studies carried out the world over. Evidently such theories describe processes only in very general terms, and inevitably local characteristics will condition the interactions of variables which the theories predict. In the case of Andean societies, however, these local characteristics are often understood to be much more than mere conditioning factors, impinging marginally on universal processes: perhaps the Andean system of reciprocity (Mayer 1974b), and the constraints on and opportunities for political power and economic complementarity accorded by the region's ecology and climate, offer better explanations of social and economic organization than would a general theory of peasant economy. In this book the reader will find arguments for both views, as well as attempts to reconcile the two.

The issue is further complicated when we remember that 'peasant specificity' is an inherent feature of any theory which accounts for the consequences of the encounter between peasant production and capitalism. Peasant economies are almost by definition 'provincial', subject to the operation of local rules of kinship, land tenure and other crucial institutions. Capitalism and markets, in contrast, are cosmopolitan, like a seamless web, constituting mechanisms which integrate rather than separate areas and groups with widely varying institutional structures.

Andean rural society presents a remarkable opportunity for studying the variety of patterns of social and economic organization which can arise even in a region which, over five centuries, has been subjected to common

1

successive forms of political and economic domination. The Inca empire stretched at its height from today's Southern Colombia to the Bío-Bío river in South-Central Chile. The Spanish empire extended over an even greater territory. And the republican states which succeeded the Spanish empire have had many features in common, especially in their international economic relations. Yet at any particular time the organization of peasant production and exchange has exhibited wide variations within the vast area, which have not necessarily coincided with national boundaries. In the period of capitalist development we observe immediately recognizable capitalist units of production – for example on the Peruvian and Ecuadorian coasts – but we also observe the proliferation of units of peasant production in many parts of the highlands, both with pronounced social differentiation, as in the more fertile sections of the Mantaro valley of Peru (Long and Roberts 1978), or with little differentiation, as in the areas described by Platt and Harris and by Figueroa in this volume (chs. 2, 3 and 5). These comparisons make a general theory of peasant economy particularly difficult to formulate, for it becomes quite clear that, just as the forms of its organization vary, so does its relationship with the capitalist system, with the accumulation of capital and with capitalist enterprises in the strict sense.

The point can be brought home if we compare the account given of the Laymi and Macha peoples of Northern Potosí, Bolivia, in this volume (Harris and Platt, chs. 3 and 2) with other accounts of the development of the Cochabamba region of Bolivia (Larson 1980). The Laymi and Macha live very near to the mining complex of Siglo XX, whereas Cochabamba is much further from it, and yet it is Cochabamba which has historically provided the labour force for these mines (Molina 1980), and it is in Cochabamba that the process of dispossession of peasant lands and enforced labour migration has been most notorious. Northern Potosí has been characterized, in contrast, by the absence of haciendas and of wage labour, by non-monetary transfers of land via inheritance and communal juridical institutions, by the prevalence of use-value over exchange-value in the circulation of goods, by the predominantly temporary character of migration, and by a comparatively low degree of differentiation within the peasantry, whether in terms of division of labour or of inequalities of income and wealth. The chapters by Platt and Harris show that the conditions which have enabled this situation to develop in Northern Potosí are as much the result of the colonial system of land administration as a survival from the pre-colonial past. Indeed, while the state has finally abolished Indian tribute, and while land tax continues to be paid in only symbolic quantities by those holding land under communal arrangements, these symbolic amounts are absolutely essential elements of the contemporary land tenure system among the Macha and the Laymi peoples. A further irony is found in the history of Northern Potosí: according to Platt, the region was a major producer of wheat for urban markets in the nineteenth century, before succumbing to Chilean and Peruvian competition, yet this dynamism did not lead to the decomposition of the peasant economy.

Although one must allow for differences between the Laymi and Macha economies, described by Harris and Platt respectively, the similarities between the two are evident and the interpretations offered by the two authors are striking examples of the problems which may arise in understanding the relationship between peasant economies and capitalism. For Harris, the contemporary characteristics of the Laymi economy are to be explained by its isolation from markets. Their products are not those most in demand in the nearby mining centres; they are able to feed themselves from their own land and their demographic growth has not placed their resources under severe strain; and national and foreign capital have not found any interesting opportunities for agricultural investment in the area. In short, for Harris, the Laymi have been fortunate, for if these conditions had not prevailed their ethnic economy would have suffered from the pressures of differentiation and outward migration. The implication is that, in general, peasant economies decompose when brought into contact with capitalist markets, a theme to which we shall return.

For Platt, in contrast, those very features of the Macha economy which appear least affected by the capitalist economy, such as the payment of wages in maize, ensure 'the reproduction of households lacking maize-production in conditions which enable them to fulfil their function within the regional economic structure' (p. 63 below), while certain apparently pre-capitalist features, such as bi-zonal cultivation, facilitate market production. Overall, he portrays a process of 'permanent primitive accumulation' whereby low prices of agricultural products result in 'unequal exchange' between the peasant production sector and the rest of the economy. The effect of these price relations is to transfer value, yet the peasantry is not therefore under pressure of separation from the land. Indeed, in the view of Bartra, who originated the idea of 'permanent primitive accumulation' (1974: 102–4), one effect of the process is to maintain a reserve of labour available in times of seasonal or cyclical demand at little or no cost to capital or the state. The peasant economy, in this view, and for all its non-capitalist organization, is an integral part of the capitalist system, and a safe mechanism for the political neutralization of the peasantry.

Even though the peasant producers of Northern Potosí migrate less than others, even within Bolivia, and seem to sell little of their produce on the market, it would be difficult to dispute this last statement so long as agreement could be reached concerning the meaning of the words 'integral part', and in particular with respect to whether those words imply a functional relationship to the whole: Platt clearly believes they do, while Harris

3

has some doubts, and thinks that the Laymi adopt strategies to avert that functionality.

The thesis of 'permanent primitive accumulation' can be thought of as a variant on the 'unequal exchange' thesis, which places greater emphasis on the productive potential of peasant units of production, and their contribution to overall capital accumulation. According to this view, peasant farmers produce at lower cost and therefore sell at lower prices than capitalists, because they use more labour and less capital per unit of output, and because most of the labour they do use is unpaid (in money terms); in this way they provide an indirect subsidy to urban consumers, thus keeping urban wages down. Furthermore, by bearing the costs of reproduction of rural labour, as well as of much urban or industrial migrant labour, the peasant family relieves either capitalists, or the capitalist state, of the burden of those costs (Vergopoulos 1978).

A different thesis is expounded by Lenin in *The Development of Capitalism in Russia*; for Lenin the incorporation of peasant economy, whatever its endogenous mechanisms, into the capitalist system, that is into commodity economy, leads to internal polarization of the peasantry, until there remain in agriculture only capitalists and proletarians. In later writings, however, Lenin was careful to say that the transition might be a very long one, but nevertheless his theory stands in opposition to the other two views mentioned since it conceives of a fundamental contradiction between capitalism and peasant economy, whereas those views claim that the two can, under certain circumstances (in particular those of dependent capitalism), stand in a complementary, even functional, relationship, though one heavily biased against the peasantry.

This volume offers some support for all these views, though not conclusive support for any one of them. Figueroa's device of presenting the *comunidad* economy in a national accounting framework offers an especially lucid view of pertinent relationships: for the six carefully sampled (and therefore representative) communities studied, he shows that although there is very little wage labour within them, they rely crucially on income from temporary migrations and remittances from migrant kin. On the face of it they remain peasant economies, and are indeed sending cheap labour to centres of capitalist production. The communities in question also exhibit hardly any investment at all, since they have no surplus left once they have replaced depleted resources. The picture fits the 'permanent primitive accumulation' thesis. The one issue which remains in doubt concerns the prices of agricultural products. Both the 'unequal exchange' and the 'permanent primitive accumulation' theses refer to their low level, but we dispose of hardly any systematic studies of prices which would bear out their contentions, except for that of Lipton (1977) which argues from a neo-classical rather than an 'unequal exchange' viewpoint, although the two seem to have several points in common.

Accepting, for the moment, that prices of agricultural products are low, the question which arises is whether this leads to exploitation of peasant producers by the capitalist sector of production, and, above all, whether such exploitation is more advantageous for that sector than the development of capitalist production in agriculture. In all probability the answer is 'no', since peasant producers buy and sell less on the market than the workers and managers of capitalist enterprises, and thus the surplus transferred by them (on an equivalent amount of land) is probably smaller. Furthermore, although small farms are often said to use land and capital more intensively than larger ones, this does not mean that they generate more surplus, since that intensity tends to correspond to a highly extensive use of labour. Much depends on crop technology, but capitalism does not have an invariable advantage in encouraging or preserving peasant production, nor, perhaps more important, is it clear what surplus is being extracted in the exploitation of unequal exchange, if indeed it is a surplus at all. One might also have difficulty accepting the implicit assumption that peasant producers are condemned to eternally stagnating income levels. It might well be the case that increasing incomes and production, and a change in the relations of production, are pre-conditions for an increase in surplus transfer from them to industrial capital.

Figueroa, in chapter 5, does not espouse either of the variants of unequal exchange, limiting himself to pointing out the integration of peasant comunidades into the national economy. Sánchez, however, adopts a stronger line (ch. 6), and uses his research to show that not only are such comunidades fully integrated into the capitalist system, but they are also penetrated by the capitalist mode of production, since apparently non-wage labour is a mere disguise for relationships which are no different from those based on wage labour. Indeed, Sánchez expresses a deliberately ironic view of the persistence of forms of exchange in which labour is remunerated in produce (crops especially). These forms are embedded in ritual kinship relations and are described by the participants in the language of reciprocity; for him their persistence is a result of a 'process of differentiation which enlarges the gap between poor and rich peasants and their general exclusion from real control of land and of production, and the obstacles to their improving their production' (p. 183 below). However, while documenting differentiation, Sánchez does not go so far as to say that the richer peasants are capitalists, indeed 'the rich are as much the victims of capitalist exploitation as the poorest' (p. 184) and in any case 'the proportion of wage labour used by the richest households . . . is of small significance compared with the number of days poor peasants must work for a wage in order to reach subsistence' (p. 189) and therefore these rich peasants are not by any means the principal employers of local hired labour. What Sánchez argues, in contrast to Figueroa yet in a study of a small area of the same region, is that wage labour is a feature of peasant economy; however, he has clearly resisted the claim that, for this reason, the local economy is merely capitalist. Similarly, while documenting differentiation he has not claimed that this is a polarization into two rural classes of capitalists and proletarians.

The comunidades of Central and Southern Peru, described by Figueroa and also by Sánchez, show a peasant economy reproducing itself with hardly any internal accumulation, and with little internal wage labour. There evidently is inequality within them, but it is not of the kind which opposes one class of employers to another class of workers. The dynamic of class formation comes from without, as the poorer members of the communities migrate, temporarily or permanently, to work for wages, and the richer members take advantage of the commercial opportunities offered by the market. These communities are providing Peruvian capitalism with ever-increasing supplies of the one 'factor of production' of which, in present structures, there is a desperate over-supply: unskilled labour. The picture of stagnant agricultural production which one gains from Figueroa's chapter is hardly consistent with the notion that capitalism exploits the peasantry by forcing them to produce more and more for less and less, which is at the heart of the 'unequal exchange' thesis. However, it is consistent with the claim that class differentiation within 'communities' is to be interpreted in a broader, national context; indeed it would seem that class oppositions have hardly any base at all in local conditions of production in these comunidades, and that the undoubted inequalities which exist within them relate to the class structure exclusively through the external links and activities of members and their close kin. One would be hard pressed to find, in these comunidades, an endogenously generated class structure.

The difficulty is further compounded by interactions between persons and groups based in different localities. Antoinette Molinié (ch. 8) describes a multi-tiered vertical complex in which labour moves between an area in the *ceja de montaña* of dynamic small-scale coffee producers (La Convención), a higher, but fertile, temperate valley (Yucay) in which haciendas co-exist with tiny smallholdings, and much higher, less fertile communities of poverty-stricken potato-growers. The interest of her description lies not merely in the physical movements between these tiers, but also in the multiplicity of types of contract which underlie those movements. A cultivator pays a money rent for a plot in La Convención, while he 'entrusts his lands' in Yucay 'to a natural or ritual kinsman' and in exchange brings 'part of his coca and fruit harvest and will also keep an eye out' for suitable marketing opportunities. That same cultivator will take advantage of ritual kinship ties with a poorer cultivator at the higher levels to buy his potatoes at less than the 'market price'; or, again, people may come from the higher tiers to work as wage labourers in Yucay for others who themselves go down to La Convención as wage labourers. In this chain of relationships it is quite clear who are the rich, middle and poor peasants, and it is equally clear that they would not all be easily found in one locality, but it is not in the least clear that the inequality which prevails within the peasantry is simply a product of capitalist development, for the inequality between the small-holders of Yucay and the *comuneros* above them is nothing new. Indeed the irony in Sánchez – who sees reciprocity as an intrinsic feature of the system of inequality in peasant society – is already present, though muted, in Murra, who sees in reciprocity the basis of Inca imperial domination. And in this volume Bradby succeeds in extracting the core of domination from that other essentially Andean concept – verticality (ch. 4).

Bradby tells us of two aspects of the changing relationships between the richer village of Huayllay and the poorer village of Carhuapata. Carhuapata has broken off the vertical relations which sustained ties of dependency between her people and those of Huayllay because her shepherds are in a position to sell their wool on the world market and thus 'appropriate their own product, rather than letting it flow back into Huayllay as surplus' (p. 114). By finding alternative exchange partners, the shepherds ceased their dependence on a single centre. Conclusion: the control of a maximum of ecological tiers, as in the title of Murra's article (1972a), depends on the control of people by ties of political and personal dependency.

The second aspect which Bradby recounts is the adoption of self-consciously 'modern' practices in the poorer community of Carhuapata while Huayllay, living on the laurels of a disappearing past, continues to revel in fiestas and anti-urban values, even though Huayllay is far more closely tied to the metropolis by numerous migrants – and there is hardly any migration from Carhuapata.

Bradby insists on the liberating features of capitalist circulation which has enabled Carhuapata to escape from the political domination of the lower level, but she is also careful to point out that 'commodity relations have not penetrated *production*' in these communities (p. 121). Nevertheless, the message that money exchange by freeing people from personal or political dependency offers them improved though perhaps not very good opportunities for accumulation, stands in contrast to the picture of growing inequality and proletarianization in the work of Rodrigo Sánchez. In Platt's chapter we are told that bi-zonal cultivation (conventionally associated with autarkic, subsistence production) is correlated with high levels of production, consumption and market participation (p. 62). This is consistent with Bradby insofar as those practising it are only 25% of the Macha population. The difficulty arises in the interpretation of the relations based on kinship and inheritance; for Bradby it is a relationship of personal dependence which may

7

even change to the benefit of the underdog with the introduction of money; for Sánchez, it is an exploitative relationship whether mediated by money or not. And for Platt and Sánchez, the rich peasants are in any case themselves exploited.

In the Andes we can distinguish at least two patterns of differentiation, in one of which the preservation of kinship or ritual kinship ties is important for the development of a rich peasant stratum, while in the other it is not. The first type refers to the situation described here by Sánchez and elsewhere by Gonzales (1979), in which wage labour on a systematic basis, and as a preponderant form of labour, is absent in all but a tiny minority of production units. These are areas in which inequality is clearly observable among peasant producers, yet there is no process of capital accumulation, no polarization of the population into opposed classes of capitalist producers and wage labourers, and so capitalist relations of production are hardly present at all. Thus in the communities on which Figueroa gives us data, the importance of internally hired wage labour is almost negligible; in Sánchez's sample of thirty-two producers he classifies seven as rich peasants, yet only four of these rely on wage labour for more than 50% of their requirements (table 6.6). And the producer with the highest annual labour input uses a total of 264 man–days: the next highest user has 189 days. In Platt's much larger sample of 500 producers in Northern Potosí, only 14% use any wage labour at all (table 2.6). In Sánchez's Andarapa sample of thirty-two the equivalent proportion is 65.6%, and the impression that inequality is more accentuated in Andarapa than in Northern Potosí is reinforced by his table 6.4, where the richest household in the sample has thirteen and a half times as much wealth as the poorest.

Sánchez does not offer data on sales, but Figueroa does, and Sánchez's Andarapa is, like Figueroa's communities, in the southern sierra of Peru. According to Figueroa's table 5.14 the production units of the southern sierra sell almost exactly half their production, whereas in Northern Potosí the equivalent figure is 17.5% (see table 2.11).

Thus in terms of both dependence on wage labour and the commercialization of production, Northern Potosí stands in contrast to the southern sierra of Peru. Unfortunately the quantitative data do not permit us to pursue the comparison in terms of inequality in general, because only Sánchez offers a distribution of land or wealth. However, certain qualitative points should be made on the way these chapters cast light on processes of social and economic differentiation among the peasantry.

In chapters 2 and 8 Platt and Molinié show the pitfalls threatening any analysis which restricts itself to one particular locality without examining land rights and labour held and performed by 'outsiders' in that locality, and by 'locals' in other localities. Although they show that such vertical relationships are structured by non-market circulation of land and goods as in the inheritance system described by Platt, this circulation is not seen to act as an obstacle to the accumulation of capital, where other circumstances permit or stimulate it. Molinié's description of relations between producers 'based' on different tiers of the Yucay vertical complex shows how they secure access to land and labour by enlisting each other's co-operation or by creating obligations through ties of patronage. Commodities circulate between each tier and urban commercial centres in a market framework, but goods move between tiers on a separate pattern, as gifts (in exchange for other gifts or favours) or on the basis of barter equivalencies which have no relation to price relationships on the 'open' market. (Similar transactions are described by Harris for Northern Potosí.) For all this, one of the important points to arise in Molinié's description, as in Sánchez's, is the instrumentalization of many non-monetary prestations, in kind and in labour, by producers trying to accumulate capital, on however small a scale.

The case of Yucay itself illustrates variations in the structuring of inequality, for within the Yucay vertical system the lowest tier is the valley of La Convención where, since 1952, a process of capitalist development has led to the formation of a stratum of capitalist farmers relying on wage labour and producing coffee and cocoa for the international market, giving rise to the second of the two patterns of differentiation mentioned above. Although there is migration between other tiers of the Yucay system and La Convención, the valley also draws seasonal wage labourers from much further afield, and we have evidence of sharp differentiation between small capitalist farmers (former direct tenants of expropriated haciendas) and others who live almost exclusively by selling their labour, and who were previously subtenants on the haciendas or have migrated in from elsewhere (Alfaro and Oré 1974). The valley is distinguished not only by the emergence of social classes but also by the availability of opportunities for accumulation which plainly do not exist in Figueroa's communities, in Sánchez's Andarapa, or nearby in the Pampa de Anta above Cuzco (Gonzales 1979). Whereas La Convención attracts migrant labour, in the Pampa de Anta richer peasants are obliged to rent out their land on a share-cropping basis in order to secure access to labour which would otherwise be drawn away by migration. This is a contrast between dynamism and stagnation, and between different types of social differentiation.

In one case we have a rich peasant stratum engaged in a multiplicity of activities in even a multiplicity of places, in the other a concentration of a small range of crops in one place; in one case we have a reliance on wage labour by rich peasants for only a proportion of their activities, while in the other they rely exclusively on wage labour; in one the language of kinship is used to obtain labour (see also chs. 3 and 6) and even to mask its dependent character, while in the other there is no such linguistic or ideological recourse.

9

It would be misleading to polarize these types of rich peasant too rigidly. The variations merely point to the existence of peasant elites with quite different locations vis-à-vis capital accumulation. They also point to a major problem in the theory of peasant economy, namely the presence or absence of a clear 'break' between the categories of 'peasant enterprise' and 'capitalist enterprise'. The issue becomes even more complicated if we speak of a 'peasant family enterprise', thus placing special emphasis on its 'family' character.

2. The 'family' character of a peasant enterprise

In the valley of La Convención (the lowest tier of the Yucay complex), in some areas of the valley of the Mantaro (Long and Roberts 1978), in many parts of the Chancay valley, all in Central Peru, and in the Ecuadorian province of Carchi (among other places), we observe the emergence of a petty bourgeois class of small and not-so-small agricultural capitalists. In La Convención, the dissolution of great estates in 1962 after a prolonged armed struggle left the way open for a process of capitalist development among small-scale producers of coffee and cocoa in a particularly fertile valley (Alfaro and Oré 1974). In the Mantaro valley there is a diversity of ecological and social conditions, but peasant producers have responded to the opportunities offered by urban growth in Huancayo and Lima by expanding wheat and milk production. In Lampián, in the Chancay valley, micro-climates and land favourable to fruit production have been exploited (Celestino 1972). In Carchi, a province of the northern sierra of Ecuador, a climate and soil particularly suitable for potato production combined with the availability of land produced a remarkably rapid development of potato production from 1950 to the mid-1970s, again among small producers, a small number of whom have as a result evolved into medium-sized capitalist farmers with herds of between ten and fifty-five head of cattle.

Under these conditions, either the peasant units of production are not 'family' units or their 'family' character has not impeded the development of many into capitalist units. One might even claim on this sort of evidence that what we describe as 'peasant units' are really small-scale capitalist units, distinguishable from larger units in degree but not in kind, for we also find close kin working for a wage. In other more stagnant areas (Southern Peru, Andarapa), even distant kin or non-kin will often only work for others if their employer defines their relationship in the language of kinship. It is in these other areas that one might find a better basis for distinguishing peasant units in kind as well as in degree, but the same nagging question would once again rear its head in another form: is it in the contrasting organization of peasant production, rather than some other factor, such as market opportunities or favourable soils, that we find the secret of their

10

different histories? And if the answer is 'no', what remains of the 'peasant' unit of production as a distinct species? If the peasant unit of production is 'the same' in stagnant and dynamic areas, then it is simply a small-scale version of a capitalist enterprise. If it is different in its internal organization, then one might have a case for saying that the peasant unit has qualitatively distinct characteristics.

One of these characteristics is traditionally said to be the family-based organization of labour. Yet not only does this raise problems of definition and delimitation, it also encounters quite straightforward empirical obstacles. The 'family' remains a curiously ill-defined category: does it refer to a type of social relationship with close kin? Does it, in contrast, refer necessarily to a concrete set of kin? Does it imply a direct correlation between closeness of kin and coincidence of economic interest or readiness to pool labour, land or other resources? Is it self-evident, in any particular society, where 'the family' begins and where it ends, and is the category consistently delimited in kinship terms even within a particular society? In the specific context of peasant production in the Andes two issues are immediately problematic: firstly, the (heavily Eastern European) stereotype of a nuclear family under the dictatorship of its male head, classically described in Gorki's autobiography, and strongly implicit in Shanin's ideal type (1973–4), has crept unnoticed into our idea of the Andean peasant production unit, and of peasant production units elsewhere. As a result we tend to treat the 'peasant family' as if each unit had one rationality and no internal economic – let alone affective – conflicts. The mere mention of this problem suffices to show that this assumption must at least be questioned and set against empirical evidence. Sánchez (ch. 6) shows nuclear families as a complex and often conflictive interaction of differential rights and obligations, and power. The chapters by Harris and Platt point to a second issue, namely the possibility that individuals only co-operate with selected partners from among their kin, and also that they may choose to have closer relations of co-operation with ritual kin (*compadres*) than with immediate affines. Indeed in Harris's chapter we are offered a picture of the Laymi as a network of kin within which individuals and households choose co-operative partners. Platt's picture of the Macha, on the other hand, is focused more on corporate alliance strategies by lineages.

These studies alert us to a possibility already hinted at, namely that one must examine the use of kinship as a language to formulate social obligations, that is as ideology, before taking for granted its effectiveness as a principle of social organization. Furthermore one might analyse in a more questioning spirit the association between family organization and non-capitalist organization of production. For it is striking that some of the cases where production is most clearly organized on the basis of the nuclear family's labour, rather than the labour of a mysteriously selected congeries of close,

11

distant and ritual kin, are precisely examples of evidently capitalist agricultural production: Southern Brazil (Lehmann forthcoming), Northern
Argentina (Archetti and Stölen 1975), the United States, and so on. Now
these capitalized family farms use hardly any permanent wage labour, but
they often depend critically on seasonal wage labour (for the Argentine
Chaco, see Carrera 1980); they use capital in the way one would expect
of a capitalist, that is, in the production exclusively of commodities and
not use-values; and they frequently go bankrupt as capitalists do and as
peasants do not (Friedmann 1978; Carrera 1980). How, then, can one claim
that family based production is peculiar to peasant – and therefore implicitly
non-capitalist–production units?

3. The variable role of money

The chapters on Northern Potosí reveal further ironies: it appears that the
Laymi people use money in precisely the opposite way from what one might
expect of a group living and producing in relative isolation from market
exchange; for reasons explained in the chapter by Harris, certain Laymi
accept cash as payment for their produce from fellow-Laymi, as a favour,
in circumstances where they would not accept cash from outsiders. This is
a favour because of the distance which has to be covered in order to buy
anything with that cash.

A slightly different, but related point, is made by Barbara Bradby when
she warns us against 'seeing the presence of money as indicative of capitalist
production relations'. Its mere presence does not signify that any accumulation is under way, at least on the basis of production.

Other contributors express the complementary view, that non-monetary
relations are implicitly governed by market exchange (what Figueroa calls
'transparent prices') and that forms of labour prestation in which money
plays no apparent role are not in essence any different from, and certainly no
less exploitative than, wage labour itself. Thus Rodrigo Sánchez argues, for
Andarapa, that exchange of labour and services between rich and poor
peasants is little different from wage labour, and occurs mainly because an
individual who gains access to others' labour by offering them administrative
and political services would be unable to obtain – let alone to legitimize –
wage labour paid in money. Sánchez is saying that the ideological description
of the transaction as an exchange of favours is not a reason for describing
it as a non-commodity relation, whereas others might say precisely the
opposite, namely that if people do not conceive such labour prestations as
wage labour then, indeed, they are not wage labour. Antoinette Molinié
describes labour prestations by poor to rich in the Yucay valley near Cuzco,
also mediated by ritual kinship relations, especially *compadrazgo*, and hardly
distinguishable from wage labour.

All this must look very puzzling; in Northern Potosí money changes hands, but not always in exchange for commodities, in Andarapa and Yucay people work for others in return for non-monetary reward yet their labour seems to be a commodity and is contributing to others' accumulation, and in Huayllay, as described by Bradby, an impoverished widow pays money wages for labour which is manifestly not contributing to a process of accumulation.

I can add a further example from field work currently being carried out in the province of Carchi, Ecuador. Here people speak of 'borrowing' a day's work from each other (*prestar el día*). A generation ago, in the early stages of peasant colonization, with shortage of labour and little commodity production, these prestations were precisely that: borrowing a day against future repayment in the form of a day's work. But now one borrows a day, if at all, usually in order to save spending the cash, and if the lender asks for his day back when one happens to be busy, one pays a peon and sends him along. If the other man does not like it – perhaps because he trusts the original partner to work with more skill or more reliability, which may be why he initiated the arrangement in the first place – there is little he can do. In this area there is a clear process of capital accumulation among small to medium-sized rural producers, and it is impossible to obtain a day's labour for anything but a wage or, occasionally, against the promise of another day's labour. Is this any different from the relationships described by Sánchez and Molinié? In all three there is differentiation and apparently some accumulation among those one could call 'rich peasants', and in all three labour is hired, as a commodity, in order to pursue this accumulation. Yet there are clear differences: in Andarapa there are limits on the hiring of labour for wages, and local workers must usually be obtained by other means, whereas in Carchi wages are by far the most prevalent mechanism. In the Yucay system the poor work for their richer and more powerful compadres for a pittance, or even for nothing, but they work for other employers, with whom they apparently have no special relationship, for a wage or, eventually, in order to gain access to a plot in the humid and fertile valley of La Convención. Labour does not, in this system, seem to be any less of a commodity in one case than in the other, and indeed it would appear that 'exploitation' is greater where the prestation of labour is embedded in a more multi-stranded relationship predicated on inequality, and described by the actors themselves in terms of kinship. This would seem to bear out Barbara Bradby's point about the more liberating character of relationships based on the impersonal medium of money as compared with transfers of labour against services or payment in kind.

If we return now to Carchi, we observe the mediation of transfers of labour or other resources by money even within the nuclear family, which may seem strange until we contemplate the alternative. In Carchi, especially in the area

13

of relatively recent colonization, it is rare for sons out of school to work unpaid for their fathers, but it is also rare for their parents to pay them a wage. The sons will participate in sowing and harvesting on their parents' land, but beyond that the fathers have to give sons some kind of participation in their enterprise if they are to gain from their labour. The usual solution is some form of share-cropping arrangement whereby each party agrees to contribute so much labour or working capital and the product is equally divided between the two parties. Ritual kinship ties do not have the same importance in Carchi as in the central and southern sierra of Peru or as in Bolivia, but the prevalence of such collaboration between fathers and sons averts the inequities which accompany labour prestations and transfers of goods based on kinship relations of subordination. In Carchi people would say that a day's labour must be counted at the going rate in share-cropping arrangements or at the very least must be counted against another day's labour, but never against ill-defined services or patronage, and once a child is out of school he cannot be expected to work with good grace free of charge even for his father. If that is the case between father and son, it would hold *a fortiori* between *compadres*.

The relationship between money and labour-as-a-commodity is further complicated when we look at Figueroa's data, since they seem to show an extremely restricted use of wage labour within the communities he studies and yet he also states quite unequivocally that barter involves transparent prices – that is, that if the goods bartered were valued at their market prices, it would be seen that the exchanges are no different from those in the market except that they involve money only implicitly. In this case the goods are commodities, but wage labour hardly exists at all as between members of these communities even though they depend a great deal on the sale of their labour outside the communities. In the Yucay valley system, Antoinette Molinié described extensive wage labour at market prices co-existing with robust vestiges of barter transfers of goods at implicit prices far out of line with those prevailing in the market. In Northern Potosí Harris describes two parallel sets of prices: one of these, governing transactions between fellow members of an ethnic group, is based on barter, but the implicit money prices are divergent from those prevailing in similar barter with non-members, and still more so from those prevailing in money transactions.

In the final analysis, the quality of labour depends probably less on the particular *numeraire* whereby its quantity is calculated than on the presence or absence of a process of accumulation in a region. It is quite clear from the data that there is hardly any accumulation in the communities studied by Figueroa, or in Northern Potosí, whereas at certain tiers of the Yucay system there clearly is accumulation, as there is in Carchi, though the data for the last have not yet been analysed in full.

4. Rent, risk and circulation of labour

This complex interweaving of monetary and non-monetary transactions is illustrated by the wide variety of share-cropping contracts observed during our research in Carchi. I use the term share-cropping to describe arrangements known locally as *al partir* or *a medias*, which are contracts between persons of similar, or dissimilar, social status and wealth, but not between big landlords and peasant producers – rather, in a broad sense, among the peasantry. These contracts vary enormously: in some cases the owner of a piece of land may provide seed and fertilizer while the partner will provide labour, oxen and pesticides, and the contract will be described in these terms, that is, input by input, rather than in money terms. The product, often potatoes, is always divided half-and-half between the partners, with the exception of the odd case in which an ageing parent has in effect passed on his or her land to a future heir but retains a small share of the product. But there are numerous cases in which all or some of the costs are divided equally between the partners; in these cases one partner is nevertheless responsible for recruiting and supervising the work-force – a burdensome task in sowings of a hectare or more – and if that partner is not the owner then it could be said that the owner receives a rental in the form of half these supervisory costs. But if these costs are the owner's responsibility then there is no rental income at all. Now, in terms of the present discussion, it may be puzzling that in the same area the same person might have a contract which requires a careful monetary accounting of all costs, including his own labour and hired labour, and also a contract with another person which distributes costs between partners input by input rather than *peso* by *peso* (or, in Ecuador, *sucre* by *sucre*). Risks are usually distributed fairly evenly, since in two-thirds of the cases surveyed pesticide costs were shared, and these vary in direct relation to the rain; expenditure on fertilizer, which is also usually shared, is decided in advance. The proportion of production marketed and the quantity of wage labour employed in production do not have a direct correlation with the monetization of the contract. The explanation lies in the balance between risk and supervision costs: if one partner pays for the pesticides he takes a supplementary risk, and the person who pays for the labour and also provides the workers, frees his partner of the drudgery, as he sees it, of *lidiar con peones* – of finding and supervising the workers. These producers are not large landlords but small and medium-scale producers, but even someone who only plants half a hectare of potatoes is likely to require wage labour at least at harvest, and probably in earlier stages of the productive cycle. Elderly persons, in particular, are unwilling to *lidiar con peones*, and are most in need of them.

In these contracts, the non-monetary character of certain calculations of cost arises from the nature of the cost (supervision) and also from the relation between risk and rent: that is, an owner may prefer to receive rent in the form of an off-loading of all or some of the risks of production onto another person. A further consideration arises when we recall that in these types of arrangement the product is invariably divided equally between the partners – the remaining features of the contract are settled on that assumption, and the division of the product is not open to negotiation. One could therefore contrast share-cropping contracts with fixed rental by saying that, from the individual partner's point of view, whereas under fixed rental the tenant bears all costs of production but the division of the expected product is uncertain, under this form of share-cropping the division of the product is certain but not so the costs of production. (Where all costs are shared equally between partners the costs for each are also uncertain, though not their division.) However, even the uncertainty regarding costs has been reduced, because it is largely restricted to expenditure on pesticides and on the labour required to spray them.

Now it is noticeable that in one of the areas we are studying in Carchi (Huaca) the prevalence of this kind of contract is accompanied by an almost total absence of multiple cultivation on several different tiers, while in the other area (El Angel) where there is some multiple-tier cultivation there is less share-cropping. It is also noticeable that more 'capitalistic' forms of tenancy, in which an owner renounces all control over the use to which his land is put, are entirely absent except as between large-scale producers or owners of some very large haciendas. Indeed, share-cropping and multi-tiered cultivation have certain features in common, namely that they both offer the possibility of risk-spreading without loss of direct control of production, in conditions where risk-spreading means cultivation in a variety of natural conditions, or engaging in a variety of productive or indeed commercial activities. Furthermore, although the people of Northern Potosí do not describe the arrangements prevailing between residents and non-residents of the two ecological tiers in the region as share-cropping, there is some resemblance between their systems and that described for Carchi. Harris describes how non-resident owners of *likina* land acquire rights to a share in production simply by the fact of 'helping out' their kin, who have usufruct of a common inheritance, in production; the quantities involved do not seem to be subject to careful weighing and measuring, but then the absence of wage labour and accumulation, and the low proportion of production marketed, mean that there is no fixed set of index numbers whereby producers could offset these costs against each other.

Some forty years ago people from Huaca in Carchi did obtain land on warmer levels in order to produce maize, but today dual cultivation has disappeared. In Carchi, the deep penetration of market exchange means that resources produced elsewhere – such as maize – can easily be bought, but the problem of risk-spreading remains, in some ways even more acutely than in an area where there is access to several tiers via ownership or usufruct. Therefore the producers of Carchi spread the costs and risks of production by contracts among themselves, since they cannot spread them among different places, and the contracts reflect the combination of the need to obtain a reasonable return in a market environment, the need to spread risks among partners, and the possibility of off-loading some of the heavier risks onto weaker (landless or land-poor) partners. The penetration of money has the effect of rendering economic transactions more anonymous, and thus less 'embedded' in more diffuse relations of patron-clientage, kinship and so on; this stimulates co-operation among people with similar qualities of physical resources and dissimilar quantities – whereas one could say that in Northern Potosí some co-operation takes place between people controlling similar quantities but dissimilar qualities of resources.

5. Verticality and political formations

The control of a maximum of ecological tiers in conditions of extreme political inequality and absence of a money economy – the conditions prevailing in the societies described by Murra in his classic article on the subject (1972a) – is yet another story. Here the control of different ecological tiers is in the hands of a dominant political authority and seems to be an essential element in the maintenance of that authority. Thus, in explaining the power of the lords of the lakeside Lupaqa kingdom even after the colonial invasion and defeat of the Inca, Murra refers to the need to invest in relations of reciprocity by offering institutionalized hospitality, even to those upon whom they were imposing forced labour (1970). The lords had to be in a position to assemble a variety of goods to redistribute, and this may have meant that they needed to gain access to a variety of tiers. Murra's account, based on various chronicles, shows that their power was not exercised over a unified territory, but rather distributed, unevenly, across a large region, so that control over resources dispersed in various places counted for more than control over a unified territory. The essence of their domination, which had been seriously undermined by 1567, was not really the complementarity of tiers or resources they controlled, but the mechanism of control over the people who worked the lords' land and produced the goods which they redistributed. Murra describes this mechanism as the Andean system of reciprocity and redistribution, and though he admits that it needs further study, he clearly believes that it was the basis of their domination. The lords provided military organization (a service?), a transport system, a land tenure system and its ritual annual confirmation. Murra first describes the provision by their subjects of seasonal labour on the land belonging to the lords, accounting for this arrangement in terms of reciprocity and redistribution. He then describes a *mita* system whereby each base unit of the Chucuito kingdom had to provide so many days' labour a year on a rota basis. This, he says, cannot so easily be explained by the reciprocity system, but Murra does not go beyond it – indeed he repeats it.

Perhaps one might seek the beginnings of an explanation in another less frequently advertised feature of Andean social and political organization, before and after the Spanish conquest. I refer to the former lords forced to fill institutional positions as agents and intermediaries between communities of direct producers and the state. *Kuraka* was the name for one, important, position of this kind, but there were many others (Spalding 1973). As the Spanish established their own system of labour control – though it retained many features of the old Inca system – so they created opportunities for such persons to make their fortunes or to make a career; they could achieve this by exploiting the Indians on behalf of the Spanish, by enforcing the mita labour obligations, by collecting dues from those who chose (and were allowed) to pay a sum of money instead of going to the mines, and so on (Sánchez-Albornóz 1978: 99–107). The Inca had not much less of a problem and presumably such intermediaries grew up in areas where they were engaged in large-scale labour mobilizations, such as those referred to by Wachtel (1978), which brought thousands of persons from the shores of Lake Titicaca to the Cochabamba valley in the last quarter of the fifteenth century and the early part of the sixteenth. (Wachtel writes of the removal of the indigenous population of the valley by Huayna Capac, and its replacement by 14 000 Indians, permanent settlers and temporary migrants in unknown proportions, from the highlands.) The leaders of ethnic groups who had to bear this weight of labour tribute, be it for military or productive purposes, must have gained some benefit from the arrangement. And even the group so often consigned without much comment to the bottom of the pile, the Uru of Lake Titicaca, turn out on close inspection to be another stratified ethnic group (Wachtel 1978).

In her contribution to this volume Barbara Bradby seeks to convert the notion of verticality into a category of analysis of social organization. Vertical control might appear to be a relation of property, but it implies a 'centralized political system with its basis in a way of controlling production on a series of ecological levels ... to appropriate a surplus ... in order to create and preserve political,' ideological and religious power' (p. 111–12). In the light of the examples quoted here, and of several articles by Murra which describe the functioning of state systems in relation to the control of human and natural resources on several tiers, it would seem that the logic of 'verticality' in conditions of extreme political inequality and a non-monetary economy is the logic of a state, its requirements in military and civilian manpower, and in production to maintain that manpower. The outposts maintained by *mitimaes* in permanent residence, producing not for themselves but for their political lords, and thus of course dependent on them for the provision of essential goods from other ecological tiers and niches, were outposts of states, large and small, from the Inca empire to the Lupaqa and down to even smaller groupings. This is radically different from the smallholders who control multiple plots on several tiers in order either to spread their risks against climatic variations, or to ensure an adequate supply of various crops for consumption or sale; and it is also radically different from the circulation of people living or producing at different tiers, or of their products, as described by Antoinette Molinié in chapter 8. The one contribution which does reproduce elements clearly parallel to those characteristic of the pre-colonial imperial and state systems of multi-tiered control is that by Fiona Wilson (ch. 7), which gives an account of the ways in which the *hacendados* of Tarma in Central Peru protected their social position in the region by cultivating at different levels and thus ensuring a high degree of autarky in the supply of their own and their workers' needs; but the main point which Wilson is making is that this very strategy reduced the hacendados' capacity for capitalizing on new opportunities for production for the world market, as a result of which they lost their social and economic pre-eminence, giving way to European immigrant capitalist farmers in the early twentieth century. Tristan Platt, in contrast, emphasizes the advantages of bi-zonal production in production for the market (ch. 2).

Ecology, then, is a conditioning factor – a truism, perhaps, but a necessary reminder. Another truism is that 'the Andes' is a diversified region, ecologically and socially. Troll (1968) gives a panoramic view of the variations in flora and in climate, from north to south as well as between altitudes. He distinguishes between the '*páramo*-Andes' and the 'puna-Andes'. The páramo highlands, to be found in Ecuador and Southern Colombia, do not allow cultivation to as high an altitude as in Central and Southern Peru and Bolivia; at the same time in the páramo-Andes night-frost only occurs beyond the upper limit of agriculture, with the result that potato harvests are not so vulnerable. In the páramo-Andes, *chuño* – potatoes preserved by dehydration and refrigeration 'using the dry diurnal temperature climate' (*ibid.*: 33) – cannot be manufactured as a form of energy storage since the temperature contrasts between day and night are insufficient; but then the climatic conditions (at least today) mean that it is not so necessary since months of planting are more flexible. The different ecological tiers are closer to one another than in the Central and Southern Andes, so that the pre-Inca societies.were able to operate apparently without establishing outposts in the way, say, the Lupaqa had to (Salomon 1978, 1980). Hence the idea of 'micro-verticality', in which ethnic groups in the Northern Andes were able to meet many of their needs without engaging in long-distance travel or establishing far-off outposts, finding suitable lands within a day's

19

walking distance from their bases. There remained certain important articles of conspicuous consumption, and others such as clothing, which these chiefdoms could not control directly, and therefore they had to engage in one of two forms of circulation: one took the form of despatching people known as *kamayuj* to work on the land belonging to another lord, and for the benefit of that lord, in exchange for access to resources under his control (Salomon 1980: 177); or they had recourse to long-distance trade specialists known as *mindalá* who evidently enjoyed special privileges in return for paying tribute in gold and like valuables to the chiefdoms where they were based. So the *caciques* of the area known today as Central and Northern Ecuador were able to establish vertical controls without establishing islands in an archipelago (Salomon 1980: 195). But as the Inca conquest advanced, the Inca strategy seems to have been, initially, to establish a legitimate position for themselves locally by setting up as 'just another chiefdom' amidst the already existing ones; and then, after gaining further military victories, the Inca imposed their own, more hierarchical system, in ways specially modified to suit local ideology and to fit in with the pre-existing system. Long-distance circulation, previously a barter circuit over which no state exercised much control, became more and more articulated to the administratively-controlled 'archipelago' system needed by an organization of imperial scale; and the kamayuj settlers came to work for the chiefs of their own communities of origin, and not under some co-operative arrangement with a host community (Salomon 1978: 986). These tactics do not contradict the general picture of the Inca empire as a system of co-option of local chiefs, or of 'indirect rule'.

It would seem, then, from the evidence provided by recent ethno-history, that although some specific characteristics of pre- and sub-Inca societies in the Northern Andes can be accounted for in part by ecology, the Inca empire was able to overcome these differences and gradually incorporate that region into its uniform administrative system – a process cut off only by the Spanish conquest.

6. Social heterogeneity and political domination

Our vision of Andean society, under the Inca and Spanish empires, and even today, is heavily influenced by administrative categories: we think of *ayllus* and their obligations to the Inca, of the caciques who saw to the fulfilment of those obligations under Inca and Spanish, of *comunidades indigenas* owing labour dues in the mines of Potosí or elsewhere, and, today, of *comunidades campesinas* with well-defined membership and rights to land, particularly in Peru: in Bolivia such *comunidades* do not exist, legally. By thinking in this way we may impose another false uniformity. For example, although the numerical importance of *forasteros* under the Spanish has always been known, Sánchez-Albornóz has shown that this category undermined an excessively static, or perhaps bureaucratic, conception of society at that time, in which tribute-paying Indians are set against their Spanish overlords in simple bipolarity. The forasteros (literally 'outsiders') were Indians who lived in communities to which they did not belong; in other words, they had escaped, or perhaps their parents had escaped, from those communities where they were formal members, primarily to avoid paying their share of the community's dues in labour under the mita system, or in money to local *encomenderos*. (Under the mita system each community had to contribute one man in seven each year to go and work in the mines at Potosí or elsewhere, or indeed in agriculture.)

Sánchez-Albornóz (1978: 27) produces evidence showing that in 1683 45% of the adult male Indians in what is today Bolivia were forasteros. They lived in alien communities with the complicity of the local chiefs, to whom they had to pay various sums in order to gain access to land, although it seems that forasteros were for a long time uninterested in obtaining secure access through membership in these communities because with this came the mita obligation. The presence of these forasteros probably strengthened the position of local chiefs, thus contributing to further social differentiation. Richer Indians could buy their way out of the system, while others fled; there remained the intermediaries, the caciques, who were under strong pressure from the bureaucracy to provide the labour, and evidently the burden fell disproportionately on those who stayed behind and were not rich enough to buy their way out. During the mining boom of the sixteenth century, according to both Sánchez-Albornóz (1978: 46) and Sempat Assadourian (1978), an Indian who fled his community and forced mine labour to work in the mines as a free labourer would earn relatively high wages. A fundamental, structural, contradiction in the Spanish colonial system – which had not been present in the Inca empire – was the conflict, especially over labour, between mining and agriculture, that is, between the mine-owners and the nascent class of hacendados in a context, of course, of catastrophic demographic collapse. The haciendas provided refuge from the mita and other tribute either by hiding people or by paying their dues for them, or paying money in lieu of the mita to the caciques responsible for providing mita labour (Sánchez-Albornóz 1978: 112). Clearly, the Indian caciques held an exceedingly ambiguous position in colonial society, and even after many of them had led the Tupac Amaru rebellion of 1780 against the abuses of the *corregidores*, they themselves, on the abolition of the office of *corregidor*, proceeded to engage in those self-same abuses (O'Phelan 1978), and were perhaps forced to do so by their structural, intermediary position. Thus we can see how colonial taxation systems, apart from dividing the population into neatly subdivided groups, also created opportunities for exploitation and enrichment within

Indian society, and for an economy and a political system in which corruption and abuse of power were not only the statistical rule, but also the expected (if not the legal) norm.

7. The meaning of '*comunidad*' in Peru and Ecuador

As in the sixteenth century, so today: a *comunidad* is not all it appears to be. Then, many of the people living in a *pueblo* were not members of an institution giving access to land (*originarios*), and therefore had no formal rights or obligations. Today, many comunidades have numerous, and active, members living away from their lands, struggling on their behalf, and on their own behalf as members of a certain status, and retaining rights to comunidad land (Smith 1975). At the same time there are people living 'in' a comunidad who are not members, that is, who do not have access to comunidad land. In other words, a comunidad is not a place nor is it necessarily a group of people living in close proximity, let alone solidarity. It is an institution of land tenure which regulates access of individuals to land. It is also a creation of the state, recreated over the centuries by the Inca, the Spanish, and the modernizing governments of the twentieth century, each for its own purposes. The Inca and the Spanish had in mind the raising of tribute in labour and, in the Spanish case, money as well. The nineteenth-century states were born under the sign of liberalism, and vowed to abolish both Indian tribute and, *pari passu*, communal land-holding, but they frequently found they could not do without the tax revenue the Indians paid (for the Bolivian case, see Grieshaber 1977: 195). Similarly, it took Peru only five years to go from the euphoric abolition of Indian tribute in 1821, at Independence, to its restoration in 1826 (Bonilla 1980: 9). In Ecuador, the *comunas* seem to be a creation of the republican state for the purpose of exacting labour dues for public works. But in much of Ecuador, as in the north of Peru (Cajamarca for example), *comunidades* as institutions of land tenure no longer exist. Platt and Harris (chs. 2 and 3) show quite clearly the close historical relationship between such institutions (though in Bolivia they are never known as comunidades) and taxation, a relationship which is not peculiar to the Andes, having been an essential feature of the Russian *mir*. More recently the Peruvian Agrarian Reform tried to establish renewed state controls on comunidades, setting conditions for membership and even envisaging forms of collectivization of production. This was not very successful for a long list of reasons, in particular because the state could not possibly control so many communities, and also because so many provisions went against almost universal comunidad practice: for example, the government wanted to exclude non-residents from member-ship, violating the time-honoured retention of rights to land by absentees. These links are valued by the resident members of the community since they provide inflows of capital, a network of urban connections, and urban representatives in case of litigation or the need to bring pressure upon government over some issue. Production is privately controlled by each household in the comunidades even though the allocation of land or its use remains to varying degrees under collective control, and the very mention of collectivization provokes strong adverse reactions among members not only because it deprives households of autonomy – which they have sacrificed to some extent under existing arrangements anyhow – but also because it would subject an independent corporate group to state control. The Peruvian Agrarian Reform also created production co-operatives – a twentieth-century answer to the sixteenth-century *reducciones* – on the coast and in the sierra, with a view to exercising control over production, and indeed a measure of political control over the producers. Unfortunately, on the whole the surplus extracted was limited, and perhaps non-existent, except in the case of the coastal sugar co-operatives. This rather depressing experience – depressing for those who seek either capital accumulation or income redistribution through moderate reformism – of a military government in the twentieth century should cast doubts on the success of state-imposed controls in earlier centuries.

Apart from these external elements contributing to the dynamic of comunidad development or decline, there are also the internally differentiating factors, some of which I have already mentioned in discussing the role of caciques and *kurakas*. Not only did they occupy a position of privilege in the colonial hierarchy, they were also able, by various quite routine abuses, to promote others and thus further a process of differentiation through the comunidad institutions, and especially through the manipulation of taxation and access to land. In Peru, in the modern period, we observe rich peasant strata developing via the opportunities provided by comunidad organization (Long and Roberts 1978), and subtly transforming the comunidad institutions. The study of Muquiyauyo by Grondín in the volume edited by Long and Roberts shows a case where the comunidad, far from being an institution regulating access to land by individual households on the basis of inherited membership, was a small-scale version of a joint-stock company, with foreseeable consequences: rich peasant dominance, separation of those able to sustain the investment required from other members, once the comunidad basis had served its political and ideological purpose, and finally collapse into debt as the over-ambitious original venture lost its political clout and thus its access to markets, credit and government support. In other cases in the same area, the comunidad institution has enabled richer peasants to marshal labour resources in construction of irrigation systems, roads, and like infrastructure, and therefore enabled enrichment and differentiation to proceed.

There are in any case numerous places where the comunidad has disappeared. In Carchi, land tenure is purely individual and governed by national legislation, though this cannot be said of the Ecuadorian sierra as a whole. The same is true of Cajamarca in Northern Peru. But the disappearance of the comunidad does not, by any means, imply the disappearance of all the practices associated with it, in particular labour levies by comunidad-elected authorities for public works. For example, in Carchi, there is a proud tradition of collective labour contributions to public works, whose most 'heroic' expression was in the construction of a highway in the 1920s, which first enabled wheeled traffic to pass through the province. That particular effort, according to our researches, was led by local political leaders and financed to a large extent by landlords who provided sustenance and drink. But there are also routine activities on a smaller scale organized by the smallest administrative unit provided for in Ecuadorian law – the *cabildo*, or in its absence, the *parroquia* (parish). If it is well organized, the cabildo establishes a rota system whereby each household in turn must send a worker when a road or water-pipe has to be repaired, or some similar job has to be done, or otherwise pay a day's wage (often in the form of a bottle or two of *aguardiente*) as a substitute. Ironically, but by no means fortuitously, this practice is particularly common in the Huaca area, where migrants from neighbouring Colombia have deprived Indian communities of their commonly-held land by various forms of chicanery. *Mingas* are much less common in other parts of the province where haciendas retain a position of dominance.

The migrants from Colombia, when they initially established themselves in Carchi in the 1930s, did so independently of the state. In a hostile environment with hardly any circulation of money they had to help each other out on a reciprocal basis or, when it came to building social goods like roads, they were able to make contributions without too much fear that 'only the rich' would profit from their labours. As money began to circulate with great speed in the 1950s so the basis of co-operation began to change and today the calculation of money equivalents ensures more or less equal contributions from all. ('More or less' means precisely that; anything more would be utopian.) Above all, the absence of a history going back to the colonial period means the absence of the institutionalized chicanery of tax-intermediaries who are also community leaders; that is as integral a feature of comunidad structure as collective control over access to land, if not more so. In the area described there is absolutely no such collective control, communal activities being restricted to public works and repairs to infrastructure, occasionally even to the church.

It is standard practice in Ecuador for the state to provide capital for such works as the building of a school or a health centre, or the repair of a road, on condition that the local people provide the necessary labour. Despite the echo of earlier labour dues, these practices are quite distinct from the control of land tenure associated with the Peruvian comunidad, and they reflect the emergence of what I would call, for want of a better term, 'modern' co-operation, in which labour, or its money equivalent at market prices, is pooled by a set of individuals or households, in order to achieve specific finite tasks of interest to them all. The cabildo plays a purely administrative role in arranging any particular common affairs these people happen to have. The comunidades of the Chancay valley in Peru, by contrast, many of which are far from backwaters of stagnation and have experienced substantial increases in commercial production, retain their involvement in land tenure, albeit as institutions at the service of the peasant elite, or even of relatively wealthy migrants. In Lampián, for example, until 1930 access to land was conditional upon fulfilment of communal obligations and land reverted to the community on the death of a member (Celestino 1972). As population pressure on resources grew, it became more and more difficult to ensure that there was land for new generations, and thus to prevent people from adopting a *de facto* individualist inheritance system. However, the continued involvement of the comunidad in land tenure enabled individuals to use their wealth to reach positions of leadership and then to take advantage of their position in order first to acquire land and later to ensure that irrigation canals built by community labour flowed near it, as well as ensuring privileged access to community-owned pasture land. Such cases – which are the rule rather than the exception – show that abuse of power and a deviation from the 'original purpose' of the comunidad are inherent features of an institution established for tributary purposes, on the basis that some members of the comunidad are superior in status to others. The 'modern' form of co-operation, in which each person has equal obligations to the creation of a collective good, but in which land tenure is absolutely individual and obligations strictly convertible into money, is the more equitable. Thus we revert to the more liberating character of anonymous monetary circulation of commodities. Not that either is egalitarian; of course, some people benefit more than others from roads and from clean irrigation canals, but the question is whether institutions place them in a position where they can engage in systematic abuse of power.

We thus see how modern forms of inequality are penetrating even some apparently 'peasant' societies, as the allocation of resources by political means is replaced by the allocation of resources via the market mechanism. Perhaps the market mechanism was always there; perhaps corruption and the abuse of power were the consequence, in colonial times and subsequently, of misguided attempts to control it. But behind the collectivist rhetoric of today, it is inequality which has 'always been there' while the institutional and ideological framework of inequality has changed. Where once inequalities were imposed by imperial systems or by flaccid republican states in need of labour or money, they are now the result of the interaction between

David Lehmann

advanced and underdeveloped capitalist economies in a unified world trading system, and the apparent continuities of Andean society are few and far between. Verticality is not what it was; community is not what it was; only great mountain ranges and the spirits they shelter – both protective and hostile – remain unchanged.

Note

Although this essay is primarily an introduction to the other papers in the volume, it also draws on field research in which I am currently engaged in collaboration with Miguel Murmis, in the province of Carchi, Ecuador. I would like to thank Olivia Harris and Tristan Platt for comments on earlier versions.

2

The role of the Andean *ayllu* in the reproduction of the petty commodity regime in Northern Potosí (Bolivia)

TRISTAN PLATT

1. Introduction

The north of the Department of Potosí – formerly the Province of Chayanta – has long been considered one of the most 'traditional' regions of highland Bolivia, supposedly 'subsisting' at the fringes both of the market and of effective state control. This apparent marginality of the regional peasant economy contrasts with the great mining complexes which have developed in its midst:[1] Colquechaca and Aullagas, during the colonial and nineteenth-century silver era;[2] and more recently the massive tin-mining centre of Catavi–Siglo XX–Uncia. This chapter represents part of a research project (see Notes), which attempted to examine the forms of articulation by which regional peasant households, grouped into a complex hierarchy of 'communities' or *ayllus*,[3] are in fact linked with both labour and product markets. This also meant examining the possibilities for accumulation that exist within the Andean peasant economy of Northern Potosí. Thus one point of departure has been the search for quantitative data in order to test the empirical basis of the dualistic scheme, which opposes the mining 'enclave' to the 'subsistence economy' of the Andean peasant.

However, the synchronic application of this dualistic model disguises what is effectively a negation of history. In contrast with the northern altiplano of La Paz,[4] Northern Potosí is remarkable for the small success which *hacendados* – above all, from Chuquisaca – had in expanding into the region prior to the Revolution of 1952. Thus, in most of the region only limited attempts have been made to apply the Agrarian Reform Law of 1953, which was designed above all as a measure for establishing a regime of individual smallholders in areas previously controlled by the *hacienda*. If we evade the complex and little studied history of the Bolivian *ayllus*, it becomes natural to affirm that, since the best farming lands were precisely those most attractive to the hacienda, the communities of 'free Indians' correspond to the regions least integrated into the market economy. From there it is a short step to the conclusion that a mass of 'traditional' communities with pitiful productive levels continue to vegetate at the margins, both of the 'capitalist enclaves', and of history itself.

Research on Northern Potosí is now sufficiently advanced for us to be able to reject such models – which still, however, dominate the thinking of both national development agencies, and certain sectors of the Bolivian Left. We are beginning to recognize the significance of the surpluses – both labour and products – contributed by the ayllus of Northern Potosí to the accumulative processes of the successive state and economic formations to which they have belonged.[5] Naturally, the precise mechanisms of surplus extraction have varied enormously in different periods. This means that present levels of sales of labour and agricultural products must be considered within a particular 'constellation' of articulatory mechanisms, which is the product of recent history, rather than attributing these levels to some mythical condition of 'original poverty'.

If we examine the situation of the Indians of Chayanta during the early decades of the republican era, for example, we find a total reversal of their present image. They were considered, indeed, amongst the richest Indians of Bolivia, and therefore those most able to support the burden of the tribute on which state finances depended.[6] For 1846 the protectionist statistician José María Dalence was able to show a higher level of wheat-production for the Department of Potosí than for Cochabamba itself, and most of Potosí's wheat came from Chayanta (Dalence 1848). The Chayanta ayllus supplied the markets of Oruro and La Paz, as well as trading their produce in the *yungas* of La Paz, and even as far as the Pacific coast. The basis of this prosperity was destroyed by the opening of Bolivian markets to the finer-milled production of the Chilean and Peruvian flour-mills, in the wake of the Chilean victory during the War of the Pacific of 1879 (Grieshaber 1979). At the same time, probably to replace the lost markets with a new source of cash with which to pay the tribute, the Indians of Chayanta seem to have begun to sell seasonal labour in the small regional mines, temporarily eclipsed by the success of the capital-intensive mines of Colquechaca, but now once again economically viable as the world price of silver declined.[7] It is possible, therefore, that the origins of the particular 'articulatory constellation' now in existence – based on the sale of seasonal labour, low out-migration, and low levels of agricultural sales outside certain clearly defined zones – must be looked for in the success of liberal economic policies in the last decades of the nineteenth century, which structured the national economy upon the export of primary materials (metals, above all) and the importation of consumer-goods.

Even before 1880, however, the regional peasant economy seems to have been unwilling to expel the labour required by the local mines on a permanent basis;[8] whereas during the present century, the new mining proletariat was formed predominantly through the importation of labour from Cochabamba, where the process of peasant differentiation was already far advanced by the end of the eighteenth century (Larson 1978). Even granted that the ratio of land to population is still far more favourable in Northern Potosí than, for example, in the northern altiplano, the apparent unwillingness of the local Indians to leave the land permanently raises important questions concerning internal ayllu mechanisms of land distribution. In this chapter we analyse these mechanisms as they operate today,[9] paying particular attention to the way in which access to maize-producing Valley lands is allocated among peasants resident on the Puna. We argue that, in analysing the capacity of an agricultural region to serve as a 'reserve army' for the needs of industry, it is necessary to examine the *structure of the supply* of labour, as this is determined – *inter alia* – by the elasticity of the mechanisms of land distribution within a 'traditional' peasant society such as we find in Northern Potosí.

An analysis of the rules which ensure access to Valley lands for some 25% of the Puna population also allows us to relate the traditional Andean strategy of 'vertical control' to internal processes of differentiation within Andean society (Murra 1972a). Historical research has shown how the seventeenth-century ayllu lords (*kurakas*) were able to develop their commercial activities on a grand scale, due to their privileged access to community labour prestations and to a wide variety of ecological levels, from the high Puna pastures (4200–4600 metres above sea-level) to the warm Valley floors (2000–3500 metres above sea-level).[10] Even in the more 'egalitarian' community conditions of today,[11] we find that those who are able to combine the agricultural cycles of Puna and Valley are those with the highest levels of production, consumption and sales.

We argue, however, that this trend towards differentiation within the ayllu is today held in check by the insertion of peasant economy within what Bartra has called a process of 'permanent primitive accumulation'.[12] This favours the maintenance of the petty commodity mode of production which has formed the basis of state agricultural policy since 1953, insofar as such a regime requires the predominance of the independent peasant household as the basis of agricultural production. Even within this negative context, however, we argue that the ayllu in Northern Potosí fulfils certain key functions for the reproduction of this petty commodity regime.

Finally, it should be noted that in this chapter we limit our attention to the 'purely agricultural' portion of the universe under study; apart from the mechanisms of land distribution, which have a more general relevance, we are here chiefly interested in the conditions which permit the peasant household to produce and sell more agricultural products. However, slightly more than half (53%) of the 500 Puna productive units sampled declared that they sold nothing, and most of these fell within the 51% who declared seasonal sales of domestic labour. Although we examine the regional factors which limit permanent out-migration, we analyse elsewhere the internal economy of the households which are obliged to sell seasonal labour to cover their cash requirements (Molina and Platt 1979).

2. The spatial distribution of resources and dispersed forms of tenure

Three areas of farming activity may be distinguished among the peasants of Northern Potosí, corresponding approximately to three ecological 'tiers' which fall away through the eastern slopes of the Cordillera de los Frailes:

(1) High Andean herding (4200–4600 metres above sea-level)
(2) Puna agriculture (3500–4200 metres above sea-level)
(3) Valley agriculture (2000–3500 metres above sea-level)

Within each tier a wide range of micro-climates must further be distinguished: together these offer the pre-conditions for the production of a wide variety of crops and animal species, although individually considered their productive capacity is highly limited. Andean ethno-botany is revealing the vast range of species, varieties and forms which have arisen in the tropical Andes, permitting the development of sedentary agricultural populations in conditions unknown elsewhere in the world (Troll 1968). The Puna ecotype is characterized by extremely unstable energy flows which render agricultural activity susceptible to high risks; crop diversification across differing tiers and micro-climates, in order to create 'multiple resource bases' (Thomas 1972; cf. Fonseca 1972), has traditionally constituted an essential strategy for surviving the uncertainties of the high Andean climate. As a result, peasant holdings have tended to consist of numerous highly fragmented parcels, frequently located at great distances from their owner's residence.

Technical experts and other 'concerned observers' often criticize this fragmentation as 'irrational', recalling as it does the typical features of the *minifundio*. Although sustained demographic growth will no doubt lead to a reduction in the size of family holdings, this process should not be confused with the acquisition of a 'multiple resource base' in High Andean conditions. In the northern altiplano, for example, government ignorance over this point has led to the redistribution of hacienda lands in integrated plots among peasant households by Agrarian Reform authorities; the result has been a period of intense litigation, as the new title-holders redistribute their land once again in order to recover their 'multiple resource bases'.[13]

In the first place, this strategy of land-use may lead the peasant producer to sow a single crop in small quantities on several dispersed parcels, in order to protect himself against hail, frost, flooding, or other highly localized hazards.

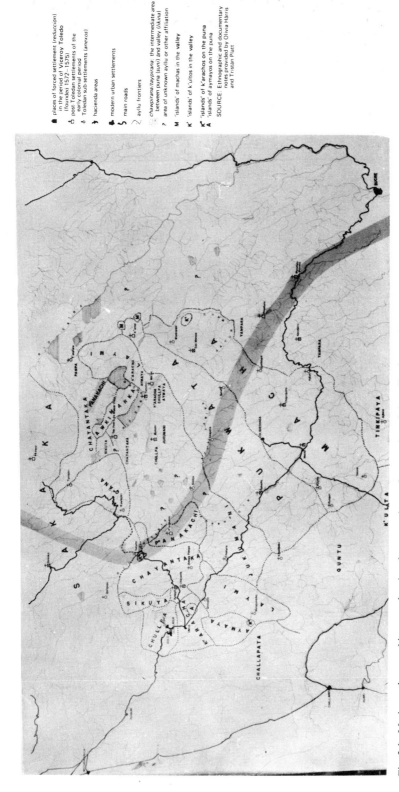

Fig. 2.1. Modern ethnographic map, showing the approximate demarcation of the ayllus in Northern Potosi.

Ecological Level			
1		High Andean Herding	**P**

Upper Limit of Agriculture   c. 4200 metres above sea-level

2 High Andean hillsides	Potatoes: *turu luk'i* *sayt'u luk'i* *aqhawiri* *luru*	*(Solanum Juzepczukii)* *(Solanum Ajanhuiri)*	**U**
	Quinoas: *t'una* *alqa*	*(Chenopodium)*	
	Barley		

3 Fields without irrigation	Potatoes: *jalq'amari* *jank'a* *lap'iya* *pipina* *pali* *saq'anpaya* *sulimana* *tuni*	} *(Solanum Andigenum)*	
	Quinoa: *jatun*	*(Chenopodium)*	**N**
	Isaña	*(Tropaeolum tuberosum)*	
	Ocas: *sapallo* *yuraj* *puka*	*(Oxalis tuberosa)*	
	Lisa	*(Ullucus tuberosus)*	

4 Fields with irrigation	Wheat		
	Broad Beans		
	Potato: *imilla*	*(Solanum Andigenum)*	**A**
	Dwarf Maize: *sara ch'isiwayu*		

Lower Limit of *t'ula (Lepidophyllum Quadrangulare)*   c. 3500 metres above sea-level.
'Intermediate Region' or *chawpirana*.

5
Valley
hill-top
	Potatoes:
	  imilla
	  runa
	  puka ñawi
		(Solanum Andigenum)	

	Lisa	*(Ullucus tuberosus)*	
	Oca	*(Oxalis tuberosa)*	<
	Isaña	*(Tropaeolum tuberosum)*	
	Quinoa	*(Chenopodium)*	
	Wheat		

	Maize:
	  jank'a
	  yuraj
			A

6
Mid-
hillside
	Potatoes:
	  runa
	  puka ñawi
		(Solanum Andigenum)	⌐

	Wheat		
	Tarwi	*(Lupinus tauri)*	
	Onions		
	Fruit		⌐

	Maize:
	  jank'a
	  yuraj		

7 River-level (with irrigation)	Chilli Peppers		⊓
	Squashes		
	Potato: *mishka*		
	Fruit		
	Sugar-Cane		<

	Maize:
	  muruchi
	  piritu		

Fig. 2.2. The vertical distribution of the principal crops in Northern Potosí

33

Second, Puna land requires long fallow periods, forcing the peasant to adopt several rotation cycles. This means that he must control a far larger area of cultivable land than that which is actually under cultivation in any one year. The fallow period may last six or seven years for lower Puna lands, and up to twenty years at the highest agricultural levels. Thus a rotation of four crops (potato, oca, quinoa, barley, for example) will require access to twenty-four plots in order to complete the cycle. Here too, other things being equal, population growth may lead to a reduction in the fallow periods, with a consequent reduction in land-productivity. Nevertheless, the rotational cycles impose a far wider distribution of agricultural activity than is the case outside the Andean region.

Finally, the optimal conditions for each of the crops which together constitute the 'multiple resource base' may be located at great distances from each other. Thus in Northern Potosí the high pastures, where camelids and the largest flocks of sheep are reared, can be as much as 120 kilometres from the irrigated fields in the warm Valleys, where chilli-peppers, squashes, sugar, maize and – in the past – cotton are cultivated. Figure 2.2 shows the approximate distribution of the principal Andean crops known today in Northern Potosí, together with certain European species which have been incorporated into the productive regime. The distribution shown is only approximate, since land quality may vary greatly from one region to another. Nor is altitude the only determinant of crop distribution. Thus the high hillsides, which are less exposed to frost, are preferred over the level fields for planting some crops susceptible to cold; on the Puna, an intense morning sun coming after a frost may destroy a crop. Each peasant must adapt his strategy to the local topography, and if he lacks the optimum micro-climate for a particular crop, he may choose to sow it outside its preferred environment in spite of the consequent decrease in productivity.

Now, we have found no cases of peasants who control *directly*[14] the entire range of ecological niches shown in figure 2.2. Herders on level 1 may have access to land on level 2, but are unlikely to control land on levels 3 and 4, though they may rent in some parcels on these levels from the farmers below. Peasants on level 3 will probably have access to land on levels 2 and 4, but not to the highland pastures, satisfying their more limited needs with pasture on fallow land or on nearby hillsides within the Puna agricultural zone. Valley peasants resident at levels 6 or 7 will normally have access to all three Valley levels, but their access to the Puna levels will depend on certain mechanisms to be analysed later. Finally, the inhabitants of the intermediate zone between Puna and Valley (*chawpirana/taypirana*) will have access to frontier lands between both zones, but not to land at opposite extremes of altitude.

However, it should not be thought that each household will only have access to land on adjacent levels. Thomas (1972) has shown how the household units living on the highest levels must search for energy sources from outside the Puna eco-system. Ecological support has thus been provided for Murra's ethno-historical thesis (1972a), which analyses the strategy of 'vertical control of a maximum of ecological levels' among pre-Colombian Andean societies. This model underlies the practice found among many highland dwellers, both herders and farmers, whereby land may also be directly controlled in the Valley: since the colonial period, this practice has been locally known as 'dual residence'.[15] Thus it is common to find a series of parcels, distributed between *discontinuous* ecological levels, all components of a single peasant holding.

Ideally considered, this model of land-holding reflects the attempts of Puna peasants to counteract climatic instabilities through the *direct* control of production in distant eco-systems (Harris 1978a). In the early stages of Andean agriculture it also facilitated economic self-sufficiency, eliminating the need to depend on other specialized groups for access to crucial products. This aspiration was consolidated in the period of the Aymara-speaking federations, and was converted into state policy by the Inca (Salomon 1978). However, we doubt that the goal of self-sufficiency plays an important role today, for reasons which will appear later, although it may persist as a nostalgic dream in some areas.

As is to be expected, the pattern of 'dual residence' affects the distribution of labour and inputs within the domestic production unit, which is the dominant form of economic organization in rural Northern Potosí. Thus animal fertilizer goes 'down' from the corrals and high pasture lands to the ploughed fields below; a flock may also be put out to pasture on lands just entering cultivation. Oxen from the Valley may be taken up to the Puna to be used as draught-animals during the highland sowing season, taking advantage of the abundant highland pastures before descending once more to the Valley. Beasts of burden – donkeys, mules, male llamas – are used during sowing and harvest to carry seed, fertilizer, tools and the crop itself between distant parcels and the domestic storehouses; they also transport the crop or other produce (particularly salt) between Puna and Valley, and to national markets. Thus the combination of inputs in the course of production is greatly eased by direct access to a wide variety of the levels distinguished in figure 2.2.

Finally, it is clear that a domestic unit with land in Puna and Valley must ensure a 'vertical' distribution of its family labour. Since the Puna agricultural calendar falls one to three months earlier than its Valley counterpart, the entire family can – in principle – move between both zones, permitting a more intense utilization of its domestic labour, with consequences to be analysed below.

3. The tribute ('contribución territorial'): legal forms of access to land

Such is the diversity of the regional resources which form the basis of peasant economy in Northern Potosí; we must now examine the legal forms which govern the distribution of these resources between the domestic units of production. In the first place, access to land is still mediated by each household's membership of a 'community' or ayllu; these institutions continue to restrict each household's freedom to dispose of its holding, not only because of the local ideology which vests an eminent right over land in the ayllu, as in pre-Columbian and colonial times, but also because the state itself (in spite of frequent attempts to abolish the ayllus) continues to use these groups and their representatives for tax-collection purposes.[16] In this section we shall be concerned with this tax as a mechanism which legitimizes each household's access to land.

Until the end of the nineteenth century, an important proportion of state revenue consisted in the tribute extracted from the Indian communities. Sánchez-Albornóz (1978: 198) has shown that, in 1838, 52.7% of all state income came from this source; even after the recovery of silver mining in 1880, the proportion was still 22.7%. At the level of the departmental treasuries, the Indian *contribución territorial* retained its importance right up to the Chaco War (1932–5) – a situation very different from Peru, where the colonial tribute had been abolished by 1850. In order to ensure this surplus extraction, the state tried to establish a relation between land and population, such that the Indian economy could reproduce itself autonomously, while still achieving adequate production levels for a portion to be appropriated by the national or departmental treasuries. Periodic registers (*Revisitas*) of the Indian population were therefore carried out until the end of the last century, confirming or redistributing household rights to ayllu land. Before the uncompleted *Revisita* of 1882–1903, Northern Potosí Indian chiefs (kurakas) would generally communicate the changes since the previous register to the tax-officials, whose intervention in internal ayllu affairs was minimal. The six-monthly tribute varied according to the tax category of each householder, whose rights were revalidated at each ceremony of payment.

The last Revisita of 1882–1903 was violently resisted by the Indian communities of Northern Potosí, as it represented a radical departure from previous practice: its aim was to implement the 1874 'Law of Expropriation', abolishing the ayllus, measuring each household plot, issuing individual titles, and recalculating the tribute as a tax on annual production. Its further aim was to create a national market in land, in order to pave the way for the expansion of the hacienda. Although none of these objectives was fully achieved, the titles issued by the land commission are still considered by Northern Potosí peasants as a point of reference so far as their rights to land are concerned. It must be remembered that in this region the 1953 Agrarian Reform has had only a superficial effect, particularly in the Puna zone, since the persistence of the ayllus in Northern Potosí makes it difficult to apply measures which were designed for areas controlled by the hacienda. In certain respects, indeed, the 1953 Agrarian Reform Law should be considered as a renewal of the nineteenth-century attempts to implement the 'Law of Expropriation': it too aimed at destroying the ayllus and issuing individual rights, as well as replacing the tribute with a new 'Single Tax' (*Impuesto Unico*). Like its predecessor, therefore, it has been violently resisted by many ayllus.

The land-tax was the subject of debate throughout the nineteenth century. Most considered it a shameful residue of colonial exploitation, and the ayllus as a block to the expansion of capitalist agriculture. Nevertheless, as often as it was abolished, state finances required its instant restoration, though under a different name (Sánchez-Albornóz 1978: 187–218). The colonial 'tribute' was successively transformed into an 'Indian contribution' (contribución indigenal) and a 'land contribution' (contribución territorial), even though the word *tributo* persisted – almost like a *lapsus linguae* – in the texts of the period. From the sixteenth century till the present day, however, the peasants have preferred to talk of the *tasa*, and I shall adopt this usage since it enables us to relate these legal dues with the distribution of the resources discussed in the last section. Thus, the term *tasa* not only refers to the tax collected by the state, but also to the land-holding over which tax payment secures control. More precisely, a tasa consists of a variable number of plots, both cultivated and fallow, lying on levels 3 to 7 in figure 2.2; herders must also pay the tasa to ensure their access to high pastures. The tasa lands stand in contrast to lands on level 2, which demand the longest fallow periods: the peasants insist that these lands, whose rotation is managed collectively for reasons we shall come to presently, are not tasa lands. They are known as *mantas*,[17] and the distinction corresponds to the better-known altiplano contrast between *sayña* and *aynuqa* (Carter 1965).

Now the traditional tax categories recognized by the colonial and nineteenth-century registers correspond to different forms of access to the regional resources on the part of each category of households. Those with greatest security of tenure were called *originarios*, descendants – supposedly – of the ayllu members recognized by the first colonial tax registers in the sixteenth century. With the passage of generations, those Indians who could show direct descent from the original beneficiaries were confirmed in the secure and inalienable possession of their land on condition that they fulfilled their obligations to the ayllu and to the state. Needless to say, with each re-registration fewer were able to produce genealogical evidence in support of their claims; other Indians might therefore be inscribed in the category of originarios, provided they received the permission of the other originarios, and agreed to pay the appropriate amount of tax. According to today's octogenarian kuraka of Macha (Aransaya, or upper moiety), the originarios were confirmed by each Revisita in the possession of both Puna and Valley lands, and had to pay $b5.00 for this dual access;[18] their further access to manta lands was considered a consequence of their possession of a tasa, not of their payment of the tax.

Besides this category of persons with land-rights supposedly *ab initio*, a second group was recognized who had originally entered the community to cultivate its surplus land, thus increasing the number of persons available to the ayllu authorities for fulfilling the obligations to the state, and protecting ayllu frontiers against encroachment by neighbouring communities. Known as *agregados*, their access was restricted either to Puna or to Valley land, and they paid $b3.00 for this more limited access to regional resources. Thus the state also had an interest in their official registration, since they helped to swell the total tax collected. Their agregado status implied less security of tenure, however, and could be used against them by originarios in cases of conflict over land. A suit brought in 1871, shortly before the last Revisita, gives us the tone of the relationship between originarios and agregados. The originario plaintiffs complained

that these ambitious Mamanis were brought here as *agregados* by our forefathers who did them the favour of registering them in our lands, since they had nowhere to live, and now with the passage of time, and though we have held on to the said lands as is shown by the presence of our animals in them, these greedy people wish to take them over and plant their crops in the corrals of our very houses ...

Indios de Tinguipaya, Colección de Minutas de 1928. In Notaría de Hacienda, Potosí.

Elsewhere in the same case, the agregados are accused of having paid the tax corresponding to the land in question: it can be seen how yesterday's newcomers are looking for a change, not only in the size of their holdings, but also in their tax status.[19]

A third mode of obtaining access to land was even less secure. Known in Quechua as *kantu runas* (*witu jaqi* in Aymara), these peasants had no rights at all to the land, beyond the usufruct ceded to them by the originario or agregado title-holders. In return for being allowed to cultivate in the margins of the title-holders' possessions, the kantu runas (literally, 'men of the margin') performed small favours for their patrons and offered services to the local priest in representation of their ayllu of residence. Since 1882 no tax was required of these 'aliens without lands' (*forasteros sin tierras*).[20]

Today, as in the sixteenth century, the payment of taxes by originarios and agregados takes place at a six-monthly meeting (*cabildo*) of the whole ayllu. Known as the St John and Christmas cabildos, they only approximately coincide with the corresponding religious festivals (24 June and 25

December respectively).[21] These cabildos are festive celebrations, with chicha and coca-leaf distributed by the Indian tax-collector (*cobrador*) for the year in question, and are presided over by the ayllu authorities. Each tax-payer is called by name to appear before the ceremonial table, and must pay his dues in the presence of other ayllu members; each person's land-rights therefore receive public confirmation at each cabildo. If anyone fails to appear, another may volunteer the required sum, thus acquiring rights to the land in question (as the Tinguipaya case cited above illustrates). In this way an agregado can gain rights to originario land with the collective approval of those present. At the nineteenth-century Revisitas, the land commissioner would ratify these changes of status, following the indications received from the kurakas and assembled Indians. As we shall see, the same mechanism might allow a nineteenth-century originario to expand his holding to include an agregado tasa.

How then has this 'traditional' situation been modified since the last Revisita of 1882–1903, and in particular since the Agrarian Reform of 1953? I have already mentioned the confused legal situation which has arisen because of difficulties in adapting the Agrarian Reform to Northern Potosí conditions. In fact, the departmental prefect reconfirmed the tributary obligations of the ayllu Indians in 1975,[22] while at the same time Agrarian Reform topographers have begun to draw up collective claims for certain communities. Today the value of the tax is purely symbolic: whereas three generations ago it was equivalent to the value of a yoke of oxen (Harris 1978a: 54), today it would scarcely buy a packet of cigarettes. Formally speaking, however, the ayllu Indians still consider payment of the tax as an important guarantee of their rights to land, although the weakening authority of the kurakas allows some stretching of the traditional rules, as the fifth generation since the last Revisita reaches economic independence.

To clarify the ambiguities which have arisen in this way, let us examine a simplified case drawn from the Macha area, which shows how holdings have been subdivided since the last Revisita in a fluctuating demographic context. The case is presented graphically in figure 2.3. Here we can see how the originario ancestor (A) was assigned two tasas, one of them an originario tasa allowing access to Puna and Valley lands, the other an agregado tasa allowing access to Puna lands only. The holding was first divided between his two sons B and C, B receiving the originario tasa and C the agregado tasa. Of B's two sons, D received the Puna section of the originario tasa, and E the Valley section. The micro-climatic diversity within each section is shown summarily on the diagram. Only in the fourth generation were the Puna lands subdivided, each beneficiary (G, H, J, K) receiving access to all the local micro-climates (a, b, c, d). It is only now, in the fifth generation, that previously uncultivated land is being brought into production by the married sons of H. Thus the marginal land of the original holding,

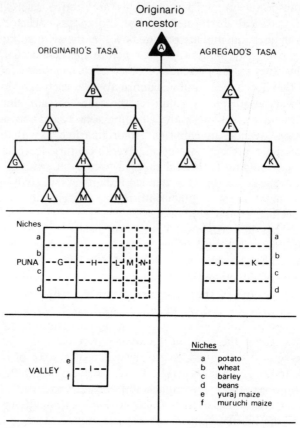

Fig. 2.3. Simplified example of the subdivision of the holding of an originario among his patrilineal descendants over five generations

previously neglected due to labour shortage and/or lack of demographic pressure is only now being cultivated by the descendants of A.

We must now ask how the various household heads represented in figure 2.3 have classified themselves with respect to their tax status. Ancestor A paid $b8.00 (according to the present kuraka of Aransaya) corresponding to the two tasas assigned to him. Once the two tasas were divided between his two sons, B and C became respectively originario and agregado: B therefore paid $b5.00 while C paid $b3.00. B's son E moved to the Valley, while D remained on the Puna paying the tax for the originario tasa: E's share of that tax was at first covered by an equal division of E's maize harvest between D and E. Only when E's son, I, had established himself permanently in the Valley, was the originario tasa formally divided, with a tax of $b3.00 on each section. As a result D became an agregado, having begun as an originario. We may suppose that this agreement between D and I was only reached once the real value of the tax had fallen, so that tenure was consolidated within each branch of the family without an increase in the real value of the tax.

Passing now to the fourth generation since A, how was the new agregado tax divided between the descendants of D? For several years, G and H were in the same situation as L, M and N (H's sons) now find themselves in: they did not formally divide the holding, preferring to sow their crops on its marginal lands, and leaving their father to pay the now devalued tax. Meanwhile they called themselves kantu runas – the term seems admirably suited to such a Chayanovian situation – men who were indeed cultivating *in the margins* of their father's holding. Only after H's death, which occurred just as his sons L, M and N were reaching their majority, did G take on the status of agregado and begin to contribute to his father's largely symbolic tax obligations. Now the fifth generation have assumed the status of kantu runas; they pay no tax, and are extending the cultivated portion of the tasa of their forefathers.

In this case we have seen how the land originally assigned to ancestor A has been fragmented in accordance with the lateral extension of the branches of his family. But since access to land is justified by reference to a single ancestor, the members of each branch have a residual right to the land of other branches: given the unequal growth of each branch, therefore, the possibility remains of reuniting portions of the original holding, according to the demographic conditions within each branch. Thus we find that I, the heir to the Valley lands, finding himself childless, approached H before the latter's death to propose joint cultivation of the Valley parcel. Similarly, the fact that F has few descendents would enable the heirs of D to extend their fields into the tasa of C's heirs, if their needs justified this move.[23]

It is possible that the mechanisms described are of great antiquity, and represent the way in which the Indian population adapted the tax categories to the requirements of the developmental cycle of each domestic group. Changes of tax category were certainly recognized during the nineteenth-century Revisitas, although naturally the bureaucratic sources do not offer so detailed a picture as can be gained through ethnographic field work. However, with the demise of the Revisitas during the present century, it is also possible that the flexibility of the tax categories in relation to the developmental cycle is the consequence of the lifting of state restrictions on the redistribution of population in relation to land available. Further ethno-historical research will be necessary to resolve this question.

Clearly, where there exists a territorial margin into which the family may expand, the use of a concept such as minifundio would be inappropriate. Where spare land does not exist, however, further mechanisms for the redistribution of land and population may come into play. Marriage strategies,

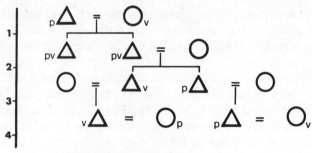

p = with access to Puna land
v = with access to Valley land

Fig. 2.4. The generational cycles of inter-zonal marriages

for example, may be designed to acquire land far away from a man's birth-place. In the foregoing exposition, we have assumed a virilocal marriage system; exogamic restrictions, combined with patrilineal inheritance of land,[24] lead to the expulsion of women from their birthplaces and their incorporation into other patrilocal groups. Such groups will seek to ensure their reproduction or expansion by continually creating new households with women recruited from other patrilocal groups. However, if a man has no male heirs, he may endow his daughters with a part of the family holding, converting them into highly desirable matches for the sons of land-scarce families. In such cases marriage will be uxorilocal and the offspring will bear the surname of their maternal grandfather. Thus the exception is brought into line with the inheritance system, in which land is also named after the family with rights to its cultivation (Willka tasa, Mamani tasa, for example).

A man with Puna lands may also choose to marry a woman with land in the Valley, in order to re-establish the pattern of 'vertical' control in circumstances where this has been lost. We have already seen how such a loss may result from the subdivision of an originario tasa between two brothers, although the kinship bond allowed each to retain access to the products of the other ecological zone.[25] But clearly an increase in their descendants will lead to a weakening of the kinship link which unites the household productive units in each zone. It then becomes possible to recreate the link through inter-zonal marriage. Genealogies collected among Valley peasants (Platt 1978a: 1106 n.6) allow us to propose the following model (figure 2.4), which shows such inter-zonal alliances as moments in a generational cycle.

According to the model, a Puna–Valley alliance will become particularly attractive after three to four generations have passed since the previous vertical marriage of the corresponding patrilineage. This is due to the gradual attenuation of the kinship ties created by the earlier marriage, or by the subdivision of the originario tasa. We may suggest, then, that at any one moment, only a quarter of the domestic units on the Puna will have access to Valley lands as well. The rural survey of 1978 offers some support for this claim: out of the 500 Puna household heads interviewed, some 25% (127/500) declared themselves owners of land in both zones. We can therefore suggest that land fragmentation is counterbalanced by mechanisms of reunification such that, at any given moment and assuming constant demographic conditions, a quarter of the Puna peasants will enjoy privileged access to inter-zonal resources.

We may therefore conclude as follows:

(1) The tasas derived from the nineteenth-century Revisitas have fragmented to the point where most peasants consider themselves either agregados or kantu runas, according to their position within the domestic cycle and the man–land ratio in their locality.

(2) The devaluation of the tax has reduced their fiscal obligations to almost nothing in real terms, although the tax payments retain their formal–symbolic importance in confirming rights of usufruct. Today, surplus is extracted from the ayllus directly through the labour and product markets.

(3) The fragmentation of holdings should not be labelled too hastily as minifundismo, since:

(a) the distribution of each peasant's holding across different ecological zones and micro-climates is characteristic of high Andean agriculture, and represents an adaptation, under given technological conditions, to high levels of climatic risk;

(b) the inheritance system permits the consolidation of fragmented holdings, in order to counterbalance the effects of uneven growth in different branches of descendants from a common ancestor;

(c) marriage strategies permit land-poor male peasants to create new holdings with their wives' lands and, in particular, to reconstitute dual control over Puna and Valley lands which the development of the generational cycle has undermined.

4. The peasant hamlet: its dynamic and economic function

Present-day family holdings have arisen, then, on the basis of the tasas assigned at the end of the past century to those peasants who, at that moment, constituted the categories of originarios, agregados and kantu runas. However, the Revisitas took as their point of departure a single chronological moment in the constant process of demographic movement and territorial redistribution. In the last section we examined certain aspects of this internal dynamic of peasant society, whose development the land commissioners were, of course, in no position to control. Thus each register offered a picture of a 'frozen' moment in this process, whose validity was soon lost as the dynamic of peasant society continued. This rupture between Revisita and reality can be understood more clearly if we consider the residential pattern of the domestic units of production.

So far the analysis has centred on the *household*, economically autonomous and therefore the nucleus of petty commodity production, and the *patrilocal group*, local expression of the patrilineal rules which govern land inheritance. The latter gives rise to peasant *hamlets*, whose size fluctuates according to local demographic movements. In the simplest model, the patrilocal group of houses is built on barren land beside the holding originally assigned to a common ancestor, and now distributed among the production units which have sprung from that ancestor. Now, at the precise moment of the last Revisita, each hamlet (or patrilocal group) was in an earlier stage of growth or decay. The land commissioners therefore assigned a variable number of tasas to each hamlet – one or two for an isolated household, a greater number for a hamlet already composed of various domestic units.

Let us consider the example presented in the last section (figure 2.3). Here, the land commissioners assigned two tasas, one originario, the other agregado, to the single ancestor (A) of the households which today occupy the same tasas. The descendants who inherited the agregado tasa have shown little population growth: today, a single courtyard is flanked by three mud-brick buildings, which constitute the homes and storeroom of the two household units headed by J and K. The descendants of B, on the other hand, have multiplied to the point of overflowing the cultivated area towards the marginal lands of the holding. Today they own ten houses, with a total of thirteen rooms, which represent the homes and storerooms of the six living families descended from B. Other hamlets are much bigger, since they were already in the stage of expansion at the time of the last Revisita; some households on the other hand are isolated since they have installed themselves only recently on unclaimed land, according to mechanisms which will be analysed shortly.

In short, we can suppose that the process of disintegration which has affected the originario holding of figure 2.3 will have developed in the past after each registration, until rationalized once more at the time of the next registration.

The formation of hamlets on the margins of cultivated or fallow land is characteristic of the Puna. There, a variable number of these residential groups, with their land, compose a minimal ayllu, or cabildo.[26] Each hamlet also claims access to manta lands. In the Valley, on the other hand, such nucleation is exceptional:[27] each household will tend to split off from the paternal residence, and construct its home alone in the middle of its maize fields.

This difference in residence patterns as between ecological zones can be

44

related to the absence of mantas in the Valley. On the Puna, the decision to open new mantas in well-fallowed areas, and the order of the crops sown each year in each manta, is co-ordinated among all the household heads of the corresponding hamlet. Traditionally, the mantas were redistributed among the households of each hamlet by the leader of each minimal ayllu (*alcalde*); today this redistribution is only vestigial, except in cases of conflict, and most households know which mantas are for their use. However, collective control is maintained over the selection of fallows, and over the direction of the rotational cycle, for reasons of security. For, as the time approaches for each hamlet to open a new block of choice fallows, a dilemma arises. From one point of view the moment should be delayed as long as possible, in order for the land to recover its optimum condition; on the other hand, if the hamlet waits too long, another hamlet may leap at the chance of cultivating such apparently abandoned resources. Most of the land battles (*ch'ajwas*) which take place over Puna ayllu frontiers are caused by conflicting hamlet claims to border mantas; this threat means that each hamlet must mobilize collectively in defence of the disputed lands. Mobilization is facilitated by the co-ordination of manta cultivation among all hamlet members, uniting individual interests in relation to a homogeneous area. Such security precautions are not necessary in the Valley, where there are no mantas.

This mechanism, like the inheritance system described earlier, shows how the ayllu ensures the reproduction of the minimum conditions for agricultural production, allowing the peasant smallholder to serve as a source of surplus and thus to contribute to the reproduction of the entire Bolivian social formation. According to the rural survey of 1978, some 10% of family expenditure is absorbed by ayllu obligations; this should be interpreted as a productive investment which contributes to guarantee the reproduction of each productive unit.

Even reducing the length of rotation cycles, however, each hamlet has only limited possibilities for expansion, and the marginal flexibility represented by the individual strategies we have examined so far may become exhausted. There exists a further solution within the dynamic of Northern Potosí peasant society. Sons without land may be expelled from the hamlet towards other more distant lands, where they will install themselves, either in low manta lands without effective owners (in this case they will try to convert mantas into tasas); or, alternatively, in the margins of the tasas of other hamlets with less population. Such solutions will lead to an increase in kantu runas or agregados within the ayllu. We have observed cases of such population 'transplants' both on the Puna, where a group of families will try to establish a new hamlet, and in the Valley, where an isolated family had to look for the approval of the ayllu dominating its new neighbourhood. Clearly, such a solution may produce serious conflicts concerning the ayllu membership of the new settlers: on the Puna we have evidence that such a family group chose to name their own tax-collector (cobrador), with the consequent creation of a new minimal ayllu, or cabildo.[28]

Further alternatives are offered, in the last resort, through the channels which articulate the Northern Potosí peasant economy with the wider society. Land scarcity may oblige a productive unit to increase the mass of seasonal migrants, although other factors, such as lack of animals, may also be relevant. This means of access to sources of money or kind has long been incorporated into the annual calendar of the Northern Potosí peasant: traditionally it has involved temporary labour in the small mines, and the waste-heaps of the larger ones; today many peasants contribute to swell the tertiary sector of the mining centres of Siglo XX–Catavi (as bearers), or the seasonal migrations towards the sugar plantations in Santa Cruz. Some will seek work in the maize fields of the same region, in order to ensure access to basic staples whose production is impossible with the range of ecological levels at the disposition of their household unit (see the case of Ravelo in the next section). The rural survey has shown that 51.6% (258/500) of the households interviewed had expelled seasonal labour during the year 1977–8, with an average period of absence of three months. Parallel to the sale of farm products, then, the seasonal sale of labour constitutes an important means of access to cash, and strengthens the subordination of the peasant household to the national markets of consumer goods and labour.

The most intense form of articulation with the labour market is, of course, permanent out-migration towards the cities or areas of colonization in the tropical lowlands. The rural survey has shown, however, that only 13% (69/500) of the households interviewed had lost members in this way, in contrast to an equivalent figure of 38% for the northern altiplano. The average number of migrants lost was 1.98, or 0.26 for the sample as a whole, in contrast to a figure of 0.8 for the northern altiplano. The comparison suggests a more favourable man–land ratio in Northern Potosí, and the continuing effectiveness of local mechanisms of land distribution.[29]

Our analysis casts strong doubts on any account of the labour market in terms of a 'reserve army' whose size would vary exclusively as a result of fluctuations in demand in the industrial centres. Equally important is the *structure of supply*, and this must be related to the specific agrarian structure under consideration. These factors would explain why Northern Potosí peasant economy has only supplied seasonal labour to small mining enterprises in the region, and was in no condition to provide a permanent work-force for the great mining centre of Siglo XX located in the same region. The mining sector had therefore to be content with a functional use of local peasant 'seasonal unemployment', and import its work-force from Cochabamba: there, already by the end of the colonial period, a polarized rural structure had developed between major landowners and a mass of landless peasants who were ready to be channelled towards the new mining centres in Northern Potosí (Larson 1978).

5. Bi-zonal cultivation and the differentiation of the peasantry

We have seen how, within a single generation, some 25% of Puna peasant households will have access to Valley lands also, on account of their position in the generational cycle of their patrilineal descent groups. These households constitute a social link between other households with land in only one of these zones. However, as the generational cycle unfolds, this linking role will circulate among units of all the various branches of each descent group. Such privileged access to regional resources carries with it an increase in ayllu obligations – the favoured households must finance fiestas in both zones (Harris 1978a: 57) – and may be thought of as circulating 'by turn' among all the branches of each descent group.

The increase in obligations for households with dual access to Puna and Valley lands reflects the eminent domain preserved by the ayllu over all land within its jurisdiction. As figure 2.1 shows, the Northern Potosí ayllu is a 'vertical' territorial unit with land in both zones: it may consist of a continuous strip or, alternatively, of two discontinuous enclaves,[30] and the precise location of a household's Valley lands will therefore depend on the Valley location of the ayllu to which that household belongs. The 'reversionary right'[31] vested in the ayllu may be seen in the ritual confirmation of land rights required of all ayllu members (above all, through participation in the ritual battle or *tinku*), as well as in the occasional expulsion of members who have violated ayllu norms and their replacement with outsiders who are settled in the vacant tasas.[32]

In the past, differential access to distant resources was related to marked differences in wealth and status (Deustua 1978). In Northern Potosí as in other Andean regions, the limited access of commoners to Valley lands was contrasted with the far more extensive control over outlying resources enjoyed by the ayllu authorities. Under Spanish rule, privileged access to community labour prestations allowed these lords (kurakas) to gain control of ayllu surpluses, which could then be converted into commercial capital to sustain their operations within the market sector of colonial society (Murra 1978a; Rivera 1978a).[33] Today, as we shall see, differential access to regional resources still affects patterns of stratification within the ayllu, although the forms of articulation with the market have clearly changed.[34]

This section will compare the economic behaviour of those producers who followed the 'traditional' practice of bi-zonal cultivation at the time of the rural survey of 1978, with that of others who did not. Our results will force a revision of the view that low levels of production and market participation are to be related to the 'traditionalism' of the Andean peasant.

Table 2.1 *Distribution of households with both Puna and Valley lands, by canton*

Canton	Households with Puna land	Households with Puna and Valley land		% with holdings on both levels in each canton
		No.	%	
Ravelo	46	27	21.3	58.7
Ocuri	41	6	4.7	14.6
Macha	98	19	15.0	19.4
Pocoata	107	10	7.8	9.3
Colquechaca	33	17	13.4	51.5
Chuquiuta	65	19	15.0	29.2
Uncia	61	23	18.0	37.7
Bustillos	49	6	4.7	12.2
Total	500	127	100.0	25.4

Table 2.2. *Distribution of households with lands on both Puna and Valley, by ayllu*

Ayllu	Households with Puna land	Households with Puna and Valley land		% with holdings on both levels per ayllu
		No.	%	
Ex-hacienda	65	19	15.0	29.0
Murumuru	14	11	8.7	78.6
Yampara	17	5	4.0	29.0
Macha	130	26	20.0	20.0
Pukwata	98	18	14.0	18.4
Jukumani	47	10	8.0	21.0
Laymi	18	9	7.0	50.0
Kharacha	52	20	15.7	38.5
Chayantaka	6	1	0.8	16.7
Chullpa	42	7	6.0	16.7
Phanakachi	1	1	0.8	100.0
Total	490	127	100.0	25.9

The 10 units omitted belonged to the Sikuya and Aymaya ayllus, none of whose members interviewed possessed any Valley lands. However, outside the group sampled, some members of these ayllus did have Valley lands.

The role of the Andean ayllu

Tables 2.1 and 2.2 show the distribution of households with dual tenure according to the county (*cantón*) in which their Puna holding is located (table 2.1) and according to their ayllu membership (table 2.2).[35] The high percentage of households with dual access in Ravelo county and Murumuru ayllu should be related to the short distances separating lands of both climatic extremes in that area. The differences in the economic behaviour of households in this and other areas will be used as a point of reference in the analysis which follows.

In the first place, it should be noted that only 49 (38.5%) of the 127 household heads with dual tenure were actually cultivating their Valley lands in the period of reference of the survey. In order to explain this apparent neglect of a highly prized resource, we must review the factors related to Valley maize cultivation.

Parallel access to Puna maize lands

A dwarf variety of maize (*sara ch'isiwayu*) can in fact be grown in protected ravines and on lower fields within the Puna zone (level 4 in figure 2.2). Table 2.3 shows that only 3 (2%) of the 127 households with dual tenure cultivated both sorts of maize at once: in other terms, of the 49 households which cultivated Valley maize, 46 (94%) did not cultivate Puna maize. This suggests that peasants on the higher Puna levels have more need of the bi-zonal pattern of cultivation than those with access to land at level 4. However, if we now consider the 78 households with dual tenure which did not cultivate their Valley lands, we find that 52 (67%) did not cultivate Puna maize either. We may conclude, therefore, that the lack of Puna maize land is a necessary, but not a sufficient, condition for a household with dual tenure to bring its Valley land into cultivation.

Household demographic structure

It has already been noted that bi-zonal cultivation requires greater labour inputs than production on the Puna alone. Further, a household's Valley lands may be up to 120 kilometres away from its Puna base: on foot, this distance may be covered by a lone traveller in two or three days, but with llamas the journey may take up to two weeks. To fill its extra labour needs, a household may hire off-farm labour, or make more intensive use of its own domestic labour. However, these difficulties may be reduced if the household possesses a favourable demographic structure.

Table 2.4 compares the distribution by sex of household members of working age (ten years and over, in our definition) in Puna domestic units with Valley lands, according to whether these units practise bi-zonal cultivation or not. It will be seen that a higher proportion of male labourers is

Table 2.3. *Classification of Puna households according to possession and cultivation of Valley land, and according to production of Puna maize*

| | Possess Valley land | | | | |
| | Cultivate Valley land | Do not cultivate Valley land | Sub-total | Do not possess Valley land | Total |
Households					
Total	49	78	127	373	500
Cultivate Puna maize	3	26	29	134	163
Do not cultivate Puna maize	46	52	98	239	337

Table 2.4. *Puna households by sex ratio of producers* and Valley cultivation*

| | Total sample | | Among households cultivating Valley land | | Among households possessing, but not cultivating, Valley land | |
Sex ratio	No.	%	No.	%	No.	%
Equal numbers	210	41	16	33	30	38
Majority of men	185	37	22	45	28	36
Majority of women	105	22	11	22	20	26
Total	500	100	49	100	78	100

$\chi^2 = 1.01$
s – 0.05 (2 degrees of freedom)
*i.e. persons over ten years

to be found in those units which cultivate their Valley lands. Inversely, households with dual tenure which do not practise bi-zonal cultivation are characterized by a higher proportion of female labourers. We may therefore suggest – the low level of significance precludes a firm conclusion – that a greater availability of male labour helps households practise bi-zonal cultivation, due to the greater need for such labour in farms with larger areas of cultivated land.

Harris (1978a: 57) has in fact suggested that bi-zonal cultivation is only possible in certain moments of the domestic cycle: the optimum situation would occur when the family has no small children (under ten years, in our definition), who would increase the difficulties of movement between Puna

Table 2.5. *Dependency ratio of Puna households, by Valley cultivation*

Number of dependants per producer	Sample		Households cultivating Valley land		Households with uncultivated Valley land	
	No.	%	No.	%	No.	%
0	197	40	22	45	25	33
0.01–0.50	168	34	12	24	32	41
0.51–1.00	95	19	9	18	16	21
1.0 and above	35	7	6	12	4	5
Total	500	100	49	100	78	100

$\chi^2 = 6.30$. Not significant at 0.05 level

and Valley, but can still count on the labour of older children. Table 2.5 evaluates the importance of dependants in households with dual tenure, according to whether such households actually cultivate their Valley lands. The results offer support for Harris's hypothesis, insofar as the number of households which cultivate their Valley lands declines as the number of their dependants increases. Unfortunately, the number of observations in the last line of table 2.5 is very small, making it impossible to reach final conclusions. However, the evidence presented in tables 2.4 and 2.5 would at least suggest that sex and dependency ratios influence the decision by Puna households with dual tenure as to whether or not they should embark on bi-zonal cultivation.[36]

Access to off-farm labour

An alternative solution to the problem of increased labour inputs, posed by the requirements of bi-zonal cultivation, may be looked for in the recourse to off-farm labour characteristic of many bi-zonal units of production (table 2.6). We may observe a tendency for households practising bi-zonal cultivation to hire in more off-farm labour than households with dual tenure which do not cultivate their Valley lands. Although production units based exclusively on family labour continue to predominate even among those practising bi-zonal cultivation, the percentage of such units which use wage-labour is nevertheless double that of the sample as a whole. Among households with dual tenure which do not cultivate their Valley lands, on the other hand, we find that the corresponding percentage is the same as the overall sample proportion.

51

Table 2.6. *Type of labour used, by Valley cultivation (households)*

Labour	Only family		Non-wage-earning* and non-family		Wage-earning† and non-family		Total	
	No.	%	No.	%	No.	%	No.	%
Cultivate in Valley	26	53	10	20	13	27	49	100
Do not cultivate in Valley	52	67	15	19	11	14	78	100
Total	309	62	121	24	70	14	500	100

$\chi^2 = 3.56$
* *ayni* and *chuqhu* (see Glossary)
† *mink'a* (see Glossary)

It is important to note, however, that 54% (7/13) of the bi-zonal production units utilizing off-farm labour came from Ravelo county where the two ecological zones of Puna and Valley are in close proximity. In this area, seasonal migration from Puna to Valley was found to be particularly important among households lacking their own maize-production, which therefore expected to be paid in kind (see 'Bi-zonal cultivation and market participation', below). In fact, 86% (6/7) of Ravelo's bi-zonal production units which utilized off-farm labour appeared in the survey results as paying their labourers with a portion of the maize harvest – as against a corresponding proportion of 77% (10/13) for the sample as a whole.

As a corollary, we would expect bi-zonal production units to sell less domestic labour than other households, and this hypothesis is strengthened by table 2.7, where we find that such units sell less labour than households with uncultivated Valley lands, or than the sample as a whole.

Access to ploughing-oxen

A further means of reducing the pressure on family labour time consists in the possession of, or indirect access to, draught animals. A total of 35% of all households interviewed, and 37% of those possessing but not cultivating Valley lands, lacked all access to ploughing-oxen. On the other hand, only 10% of those practising bi-zonal cultivation were in a similar position: the rest could dispose of animals at least through loan or hire. Moreover, 59% of the bi-zonal production units owned their own pairs of oxen, in contrast with only 32% of the households which did not cultivate their Valley lands.

Table 2.7. *Sale of labour and Valley cultivation*

	Never sell		Sell seasonally		Sell regularly		Total	
	No.	%	No.	%	No.	%	No.	%
Households cultivating Valley land	26	53	21	43	2	4	49	100
Households possessing, but not cultivating, Valley land	28	36	42	55	7	9	78	100
Total	196	39	258	52	46	9	500	100

Evidently possession of, or access to, a pair of oxen facilitates bi-zonal cultivation; and this, together with the information presented concerning the use of off-farm labour, might suggest that bi-zonal cultivation is to be related to higher levels of wealth. Before considering this hypothesis, however, we shall examine one further variable which may affect decisions as to whether or not to cultivate in both zones.

Indirect access to maize through kin relations

Survey techniques are inefficient methods of quantifying non-market spheres of exchange, although such spheres are of undeniable importance within the set of mechanisms which permit the reproduction of Northern Potosí peasant economy (see 'Bi-zonal cultivation' below, however). Here we use an indirect indicator of the importance of non-market exchange relations. Of the 500 households interviewed, 79 (16%) declared that their relatives were 'owners' of Valley land. Of these, 43 (57%) also had Valley lands of their own. However, of the 79 units with *indirect* access to Valley products, only 18 (23%) were themselves producers of Valley maize. This suggests that membership of an extended kin-group, other members of which have access to Valley lands, reduces the need to ensure domestic production of maize – a conclusion already presupposed in figure 2.4 above, which has been constructed on the basis of non-survey information. Once again, however, it is instructive to contrast the situation in Ravelo county with that which obtains in the rest of the study area. Table 2.8 suggests that the existence of vertical kin relations is an irrelevant variable in Ravelo, possibly due to easier movement between nearby zones in that area, whereas in other counties a well-endowed kin network can spare a household the need to use its distant Valley resources.

Table 2.8. *Puna households with own land and relatives in the Valley, according to Valley cultivation*

	Ravelo		Other cantons	
	No.	%	No.	%
Cultivate maize	10	91	8	25
Do not cultivate maize	1	9	24	75
Total	11	100	32	100

$\chi^2 = 15.46$, significant at 0.001 level

Levels of gross farm production: indices of inequality

Different criteria may be used to determine levels of wealth within the Northern Potosí peasant economy. For our present purpose, we shall use an index consisting of the value of household agricultural production and animal sales over a one-year period, calculated at April 1978 prices. We omit, therefore, the value of unsold animals, which can be better conceptualized as self-reproducing capital and a form of savings, rather than constituting part of annual production.

Table 2.9 shows a clear correlation between gross farm production, defined in this way, and bi-zonal cultivation. Here we can see that 64% of the sample is concentrated in the category of 'middle peasants' (groups 2 and 3 in table 2.9), whereas in the polar categories (groups 1 and 4) we find a reduced number of 'rich peasants' (15%) and 'poor peasants' (21%). A similar distribution is to be found for households with uncultivated Valley lands, as it is for the sample as a whole.

In contrast, the situation among households practising bi-zonal cultivation is completely different: the smallest number of households is to be found in group 1, and the percentages rise consistently, finally reaching 41% of the total concentrated in group 4. We may conclude that bi-zonal cultivation is to be related positively with higher levels of wealth.

The question which now arises is whether higher levels of production are the *result* of bi-zonal cultivation, or whether these levels are the *precondition* for engaging in Valley maize-production. In the light of our previous analysis of the variables associated with Valley maize-production, we can propose two possible answers to this question, which may serve to orient future research.

Table 2.9. *Households by gross agricultural product and Valley cultivation*

Gross agricultural production (in pesos)	1 0–2500		2 2501–5000		3 5001–10000		4 10000 +		Total	
	No.	%	No.	%	No.	%	No.	%	No.	%
No access to Valley land	87	23	137	37	105	28	44	12	373	100
Cultivate Valley land	3	6	11	22	15	31	20	41	49	100
Possess but do not cultivate Valley land	13	17	31	40	21	27	13	17	78	100
Total	103	21	179	36	141	28	77	15	500	100

$\chi^2 = 33.71$

In our first model, households which have recently gained access to Valley lands by inheritance or by marriage must decide whether to cultivate them or not. To bring in off-farm labour, they would already have to be in the category of 'rich peasants'; at this stage, therefore, only those households with a favourable demographic structure will be in optimal conditions for cultivating their Valley lands – conditions which would be further improved if they had access to draught-animals. Alternatively, membership of an extended kin network, whose other members can offer indirect access to Valley products, may lead households with dual tenure to postpone the cultivation of their Valley lands. In such circumstances, they may be obliged – like many households without access to Valley lands – to sell seasonally a part of their domestic labour, in order to compensate for deficiencies in their farm-production with alternative sources of necessary cash.

In the second model, the productive levels achieved through bi-zonal cultivation permit the hire of off-farm labour, and thus allow the expansion of production even without a favourable demographic structure. These productive levels may have been reached precisely through the strategies outlined in the first model, or through the intensification of labour-use within the household. Other paths to wealth – for example, trade – may also permit the consolidation of the new productive levels through the employment of day-labourers or *mink'as*.

Now the survey showed that 11 of the 20 'rich peasants' who practise bi-zonal cultivation are to be found in Ravelo, where they constitute more than half of all 'rich peasants' in that county (11/21). Since this canton also shows the highest percentage of households using hired labour, we can suggest that the second model is more applicable in Ravelo, while the first model is more applicable in the rest of the study area. Such an interpretation would also take into account the relative lack of seasonal labour migration from Puna to Valley in the other cantons.

We can see, therefore, how the opportunity to cultivate Valley lands constitutes one of the principal mechanisms of social differentiation in Northern Potosí – as indeed it was in previous modes of production. During the colonial period, the ayllu lords of Upper Peru succeeded in becoming a privileged stratum of traders by virtue of their access to land and labour prestations both on the Puna and in the Valley, and further afield as well. Today we find that differential access to regional resources, offered by the ayllu to a small number of its members, allows these households to achieve exceptionally high levels of production, and even to hire in non-family labour, thus giving rise to an 'embryonic class structure' among local petty commodity producers. However, this interpretation only indicates the potential of the system, were it not subject to the limitations imposed by the process of 'permanent primitive accumulation'. This process requires a constant transfer of peasant surplus labour to the urban and mining centres, constituting a brake on the accumulation of capital among the peasantry.

Bi-zonal cultivation and market participation

We have already referred in section 2 of this chapter to the common belief among Andean ethnographers that households practising bi-zonal culti-vation are able to cover their consumption needs more exhaustively with their own production, and are therefore located on the margin of the market economy in pursuit of the 'traditional' ideal of economic self-sufficiency. As we have indicated above, the importance of the autarkic ideal in the past is undeniable; however, its over-hasty projection towards the present would lead us to predict that households practising bi-zonal cultivation are those with the smallest volume of agricultural sales, the smallest participation in the consumers' market, and the largest proportion of total production going toward domestic consumption. This hypothesis is not supported by our results. Instead, these show higher levels of agricultural sales for house-holds practising bi-zonal cultivation. We must therefore conclude that a more diversified productive base across ecological zones creates conditions for higher levels of marketed production; or – in more anthropological terms – that the 'vertical control of a maximum of ecological levels' enables the Andean peasant household to fulfil more effectively its modern role within the petty commodity regime, and to ensure through agricultural sales its access to the cash necessary for its reproduction.

Let us first compare levels of maize-consumption among households

Table 2.10. *Average maize consumption per household in each canton surveyed, by mode of acquisition of maize consumed*

Canton	Own production	Day wages	Barter	Purchases	Rent payment on land	Total consumption	No. of units	Average consumption per household
Maize producers								
Ravelo	636	24	—	71	—	731	21	35
Ocuri	222	—	—	—	—	222	6	37
Macha	528	24	3	76	—	628	25	25
Pocoata	2618	12	—	293	—	2926	94	31
Colquechaca	190	—	—	16	—	206	8	26
Calacala	825	—	8	79	4	916	42	22
Uncia	582	—	—	—	—	582	9	65
Bustillo	18	—	—	104	—	122	4	31
Sub-total	5619	60	11	639	4	6333	209	30
Non-maize producers								
Ravelo	—	576	10	229	—	815	25	33
Ocuri	—	48	43	216	—	307	35	9
Macha	—	24	358	528	—	910	73	12
Pocoata	—	48	12	36	—	96	13	7
Colquechaca	—	24	38	296	—	358	25	14
Calacala	—	24	16	177	—	217	23	9
Uncia	—	—	10	354	—	364	52	7
Bustillo	—	—	89	243	2	340	45	8
Sub-total	—	744	576	2085	2	3407	291	12
Total	5619	804	587	2724	6	9740	500	20

which practise maize-production with the equivalent levels among house-holds which do not produce their own supplies of maize. In table 2.10 we have combined production figures for Valley and Puna maize (*sara ch'isiwayu*), with county totals broken down according to source. We can observe how maize-producers (42% of the sample) enjoy far higher levels of maize-consumption than non-producers: average household con-sumption during the year of the survey reached 30 *arrobas* (1 arroba = 25 lb) for the first group, while falling to 12 arrobas for the second group. The exception is to be found among the non-producers of Ravelo, whose consumption levels are virtually the same as for the producers of the same county. We shall return shortly to this apparent anomaly.

However, higher consumption levels among maize-producers do not result in lower levels of sales. Table 2.11 shows the allocation of maize-production between consumption and sales according to the type of maize produced. Although the proportion of the Puna maize crop which is consumed is slightly higher than for the Valley maize crop (80% against 73%), average household consumption of Valley maize is nearly double the equivalent figure for Puna maize-producers (39 arrobas against 22.5 arrobas). At the same time, Valley maize sales represent 22% of total production, with average household sales reaching 12.5 arrobas; on the other hand, the 4 arrobas of Puna maize sold on average by each production unit only represent 14% of total production. We may conclude that the higher production levels characteristic of Valley maize-producers permit them both to consume more and to expand sales.

This conclusion is reinforced if we analyse agricultural production as a whole. Table 2.12 compares the values allocated to consumption and sales, both for the two types of maize-producers, and for households which do not produce maize of any kind. The maize-producers can be seen to achieve far higher levels of sales than is the case for non-producers, as well as enjoying higher levels of average household consumption. But the average household production of Valley maize-producers can be seen to be far higher than that of the rest of the sample, and explains how these bi-zonal units of production can achieve both the sale of greater absolute values on the market and higher levels of average home consumption.

To conclude this section, let us return to the anomalous levels of maize-consumption enjoyed by non-producers of maize in Ravelo county, since the explanation will lead to some theoretical observations about the pheno-menon we have termed 'embryonic differentiation'. In terms of agricultural production, Ravelo is one of the most prosperous areas in Northern Potosí: average household production reaches 10 139 pesos in value, which means that the 'rich peasant' (group 4 in Table 2.9) constitutes the county average. An average of 25% of household production is placed on the market. If we now consider the 25 households without maize-production in the county,

Table 2.11. *Total Valley and Puna sales and consumption of maize production, in arrobas*

Product	Sales			Consumption			Total production			No. of producers
	Amount	%	Average	Amount	%	Average	Amount	%	Average	
Puna maize	676	14	4.15	3696	80	22.67	4639	100	28.46	163
Valley maize	611	22	12.47	1924	73	39.26	2730	100	55.71	49

Total production amounts to more than the sum of sales and consumption because a portion is put aside as seed.

Table 2.12. *Sales and consumption of total agricultural production, in pesos, according to whether households produced Puna or Valley maize*

Producers of	Sales			Consumption			Total production			No. of producers
	Total	%	Average	Total	%	Average	Total	%	Average	
Puna maize	200 781	21	1 232	671 784	69	4 121	976 662	100	5 992	163
Valley	90 423	20	1 845	286 031	62	5 837	464 130	100	9 472	49
No maize	136 757	11	470	892 966	69	3 069	1 294 848	100	4 450	291

The number of producers exceeds 500 because three producd both types of maize.

we find that these too achieve an average household production of 9677 pesos, of which 23% is sold. These figures are very similar to those achieved by the bi-zonal production units, and Ravelo seems therefore to constitute an exception to the conclusions we have just reached.

The situation can be better understood if we consider the source of the maize consumed by non-producers, as shown in table 2.10. As we have already shown, the use of off-farm labour is particularly common in Ravelo, it being generally remunerated with a portion of the harvest. These results are confirmed in table 2.10, where the exceptional levels of maize-consumption enjoyed by non-producers are seen to come from the sale of seasonal labour in the fields of the maize-producers. The high levels of sales achieved by non-producers of maize in Ravelo would seem, therefore, to be facilitated by their easy access to a 'wage' in maize, which allows them to achieve similar consumption levels to those of maize-producers.

It is clear that the equalization in levels of maize-consumption is the result of the sale of wage-labour by the households lacking maize-production, and this sale constitutes one criterion for detecting the 'embryonic differentiation' of the Northern Potosí peasantry. However, in the conditions imposed by the system of 'permanent primitive accumulation', this process does not lead to a separation between the sellers of labour and their land. On the contrary, it is precisely through the sale of labour that they are able to achieve levels of marketing and consumption roughly similar to those of the maize-producing households. The 'wage in maize' then begins to resemble the classic Andean mechanisms of redistribution of surpluses in exchange for labour prestations. The result of the 'wage relationship' is the reproduction of all the households in the county, whether or not they have access to home-produced maize, in adequate conditions for them to be able to fulfil their function within the regional economy. We therefore propose that the conceptual ambiguity reflects a real contradiction, and that the 'redistributive' aspect of the phenomenon should be emphasized insofar as the regional economic context requires the maintenance of household-based peasant production and inhibits the polarization of the agrarian structure into opposed classes.

6. Conclusion

We have seen that certain features of Northern Potosí ayllu organization are directly functional for the reproduction of small-scale peasant production within present-day Bolivian capitalism. As was pointed out in the Introduction to this chapter, a historical perspective confirms our rejection of models which relegate the ayllus to a 'pre-mercantile' status, and see growth of market participation among the Bolivian peasantry as typical of regions previously occupied by the hacienda. If today's levels of sales in Northern

Potosí are generally low, this should rather be attributed to state commercial policies which have destroyed the favourable marketing conditions once enjoyed by the region's ayllus.

In the juridical vacuum which prevails in Northern Potosí, the petty commodity producer is articulated both with the regional market economy (thus contributing to the reproduction of the mining work-force) and with collective systems of land-holding within the ayllu: individual property of land – normally considered a definitional feature of the petty commodity regime – does not exist. In this chapter we have isolated the inheritance and marriage systems as mechanisms which allow the redistribution of land among ayllu members, according to contrasting demographic conditions within different patrilocal groups. We have also shown how payment of the colonial tribute (tasa), mediated by the ayllu authorities, still constitutes an essential element (in spite of its trivial monetary value) in the validation of land rights: Agrarian Reform titles have still to be issued to most Puna ayllus. The virtual absence of a land market means that access to land can only be guaranteed if households effectively demonstrate their membership of the corresponding ayllu. Without delving here into the ritual and ideological correlates of membership, we have argued that the 10% of household expenditure dedicated to community fiestas should be conceptualized as a productive investment necessary for retaining rights to land.

Our data suggest that the generational cycle within each patrilocal group offers certain households the opportunity for bi-zonal cultivation in Puna and Valley. Thus a dynamic towards social differentiation can be observed within the ayllu itself, regardless of the economic formation to which it belongs, in the complex of mechanisms which reconcile local demographic movements with the different areas of land available to different hamlets. The survey results show a clear correlation between bi-zonal cultivation and high levels of production, consumption and market participation. A factor which underlay the commercial accumulation of the colonial ayllu lords continues, therefore, to offer similar opportunities to some 25% of the present population, although the realization of this potential is largely blocked by the process of 'permanent primitive accumulation' at the regional level.

Obviously, the consolidation of bi-zonal cultivation by certain households cannot be explained simply by reference to household demography or a more intense usage of domestic labour: more important would seem to be access to off-farm labour characteristic of the 'embryonic class structure' in certain counties. However, our analysis of the 'wage in maize' has shown that it would be equally incorrect to postulate a growing mass of landless peasants due to the increase in regional 'wage labour'. In Ravelo this productive relation can also be conceptualized within the 'redistributive' framework of traditional Andean labour relations (mink'a), since in fact it en-sures the reproduction of households lacking maize-production in conditions which enable them to fulfil their function within the regional economic structure. This is, of course, perfectly coherent with a model of agricultural development designed for a country with extremely low levels of capital investment, and based on domestic production relations and the predomi-nance of the 'middle peasant'.

The significance of two interesting clauses in the 1953 Agrarian Reform Law will now become apparent. The first prohibited the sale of parcels assigned to peasant households, thus inhibiting the development of a land market. The second prohibited the tenure of land outside the zone of permanent residence, thus opposing the practice of bi-zonal cultivation and eliminating a traditional opportunity for accumulation among the highland peasantry.[37] Thus, the populist rhetoric of the National Revolu-tionary Movement (MNR), which directed the 1952 Revolution, has diverted attention from the real effects of the Agrarian Reform. Both clauses are entirely coherent with the model of 'permanent primitive accumulation', based on the institutionalization of the petty commodity regime, which was an essential element within the new structure of depen-dency created by the MNR from 1952 onwards, and consolidated by succes-sive military governments since 1964.

Notes

This article is part of a larger 'Report on the urban-mining centre of Siglo XX and Catavi, and its rural context', prepared by a multidisciplinary team between 1977 and 1979 under the direction of Antonio Birbuet. The statistical information here presented is the result of a survey carried out during April and May of 1978 among 500 peasant households in the Puna region of Northern Potosí. The methodological basis of this survey is included in the Report, but is omitted here for reasons of space. I am most grateful to Sr Birbuet and his team for their collaboration during the period of research, and in particular to Sr Ramiro Molina, my partner in the Rural Department of the project. I would also like to thank Olivia Harris and Jorge Hidalgo for their comments on an earlier version of this chapter, as well as John Beard, Guido Pinto and Daigh Tufts for their help on the statistics. Other material used corresponds to field and archive work carried out by the author between 1970 and 1976, with particular reference to Ayllu Macha. This bias will have to be corrected for the other regional *ayllus* through future research, and such studies are already under way for Ayllu Laymi (Olivia Harris) and Ayllu Jukumani (Ricardo Godoy).

1. This contrast is striking enough to be taken as the point of departure for an import-ant study by Harris and Albó (1975).
2. The rise and fall of the nineteenth-century silver boom has been studied by Mitre (1977, 1978).
3. Some of the complexity of the regional ayllu system can be seen in Platt (1978a, 1978b) and Harris (1978a).
4. See the pioneering study by Silvia Rivera (1978b) on nineteenth-century *hacienda* expansion in the region of La Paz.

5. See Murra (1978c) for the privileged position of the Charka warriors within the Tawantinsuyu (present-day ayllus can be shown to have constituted components of the pre-Inca federation of the Charka and Karakara). For the pre-Toledan tribute-system, see Platt 1978a: we have termed this system, in which peasant surpluses were concentrated in the hands of the ayllu lord (*kuraka*) for subsequent sale in the colonial markets, 'administered conversion'. The growth of 'forced commercialization' – to borrow Kula's term (Kula 1974) – is tentatively attributed to the forced sales (*repartos*) of the eighteenth-century *corregidores* (Harris 1978a); the structure of household consumption may also have been modified by the wages in kind issued by many nineteenth-century mining companies (see Mitre 1977: 207). For the importance of ayllu market relations during the nineteenth century, see Grieshaber (1979).

6. See 'Gobernador de Chayanta al Sr, General Presidente del Departamento de Potosí de Agosto de 1825', cited in Grieshaber (1979).

7. I am grateful to Ricardo Godoy for information on the rebirth of small mining in Northern Potosí from 1880.

8. Aramayo (1861) comments on the transition to a work-force in the large mines made up of 'cholos'. The absence of a population of cholos near Colquechaca suggests a wave of immigrants: the word 'cholo' itself suggests a possible origin in Cochabamba, where the quantity of landless peasants already present at the beginning of the nineteenth century (Larson 1978: 48–9) may well have supplied labour to the new mining centres, in anticipation of the better-known wave during the tin era (Harris and Albó 1975).

9. Certain key features of today's inheritance system can be shown to be valid for the mid nineteenth century. See the comments of the Apoderado Fiscal for Chayanta in 1877 on the right of women and minors to inherit land where no male heir was available (cited in Grieshaber 1977).

10. For the commercial development of the seventeenth-century ayllu lords, see particularly Murra (1978a) and Rivera (1978a); compare, for the Province of Chayanta, Platt (1978b) and the important document reproduced in Urioste Arana (1978).

11. The decline of the ayllu lords has accelerated dramatically since the Revolution of 1952, when their access to community labour dues was finally abolished.

12. Bartra 1974: 102–4. By 'permanent primitive accumulation' is meant a constant transfer of value from the peasant sector which does not however lead to the expropriation of the peasantry. Bartra mentions the mechanism of 'unequal exchange', which results from the national policy of low prices for agricultural products. In this context should be mentioned the results of a further survey, carried out as part of the project mentioned in the Notes (above) on the sources of the capital invested by local intermediaries in the purchase of lorries. These sources are predominantly previous mining activities, not agricultural ones. We also noted the trivial development of credit relations between intermediaries and peasants. Two 'classic' mechanisms of land expropriation are therefore absent in Northern Potosí, freeing the ayllus from a traditional threat. Thus, the community, petty commodity production, the forms of commercial and usury capital, and the price structure are all elements within an economic system which permits the systematic extraction of peasant surplus-labour, without separating the producer from his principal instrument of production: the land.

13. See Delgado (1967). In some cases the Agrarian Reform maintained the tenancy pattern found under the hacienda regime, characterized by inequalities in the size and location of the parcels. On the other hand, in Ancoraimes, an attempt was

made to concentrate holdings, on the basis of an 'equivalence index' which proposed relations of commensurability between the different types of cultivated land. This policy provoked strong resistance among all the peasants (not only those directly affected), such that the new Reform-sponsored distribution was collectively rejected by the community. The Agrarian Reform was therefore obliged to revise its policy, and confirm the previous distribution of parcels.

14. Strictly speaking we are here talking of *possession*, not *property* rights: individual property is limited by the ayllu's eminent right over all its members' land (see section 3).

15. Thus in 1779 the priest for San Marcos de Miraflores (a Valley parish of the Macha ayllu) lamented, 'the small experience I had of doing similar work (the reconstruction of a chapel) with ayllu Indians who have dual residence in Puna and Valley'. *Libro de Fábrica de esta Santa Iglesia de San Marcos de Miraflores, que corre desde el día siete de septiembre del año 1779.* Document consulted in the Parish Library of San Pedro de Buena Vista, Provincia Charcas. Compare Harris (1978a: 57) for the concept of 'dual residence' among today's Indians of Ayllu Laymi.

16. It has been pointed out that Spanish mercantilism maintained the convergence of tax and rent that seems to have existed under the Inca, insofar as the Spanish king succeeded to the Inca's 'eminent right' over all land within his domain (Platt 1978a). However with the emergence of the *criollo* republic in 1825, these two concepts were opposed to each other: while the white government insisted that the ayllus occupied land which had been 'usurped' from its real owner, the state, and that the tribute was really a rent on state land, the Indians themselves insisted that the land was securely theirs so long as they fulfilled their obligations to the state, chief among which was the payment of tax (tasa). In what follows, I prefer to talk of 'tax', since the obligation to pay this traditional due has recently been confirmed by the departmental prefect, in the wake of continued ayllu resistance to change over the last 100 years. This does not, of course, prevent fiscal officials in Potosí from claiming that the tasa is 'really' a rent on state land (*alquiler*).

17. Probably from the Aymara *mantaña* – 'enter': each year the peasants 'enter' a new block of fallows whose turn for cultivation has come round.

18. Until the recent prefectural reconfirmation of the tasa, originarios had to pay $b5.00 and agregados $b3.00. At the end of the last century, however, originarios were still paying $b9.60 and agregados $b7.00, as had been the case at least since the Revisita of 1816 (*Revisitas*, Archivo Nacional de Bolivia, Sucre). This inconsistency in the kuraka's testimony should not lead us to deny it all value: although no Revisita suggests that the originarios had access to Puna and Valley lands, the kuraka is clearly convinced of this element in the definition of the tax categories. Given the little interest, and control, of the land commissioners over internal ayllu processes of land distribution, I tend to accept the kuraka's opinion, while recognizing the necessity for reconciling it with the Revisita evidence through future studies of the registration process.

19. Changes in tax status were common throughout the nineteenth century, as is shown by the Acts of the Land Commissioners (*Revisitas*, Archivo Nacional de Bolivia, Sucre); in fact, the commissioners normally simply ratified the decisions of the kuraka and his ayllu.

20. See, however, the prefectural decision (*Resolución Prefectural No. 16/75 de 30 de septiembre de 1975*) which 'disposes the readjustment of the rate (tasa) of the territorial contribution (contribución territorial) in the whole Department of Potosí': here, originarios are obliged to pay $b20.00 annually, agregados $b15.00, and *eventuales* (kantu runas) $b10.00.

21. See Platt (1978a) for the irregularity of the tax payment in the sixteenth century. Compare, too, Viceroy Toledo's instructions to corregidores: 'the tribute must be collected and placed in the Community chest, half throughout the month of May and until mid-June, the other half in the months of November or December'. In *Cajas Reales 18*, Año 1575, pp. 214ff, Casa de la Moneda, Potosí.

22. Compare n.20 above. The payment of the new rates is still very uneven, and many ayllus still insist on paying the previous quantities. However, some appear in the departmental accounts as paying as much as $b80.00 for access to four tasas de originario. In other parts, the ayllu still resists the payment of $b10.00 by kantu runas, who were freed of tax obligations by the 1874 Law of Expropriation.

Revising the fiscal accounts, however, it is interesting to observe how many originarios have suddenly appeared on the scene since the prefectural decision: before, I had been assured by ayllu authorities that most Indians were today either agregados or kantu runas. The acting kuraka of Macha (Aransaya) has explained to me that many are now preferring to pay the originario tasa in order to guarantee their rights to land. Once again, we can see the freedom with which the Indians manipulate the tax categories according to their perception of their interests.

23. Recently a Macha land-holder has provoked the indignation of his numerous neighbouring 'cousins' (*primos*): instead of ceding his surplus land to the land-scarce branch of the patrilineage, he has preferred to hire in day-labourers in order to utilize the whole extent of his inheritance. Such a practice may anticipate the context of future conflicts in Northern Potosí.

24. The transition to patrilineal inheritance, imposed by the Spanish, has been analysed for a Pakaxa town in Rivera and Platt (1978). However, it should be emphasized that we are here dealing with the *predominant* model of *land* inheritance: in other contexts (for example, the inheritance of animals or other moveable goods), bilateral models have more importance. Compare n.13 above.

25. Compare a similar situation in the case of a peasant from Cabildo Umajila (Ayllu Macha, Urinsaya) in 1926:

'I have an agreement with my sister and nephews to deliver to them all my shares [*acciones*: fractions of the originario ancestor's holding], together with the corresponding obligations to the State – such as serving as tax collector, courier and other turns (*tandas*) – while I renounce these obligations, since I have other lands in the Valley, my second resisdence, which I shall only be able to leave occasionally, but meanwhile my share will remain in the power of my mentioned relatives. In exchange, they will be bringing certain Puna products, such as *ch'uñu*, to my Valley residence.'

In *Protocolización de 1942*, Notaría de Hacienda, Potosí.

26. The minimal ayllus, or cabildos, constitute the lowest level in a whole hierarchy of larger ayllus, which will not be treated here. See, however, Harris 1978b for Chayanta, Platt 1978b for Pocoata, and Platt 1978c for Macha.

27. We here refer only to the nucleating processes generated by peasant socio-economic organization: other urbanizing processes have given rise, naturally, to towns superimposed upon the residential dynamic of the rural economy (such as the Toledan *pueblos de reducción*, and the mining centres shown in figure 2.1).

28. The Indian tax-collector (cobrador) is named by turn from among the householders of his cabildo, which is made up of various hamlets and their land in Puna and Valley.

29. Data for the northern altiplano are to be found in Urioste (1977). An analysis of Northern Potosí seasonal migration, which relates off-farm monetary income to global levels of wealth, can be found in Molina and Platt (1979).

30. The map shows what I have termed the 'maximal ayllus' of Northern Potosí: these are made up of a hierarchy of lesser ayllus, of which the cabildo, made up of several hamlets, is the smallest. At this level, the cabildo or 'minimal ayllu' is generally made up of two enclaves, one in each ecological zone, even within the continuous strip of certain maximal ayllus (for example, Macha and Pukwata).

31. The importance of Gluckman's (1943) analysis of Lozi land-tenure for understanding Andean systems of land-tenure was first pointed out by John Murra (1975: 299–300, for example). We have found the concept of a 'hierarchy of reversionary rights', homologous with the hierarchy of ayllus, particularly useful.

32. Thus we should avoid extending towards Northern Potosí the generalization proposed for the whole of Peru by Rodrigo Montoya (1971: 77), which denies the relevance of 'collective ownership' for all irrigated lands.

33. For the case of a Pukwata lord during the seventeenth century, see Platt (1978b) together with the document reproduced in Urioste (1977), in which several Pukwata Indians denounce the accumulative practices of their lord.

34. The seventeenth-century lords were also the colonial tax-collectors, and their entry into the market at first expressed the mechanism of 'administered conversion' through which they acquired the cash necessary to pay the tribute (see Platt 1978a). Today, on the other hand, entry into the market is in the hands of individual householders, and the cash acquired goes towards buying consumption goods or (in Ravelo) modern agricultural inputs (insecticides, fertilizers) which are not produced within the household economy. The market has thus assumed a direct reproductive function with relation to most domestic units of production.

35. Here we only present maximal ayllu membership, omitting the cabildo membership of the families interviewed. Harris (1978a) indicates that the main dwelling of bi-zonal cultivators in Ayllu Laymi is normally in the Valley. For survey purposes, we have omitted this variable, which does not affect the interpretation of the results.

36. As a hypothesis, we may see here an interesting convergence with the views of the Macha kuraka cited above. If we assume that bi-zonal cultivation is characteristic of the originario, and that 'originario' used to be a *stage in the developmental cycle of the patrilocal group*, rather than an absolute and rigid category, it becomes natural that our results should find a correlation between bi-zonal cultivation and the demographic features of the peasant household. We may even consider inverting the terms of the definition: originario is above all a fiscal category and carries no assumption about the processes of formation of the production unit so categorized. It may even be fruitful to investigate whether 'originario' – in certain circumstances at least (such as extreme demographic pressure) – may not have been the name given to households in a given stage of the cycle by the kuraka charged with supplying the demographic information required for drawing up the tax registers.

37. An indication of the dramatic decline in levels of household maize-production and consumption, which shows the devastating effects of colonial accumulation on the Andean peasant economy, is found in the letter sent to the king of Spain on 12 February 1608 by Francisco de Alfaro, with reference to an application entitled *Pleito sobre las tierras de los yndios de macha* (Gandia 1939: 387–8):

> 'ay probado que siembran los yndios a seys y aun a diez cargas de senbradura de maiz y la sentençia que oy ay aun no les dexa a carga de senbradura – y advierto a vuestra magestad que una carga en esta tierra se diçe media hanega de suerte que una hanega es dos cargas y dizese carga respeto de los carneros de la tierra que cargan solo media hanega.

> 'el obispo de quito que fue el comisario en la ynstrucion que dio al corregidor para repartir las tierras mando diesen a los yndios raçon de tres cargas de

senbradura de maiz a cada uno ... don Pedro oçores que tubo la comision de tierras despues del obispo mando dar a dos cargas de senbradura de maiz a los yndios yanparaes ... y ... el liçençiado matienço oydor desta audiençia ... les hallo faltos de tierra y quito a los yndios de caracara una chacara para dar a los machas y los machas avian de dar mil pesos quatroçientos luego y seysçientos a tributo para los caracaras y esta chacara se dio de balde a la suegra del liçençiado calderon oydor de esta audiençia y la posee oy su hija casada ...

'los yndios particulares sienbran a tres cargas y el que menos diçe a dos vea vuestra magestad como con menos de una tendran harto y la raçon natural es tan concluyente que no es menester otra y asi digo que tenian los yndios algunas tierras buenas y las mexores se dieron a españoles que todos tenian mucha mano y asi escogieron y a los yndios quedaron las peores que apenas acuden a veynte y çinco pues presuponga vuestra magestad que las tierras an menester año y vez de suerte que para senbrar una carga an menester tres y que teniendo aun no una no senbraran almudes y quando cada uno dé de cosecha quatro hanegas que sale casi a çinquenta suplico a vuestra magestad advierta que una casa de un yndio tributario uno con otro son quatro personas marido y muger y dos hijos y los dos quiere que coman por uno de suerte que en cada casa pongamos tres personas cada uno a menester por lo menos hanega y media cada mes de suerte que no tienen cosecha para comer dos meses demas de que su vino es la chicha que se hase tanbien del maiz ...'

From the somewhat confused text, we can extract the following information:

(a) Each peasant household 'traditionally' had access to sufficient land to sow 3–5 *fanegas* (6–10 llama loads) of maize. One fanega = 7 arrobas = 175 lb.

(b) After the late-sixteenth-century 'redistribution' of lands by the Bishop of Quito, each household retained land sufficient to sow only $1\frac{1}{2}$ fanegas (3 llama loads).

(c) Given that each piece of land had to rest for two years, the area annually available to each household was only enough to sow $\frac{1}{2}$ fanega (1 llama load).

(d) This allowed each household to harvest 50 arrobas annually.

(e) If we suppose that the average household is composed of a couple and their two children (in Alfaro's calculations, equivalent to three adults), and that each adult will require 18 fanegas per year, then each household will require 376 arrobas a year.

(f) Thus, after the alienation to the Spanish of large extensions of ayllu Valley land, each household could scarcely cover an annual consumption calculated at 378 arrobas per year, without including requirements for seed, corn-beer, etc.

Today, however, we have seen that Macha bi-zonal units of production only reach an average household consumption of 25 arrobas per year, while households without access to home maize-production only consume 12 arrobas per year. Clearly, then, the Northern Potosí peasants have suffered a brutal reduction in their average levels of production and consumption, as a result of their incorporation into Spanish and republican processes of primitive accumulation. The 'traditional' peasant, as he exists in the 'developmentalist' mentality of rural extension agents and large sectors of the Bolivian Left, is an ideological fiction. In the sixteenth and seventeenth centuries the Andean peasant could still achieve extremely high production levels, which were gradually eroded as mercantilist mechanisms of surplus extraction brought the pre-Colombian inheritance into a state of crisis. What is surprising today is the capacity of the Andean rural economy of Northern Potosí to continue functioning within the constant process of 'permanent primitive accumulation'. Thus it is not a matter of a 'traditional' agricultural sector which has shown itself conservatively resistant to attempts to raise its productive levels, but rather of an Andean peasantry which – in spite of deteriorating conditions of production – still performs an essential role in supplying farm produce to the tin mines of Llallagua and Siglo XX. (I am grateful to Thierry Saignes for calling my attention to the document of 1608.)

Murra (1978b: 78) has pointed out the impoverishing effects of different Agrarian Reforms on the Andean peasantry. Our results support his observation, and also suggest negative effects on levels of sales and capital accumulation among the ayllu Indians. We refer, of course, to the accumulative potential already existing within the peasantry, but ignored by the Agrarian Reform. However, we do not deny that in certain privileged areas (the lower valley of Cochabamba, for example) the level of sales may have risen after the Agrarian Reform, although – and this agrees with our Northern Potosí results – in close relation with an improvement in levels of domestic consumption (see Albó 1976: 32).

3

Labour and produce in an ethnic economy, Northern Potosí, Bolivia

OLIVIA HARRIS

1. Introduction

As winter advances and the earth dries out, the river-beds of Northern Potosí, which are a swirling trap for unwary travellers during half of the year, become an avenue of communication between the treeless highlands and the precipitous intermontane valleys that lie to the north-east. Hundreds of llama trains, donkeys and mules wind their way down in search of valley maize; the drivers stop for refreshment at temporary shacks that have been set up in the river-beds to sell bread and chicha to the travellers, and at night build huge fires in sheer exuberance at the quantity of wood. Families who for months have used virtually anything that will burn to keep their hearth alight now have the luxury of selecting only wood that has a pleasant smell. And when they return along the same route, a week, a month, two months later, they are so heavily laden that the journey takes twice as long as the downward one. Not only the animals are loaded to capacity: women will carry two or three large squashes in addition to the normal pack, and men bring ploughs or rafters on their shoulders.

The journey is hard. While the highlanders enjoy the change of scenery, the warmth and a different diet, they have to travel through the territory of little-known and sometimes hostile groups. Everyone knows stories of others who have been attacked or robbed on the way, and even though today such experiences are rare, there are plenty of other rigours to be faced. Night and morning they chew coca and make offerings to the guardian spirits of the mountains (*kumpriras*), not only to safeguard their journey, but also to ask help in obtaining all the valley produce they require.

Lorries also make the journey from the mining centres in the highlands down the river-bed beyond San Pedro de Buenavista. The lorry-owners, mainly townspeople, may themselves trade in maize, or they may hire out space in the vehicle for transport. But in spite of the relatively greater ease and speed of travelling by lorry, most peasants continue to travel on foot, using their own pack-animals and staying with their kin in the valley region.

Money has circulated widely throughout the Central Andes since the mid-sixteenth century, but the rural economy of Northern Potosí is today only very partially integrated into the market. I shall here describe the processes of circulation which persist alongside, and in complex articulation with, the market.

Contemporary patterns of circulation have to be understood in the light of the ways in which Andean societies have historically made use of the dramatically varied landscape. As Troll demonstrated, the zonation of the Andes compresses in a small area an extraordinary ecological variation that takes a quite different form from that found all the way from the North Pole to Panama (1968). Murra has shown that this ecology was, in the Central Andes, exploited in a particular way by vast polities, such that a single administrative unit embraced far-flung households and resources in outliers many days' journey from the nucleus. Circulation of goods from these different climates was administrated in such a way as virtually to preclude the existence of markets (1972a, see also 1956). Human adaptation in the Andes has thus incorporated a fine degree of ecological and geographical specialization, without thereby involving the indigenous development of a market system for the exchange of such specialized produce.

For the pre-Columbian polities we can assume a large-scale administrative capacity, but the intervening centuries have witnessed the alienation and splitting up of ethnic lands. Some writers have argued that it is particularly the cutting off of the nucleus from its more distant outliers that led to the 'peasantization' of the native Andean population. Through this process resources that were formerly controlled and exploited directly by each group became obtainable only from outsiders, and for money (Webster 1971, Fonseca 1973). In addition, dues in labour, kind and money to the state, church and local land-owners produced profound changes in the structure of freeholding ethnic organization. The groups that exist today in Northern Potosí are only fragments of the polity of Charcas whose ethnic lords held sway four centuries ago over the whole region (Espinoza 1969; Platt in prep.). The Laymis, whose economy I shall describe, are Indians of Chayanta, part of the former Charcas, as many colonial documents testify, but Chayanta as a unit persists today only in the religious organization of a crumbling town that is known to historians as the administrative capital of a once-important colonial *corregimiento*.

Along with these transformations there are also continuities. The smaller-scale units still control much of the land they were working in the sixteenth century,[1] and are still important for economic organization. We know that Chayanta, along with many areas, was the scene of major shifts in population throughout the colonial period, as some of the original land-holders left to evade the burdens imposed by the colonial state, or to work in Potosí, and were replaced by successive waves of newcomers – *forasteros*.[2] In spite of such changes, the fundamental disposition of the ethnic groups themselves has to some extent persisted. Ethnic organization involves reversionary rights in the land worked by members of the ethnic group, and attendant political and ritual institutions.

The characteristic form of peasant economy is one in which each household has access to the means for its own subsistence and relies on the market for whatever goods it cannot produce. Correspondingly, discussion of exchange in peasant economies tends to focus on labour and forms of co-operation, and the distribution of means of production, particularly land and livestock. What makes the indigenous Andean economy of particular interest is the persistence of product-circulation outside the market on a large scale. I have used the term ethnic economy to designate the Laymi case, since its salient characteristics derive from the organization of the ethnic group. This is not to suggest that all product-circulation outside the market is thereby to be subsumed within the confines of the ethnic group.[3] Neither is it to assign a grand theoretical status to the ethnic economy. In order to understand the workings of economic systems not dominated by the commodity form we have to proceed inductively, rather than use deductive categories (Friedmann 1980). It is through an examination of the circulation of labour and produce among the Laymis that the importance of ethnic boundaries emerges. These boundaries are not solely economic, nor are they absolute; but in view of the emphasis placed on the household enterprise and the peasant community in discussions of the rural Andes, it is worth insisting that the Laymi economy is reproduced at the level of the ethnic group as a totality in order to point up its unusual features.

2. Land tenure and the ethnic group

The Laymis – Aymara-speakers – today number roughly 8000 souls, of whom about two-thirds live in the highland *suni* (between approximately 3800 and 5000 metres) and the other third in the temperate *likina* (2000 to 3500 metres). In both zones households have a broad subsistence base including a variety of both indigenous and Old World crops and livestock. In the suni llamas and sheep are reared, and the staple is a rich variety of tubers, together with some beans, wheat and barley; in the likina the main crops are maize and squashes, with some wheat, beans and certain breeds of potato and *quinoa* that prosper in the warmer climate. Goats and some sheep are reared. These two 'tiers'[4] of Laymi territory are separated by a journey of several days, which can take as long as two weeks with laden llamas (see map, figure 2.1); in consequence there is a radical dualism in the way Laymis experience and represent their ecological setting, which treats all the intermediate gradations as a 'centre' through which they have to pass when travelling between suni and likina.[5]

Today most of the Laymi population lives in hamlets dispersed across their whole territory. A small proportion inhabits the early *reducción* town of Chayanta in the highland suni, sharing it with five other divisions of the Chayanta Indians.[6] Several hundred others live in two villages close to the road that leads from Oruro to Sucre. One of these – Qalaqala – can perhaps be termed the Laymi capital, since the two major authorities of the ethnic group normally reside there. The church, built in the early eighteenth century, was for a long time adjunct parish to Chayanta (*vice-parroquia*), and the village thus concentrates a degree of both political and ceremonial organization for the whole ethnic group. It is not clear at what historical juncture the higher, more inclusive level of Chayanta ceased to operate as a political unit, but today the two *segundas mayores*, one for each moiety, are the highest authorities for the suni Laymis. They collect the tax paid by land-holders and deliver it to the departmental authorities in Potosí; they also arbitrate disputes between members of their own moiety or jointly between moieties, and represent their suni moiety members to the administrators of Bustillos province. Below them in the political hierarchy, the Laymi suni is divided into smaller units – *cabildos* – each headed by a *jilanqu* who is elected annually from among the land-holders, and who is responsible for collecting the land-tax and settling local grievances.[7]

Until 1953 this political structure embraced also Laymis living in the likina. Although they are within a different province (Charcas), and had separate corvée obligations in the local valley towns, their tax too was paid to the segundas mayores in the suni, and their own local jilanqus were answerable to the moiety authorities. However, when the land-tax was abolished by the 1953 Agrarian Reform, likina cultivators ceased to pay it while those in the suni continued.

The authority system, structured as it was around tax-collection, therefore continued in the suni, while in the likina it was replaced by a provincial branch of the peasant union, the National Federation of Peasant Workers. The suni authorities no longer have any jurisdiction over the likina. This formal separation of the two tiers will in the long term no doubt have wider organizational implications, but for the moment the memory of their former unity is strong, and reinforces the economic and cultural integration which is still very much a reality.

Why then do suni cultivators continue to pay land-tax, albeit at a rate that inflation has devalued to a purely symbolic amount? A long historical association exists between the organization of taxation and the communal rotation of cultivation between open fields, known locally as *mantas*. As Sánchez–Albornóz argues, this integral relationship between tax-payment and the system of tenure which prevails in the highlands underlies the fierce resistance that met repeated attempts by Bolivian governments to alter taxation and create individual rights of tenure throughout the nineteenth century (1978: 187–218). More recently it has aroused opposition to the attempts of the Agrarian Reform Council to individualize land-owner-ship and impose a uniform tax for all smallholders.[8]

Each hamlet possesses a series of mantas which are divided into parcels worked by each household. The order of rotation is agreed on by the community parliament (Aymara: *paylamintu*) and this careful co-ordination of cultivation allows maximum use of fallow land for pasture by concentrating agriculture in agreed fields. It thus protects the crops against the ravages of livestock and ensures the reproduction of a mixed subsistence base. It also allows a maximum scattering of parcels for each household, exploiting to the full the extreme variety of micro-climates within a small area, and spreading the real risks involved in agriculture at this altitude.

As tends to occur with open-field systems over time, the parcels in each manta are owned by particular individuals who hold the titles to the land. The distribution of parcels, however, has none of the rigidity of a system of private property. Each estate is large, known either as an *originario* unit, corresponding supposedly to the 'original' inhabitants, or as an *agregado* unit whose smaller size indicates an associate member of the hamlet. However, today any distinction in terms of origin has been forgotten, to the extent that a single individual may hold simultaneously an agregado and an originario title; their only significance is in terms of size, which has remained unaltered for nearly a century. Nonetheless each unit is larger than the needs of a single household, sometimes considerably so. The title-holder is responsible for paying the tax and allocating the various community obligations that derive from possession, but he, or occasionally she, must share out the parcels among the members of the agnatic kin-group, in quantity and quality sufficient to guarantee subsistence to each household. While most households have access to land through agnatic links, there is also a category of landless households for whom direct rights to land through kin ties have lapsed over the generations. These landless households borrow parcels from land-holders, and by strategic use of the ritual kinship system try to ensure preferential treatment from those who have land to spare.

The combination of large holdings and fallowing makes possible the flexible allocation of parcels each year, according to need and household size. This is not to deny that the actual title-holders and their immediate kin generally have more access to better land than others, but individual rights are circumscribed by the obligation to lend out parcels to those in need. The local parliament is involved directly in re-allocating estates when owners die without leaving a direct heir, and continued tenure is guaranteed explicitly by the services and obligations that each household performs for the community. While there is some sanction against a recalcitrant title-holder who refuses to lend to landless households, the fact that this system persists is itself eloquent testimony to the absence of a market in land, and to the low degree of commoditization of its fruits. In many cases the owners do not even charge the two days' labour rent per year that they are entitled to. The Laymi manta system is similar to that described by Platt (ch. 2), to the *aynoka* system of Irpa Chico near Lake Titicaca (Carter 1965) and the *laymi* system of Espinar in Southern Peru (Orlove 1977); but it differs from the former two in the greater overall significance of mantas in Laymi agriculture. Whereas in the systems described by Platt and Carter individually held parcels outside the system of community rotation are the basis of household subsistence (known as *tasa* in Macha, and *sayaña* in Irpa Chico), such parcels have little significance for the Laymi economy.[9] All pasture land is held communally by the hamlet, again in contrast to some other regions where a proportion of pasture is possessed by individual households (e.g. Preston 1974).

The striking difference of tenure between the suni and the likina derives from the absence of fallowing in the lower tier. Here land is more productive and cultivation continuous. Each house is situated beside its main maize field, with other parcels above and below this level. Due to the different conditions of production the valley holdings are more individualized than the highlands, and in many regions of the Andes the valleys have indeed split off from their highland counterparts and turned to the production of cash crops.[10] However, though tenure in the Laymi likina is individualized, parcels are still distributed to those without adequate land through ties of kinship and ritual kinship. Tenancy or share-cropping arrangements are not found, and those who borrow land pay no rent. Thus in spite of the absence of fallowing, land is still distributed to needy households, and rights to land are guaranteed by the performance of community dues.

The continued existence of these systems of tenure depends on many factors, particularly the absence of conditions which have transformed so many other rural communities. There is no class differentiation within the ethnic group. Even the hereditary office of *kuraka* with its attendant privileges has disappeared (though it persists in some of the neighbouring groups). Offsetting these negative conditions are positive ones, of which perhaps the most important is the prevailing endogamy. It is through their marriage practices that one can begin to understand the remarkable continuity in organization and land-holding among the ethnic groups of Northern Potosí, in spite of the massive depopulation and internal migration that occurred in past centuries (Grieshaber 1977, Sánchez–Albornóz 1978). The Laymis are numerous enough for endogamy to be possible, even with marriage rules that forbid a union with anyone to whom a kin link can be traced. These rules have the effect both of spreading links very widely within the group, and of guaranteeing the common kinship by which they retain their collective identity over time, divided as they are across such a wide area by many intervening, sometimes hostile, groups (Harris 1976).

75

3. The circulation of produce

In the organization of Andean polities prior to 1532, their direct access to a number of different ecological zones appears to have been orchestrated and administered by ethnic lords – kurakas (Murra 1972a). While we know very little about the ways in which produce may have circulated at the local level, the concept of redistribution has been used by some to describe the system (e.g. Wachtel 1974). Certainly local kurakas controlled resources of various ecologies (Murra 1978b), such that we can suppose at least a degree of centralization both of administration and of produce. The contemporary organization of the Laymis is however striking for the virtual absence of a centric pole of organization or redistribution.

This lack of centricity does not mean that their economy is simply an aggregate of households. The identification of economic units or enterprises in a non-commodity economy can never be more than partial; and it is closely related to the contrasting ways in which labour and goods are circulated and exchanged. In particular, the point at which relations of sharing, common ownership, and distribution according to need give way to stricter calculations of equivalence and limited toleration of delay in completing an exchange, is normally identified as the boundary of the unit.[11] In the Laymi economy the individual household in some respects is such a unit. For example it has rights to the use of land, initiates production and shares consumption; in market relations the unit of exchange is often the household; the division of labour by sex and age is organized in such a way that ideally each domestic group can perform the tasks necessary for subsistence. On other criteria the local land-holding community is the significant economic unit. At yet another level, the generalized circulation of produce and of labour extend beyond the local community and its constituent households to embrace the ethnic group as a whole.

The ethnic group is not of course autarkic. Many of the forms of exchange that exist between Laymis are also found with non-Laymis, and some exchanges link them directly with international capital. For example, there is a form of direct exchange of use-values by which townspeople are able to obtain agricultural produce and livestock at favourable rates, giving bought items such as coca, alcohol, clothing, bread and matches in exchange. Similar forms of barter are observed between Laymis themselves. They may buy commercial goods to exchange against crops they cannot produce themselves, in cases where the producers refuse to accept cash. Such transactions occur frequently between the two tiers of Laymi territory; but within the suni also, people residing round Qalaqala sometimes travel to the uplands to obtain the better-quality potatoes that are thought to grow there. In all these instances, however, there is a marked difference between the exchange rates offered to outsiders and those amongst fellow Laymis, that signals a contrast in meaning and social universe. This difference is the more striking since the advantage does not always go the same way. For example, in the cases where suni dwellers obtain potatoes in exchange for bought goods, fellow Laymis give more commodities than townspeople for the same measure of potatoes. Conversely when highlanders go to the likina to obtain maize, a member of the ethnic group will get more grain in exchange for the commodities he has brought than will an outsider. In the former case the outsider does better than a fellow-Laymi; in the latter case the reverse is true. But in both cases the difference in rates is explained in terms of the behaviour proper between members of the ethnic group.

In these examples, many factors go to determine the rate of exchange, but since one side of the exchange derives from the market it is possible to translate the transaction into monetary terms. There is, however, another form of direct exchange of use-values in which the two sides mutually exchange what they themselves have produced. Here the rates of exchange cannot without distortion be translated into monetary equivalents, since they derive from the concrete qualities of what is changing hands. For example, earthenware pots are exchanged against the amount of grain or *ch'uñu* (dehydrated potato) which they contain. When quality cloth is sought by likina households they offer in exchange the cloth's capacity in maize grain. For example if a poncho is exchanged, the slit for the head will be sewn up temporarily so that the poncho itself can be filled to its full capacity with grain in payment. Such exchanges are made both between Laymis and with members of other ethnic groups, but preference is always given to fellow-Laymis. That is, exchange is permitted with outsiders only when they offer goods not available within the ethnic group. This applies particularly to the traditional routes by which Laymis obtain salt and pots from the direct producers in exchange for agricultural produce, for neither salt deposits nor potting clay are found within Laymi territory. They also exchange with neighbouring ethnic groups to obtain crops they cannot produce themselves – *ají* in the likina, quinoa in the suni.

The fact that measurement is by volume rather than by weight in exchanges between direct producers is itself an index of the degree to which monetary equivalence in exchange is avoided. Indeed the only moment at which measurement is by weight is the very point at which cash enters the ethnic economy, that is, when potatoes are sold for money in the mining centres. Fonseca has demonstrated how the shift from measurement in volume to weight occurs as profit (rather than direct consumption) becomes the goal of one or both parties to the exchange (1973: 115, 132).

The contrast between members of the ethnic group and non-members is not frequently in these cases related to exchange rates, since Laymis will rarely accept from outsiders indigenous products that they can produce themselves. The exchange system with outsiders is premised on both parties

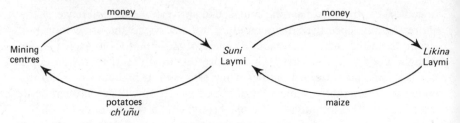

Fig. 3.1. Circulation of money in the Laymi economy

requiring the product of the other. Salt and pot traders come from areas where agriculture is much poorer than in the fertile territories of the Laymis. With outsiders, Laymis feel under no obligation to exchange and only do so if they specifically require what the other side is offering. Between Laymis, however, the definition of wants is affected by social obligations to circulate their produce.

This can be illustrated by the way that money circulates. Most cash enters the Laymi economy through the sale of potato and ch'uñu (by weight) in the mining centres. Some suni Laymis will take this cash to obtain maize (by volume) from kin in the likina (see figure 3.1). The fact that money enters the ethnic economy mainly by this route can be explained partly by the greater access to the market of the suni,[12] the obvious convenience of carrying cash rather than crops in making the long journey to the likina, and the more limited circulation of cash in the likina. This in turn is due partly to distance from markets, but also to the greater fertility of the temperate lower region, making possible for example the breeding of livestock that in the suni must be acquired by purchase (donkeys, cattle). Indeed likina cultivators claim that they would rather dispense altogether with cash payments and exchange maize only directly for other use-values. They accept cash, they say, as a favour for their suni kin for whom this form of transaction is more convenient. Even so, there comes a point where cash is no longer acceptable, so that those from the suni who require more valley produce must offer direct use-values. It is virtually impossible for those outside the ethnic group to obtain Laymi maize for cash, or indeed to obtain any Laymi produce for money within the territory of the ethnic group. Tubers are only sold for cash in the mining-towns; maize is only exchanged for money to fellow-Laymis.

The resistance to cash was exemplified by the difficulty I had in buying things when living in Laymi hamlets. This applied not only in cases where cash sales were unusual or disapproved of, for example for woven cloth; but also in the case of eggs which were habitually accumulated by suni people and taken to the mining centres to sell for cash. There was, it seems, a marked difference between selling for money at home and selling for money in the mines. The explanation I think is two-fold. On the one hand money obtained through the sale of produce almost always has a specific destination; for example, in the case of eggs it will be used to obtain luxury foods such as sweets, oranges and bread. The cash should be reconverted as rapidly as possible into articles of consumption – to make the sale as like barter as possible, and to circumscribe the degree to which money can become abstracted from the particular object it is destined to buy. Second, there is a marked reluctance to increase the amount of cash actually flowing within the confines of the ethnic group itself, partly because of the uncertainty of inflation of the Bolivian currency. Also, the complex system of debts and credits between Laymis themselves depends on there never being sufficient cash to cancel all debts at once.

While likina residents do require some cash (particularly to spend at religious feasts and pay for masses), and while cash does circulate within the ethnic group, its use is strictly curtailed, and purely commercial relations are rare. Moreover, only a small number of households obtain the maize and other likina products they require exclusively for cash, or even the direct exchange of use-values. In such transactions the return is immediate and involves no long-term obligations; but even these individual acts of immediate exchange have to be understood in the context of other, more enduring ties that underwrite them. For the majority of households, returns are not immediate, nor is there strict book-keeping of equivalencies. Instead householders from one tier will travel regularly to the other, taking with them their most favoured produce: from the likina good quality yellow maize, dried squash, maize flour, hominy, wild peppers and honey; from the suni wool, ch'uñu, ch'arki, quinoa flour, coca-leaf and alcohol (the last two are treated in this instance as suni products since it is tubers that 'produce' the money with which they are bought). They offer these to households where they have relations of largesse, or where they hope to establish such relations. The gifts are conceptually separate from whatever produce the travellers acquire; they are used to call forth the generosity of their hosts. Each side is committed to a belief in its own superior generosity; and it is degrees of largesse that partners compare rather than precise calculations of what is transferred. In particular, relative need is taken into account, including the quality of the harvest, whether a particular household has to sponsor a feast or commemorate the dead, and how many other calls there are on the producer's resources.

In such relationships, access to the produce of the other ecological tier is often reinforced through working for the host. As in Fonseca's account of links between ecological zones in Huánuco, the labour input of highlanders in search of maize, the returns on this labour and the long-term social relationships that are therby maintained underwrite a system of inter-zonal exchange based on conventional and stable rates (1973: 119ff). For the

79

Laymis labour inputs between suni and likina have a more explicit meaning. Such are the cases where kin (usually full siblings, or parents and children) share a single holding that spans both zones, and divide it up so that each household is primarily responsible for cultivation and community obligations in a single tier, but retains full rights of access to the other. The shared rights in the land the ambivalent: those who do the work of cultivation will treat the crops as their own; yet when they go to visit their kin in the other zone they will also assert their rights to crops in which they have invested little labour. It is more the *fact* of working than the precise amount of labour given which defines the relationship and guarantees continued rights of access, so that at least one person will arrive for the harvest, or a child will be loaned to the household of the other tier to look after the family flocks.

There is a variety of arrangements for maintaining access to the produce of the other tier, but over and above these, about a quarter of Laymi households cultivate simultaneously in both likina and suni in spite of the distances involved. This double cultivation is made possible by the complementary timing of intensive agricultural activity in each zone, and by frequent travel between them. Double cultivation uses household labour more fully and productively throughout the year than cultivation in a single zone (Platt, ch. 2 above), but not all households have the minimum labour resources required. In some instances it is not clear whether one should talk of a single household enterprise cultivating in both tiers, or two distinct enterprises that co-operate closely. In any event households practising double cultivation rely on the help of neighbours and kin to cover for them during the absence of some or all members in the other tier; this practice illustrates how misleading it would be to treat the bond between likina and suni simply as one of product circulation. While those living in a single tier treat the residents of the other – even close kin – with suspicion (based at least partly on the ambiguous nature of the exchanges that are their mutual interest), those practising double cultivation are neighbours, and thus bound in sets of mutualistic relations, in both zones. While they rely on the assistance of kin and neighbours in both, the communities in which they cultivate are also able to make extra demands on them because of their higher productivity. They are expected to be more generous than others, and the feasts they hold in both tiers must be lavish. What is more, they travel throughout the year, carrying news as well as produce, and are thus an important means of communication in a world that for many Laymis is viewed as a fundamental opposition between the known and the unpredictable, the secure and the exotic.

In Laymi organization today, despite the distance between them, the produce of each tier is not distributed simply through exchange. The degree to which *all* the different forms of circulation – barter, sale, largesse – together with double cultivation, form a single system founded in the common kinship and cultural forms of the whole ethnic group can be illustrated by a process which has evolved over the last twenty years. Two hamlets to the extreme north-east of likina territory have been gradually seceding from the ethnic group and integrating themselves with their northern neighbours – the Pampas. The secession was an all-embracing one: not only were economic links with suni Laymis gradually severed, but also kinship ties were brought to a stop by ceasing endogamous unions in favour of marriage with the Pampas. Finally a variety of cultural identifications with the rest of the ethnic group such as the style of music were renounced, and Aymara as a first language was replaced by Quechua, the *lingua franca* of the valleys. Those households with suni lands abandoned them. In the words of many Laymis, these hamlets have now become Pampas, thus confirming the integral connection between endogamy, cultural practices, and the many-stranded system of economic links between ecological zones that together define the ethnic group today. Moreover, the links do not involve merely the movement of produce; apart from those practising double cultivation most adults have resided in both zones, or at least visited for an extended period. Some marry into the other tier and feel homesick for the landscape they have lost. For many, the occasional periods spent away staying with kin are like a holiday, vivid and pleasurable in the abrupt alteration of the basic condition of life.

This history also clarifies the importance of proximity to markets. The two hamlets which were breaking with their Laymi kin were within reach of Torotoro, the pueblo to the north-east which with the completion of the road became the furthest reach for lorries in search of maize for the insatiable Cochabamba market. They ceased to depend on suni Laymis for cash, wool, and other highland products. The presence of cash in inter-zonal exchange within the ethnic group should not, then, be seen as an index of breakdown of the system, but a necessary use-value whose effects are restricted and controlled precisely by limiting its currency to exchanges between Laymis.

This apparent paradox by which the impersonal medium of money is restricted to relationships which are not exclusively economic but founded in a complex of social bonds, while exchanges with strangers and outsiders take the supposedly more primitive form of barter, is a way of preventing cash from dissolving other types of economic relationship. If this is so, we must question the assumption by which a scale of reciprocity ranging from unstinting generosity to immediate exchange of equivalents is directly correlated with a scale of social relationships ranging from close kin through to strangers. This model, persuasively presented by Sahlins (1965), has been found useful in other Andean regions (e.g. Mayer 1974a). In understanding the Laymi economy it has limited value. While there is an ideology that close kin should show uncalculating generosity to one another, the reality is otherwise: in practice the most successful and enduring relations of largesse are often between more distant kin. Ties of ritual kinship are also very important, both in the consolidation of existing economic relations, and in initiating new ones. Long term relations of largesse, with little exact calculation of return, may unite households related only through ties of *compadrazgo*; conversely exchange for cash may occur between full siblings. Even the ties derived from working a common land-holding are not restricted to close kin; if they do not wish to work a particular holding, it will be loaned to more distant kin, or non-kin.

Common kinship, reproduced through endogamy, is a pre-condition for the continuance of the ethnic economy in its present form. However, this does not entail the reproduction of specific kin ties or particular corporate coalitions. Existing structures are oriented rather to maximum flexibility. Which ties are activated in the circulation of produce and cash between suni and likina will depend on what other calls there are on a particular household. Given the demographic distribution between the two zones, with about two-thirds of all Laymi households in the suni, each likina household must supply on average two to three suni households with the maize they require. When maize is scarce suni people will need to exploit as many links in the likina as possible in order to meet their needs; even when maize is plentiful some likina producers will hold back in the knowledge that there are likely to be many further calls on their supplies that they cannot refuse. Ties of kinship serve to spread demand as wide as possible, rather than to provide exclusive access, and most households are partners in a variety of inter-zonal relationships.

4. Dependence and interdependence between suni and likina

So far the discussion has focused primarily on the ways in which suni households obtain maize from the likina. This is in fact the single most important form of circulation between the two tiers of Laymi territory, and it raises the issue of the relationship between them. Within the over-arching structure of the ethnic group there are also radical differences and oppositions between them. Likina residents claim with some justification that the suni needs them more than they require suni products. In the short term this is true: maize is essential for all ritual feasts, whether of a household or a whole community. The wood used in construction comes exclusively from the Laymi likina, and major instruments of production such as ploughs and looms are made by likina craftsmen. The dependence of likina households on suni products is less marked. Most plant some potatoes and other tubers on the upper, more exposed slopes above their maize fields. Many also rear sheep which cover at least some of their needs for wool. When we further take into account the demographic imbalance between the two zones and the preferential prices at which maize is exchanged for cash, there seems to be some basis to the complaints of likina people that they give to the suni far more than they receive.

Nonetheless while likina requirements for highland produce are less immediate than the suni's for that of the lower zone, overall their needs for wool cannot be met adequately from their own sheep. Llama wool, used particularly in the weaving of blankets and sacks, necessarily comes from the suni, as do the llamas that must be sacrificed for certain rituals (notably feasting the souls of the recently dead). Suni people are better weavers (just as likina people are skilled carpenters), and most likina households obtain some cloth or clothing directly from suni producers. Again, the ch'arki, ch'uñu, and quinoa flour that come from the suni are much appreciated additions to the likina diet. We see in these examples the way that cultural preferences and ritual obligations sustain the needs that each tier has of the other.

On another level, while most Laymis can be classified as residing un-ambiguously in only one of the two zones, the possibility of changing their residence, coupled with the rights of tenure that many have in both, gives them a flexibility of social organization rare in the contemporary Andes. It allows elasticity in allocation of land, which can in this system be matched to available labour without either the extensive negotiations involved in making over rights to land in perpetuity, or the extraction of high rent that frequently accompanies share-cropping arrangements. This flexibility is also advantageous in times of persistent illness, epidemics, crop failure, warfare and disputes. As many life histories testify, a change of residence, and the possibility of initiating cultivation for a short or extended period in the other tier, may be the key to survival, and certainly make it possible to resolve immediate problems without a complete break from the land.

The relationship between likina and suni raises many questions beyond the scope of the discussion. Historical evidence suggests that in Qullasuyu the nucleus of power was usually in the highlands.[13] The idea that the suni extracts from the likina, rather than making balanced exchanges, gains support both from the location of the highest political authority of the Laymis in the suni, and the symbolic representation of the relationship between the two tiers. Laymi cosmology portrays the likina as the more productive region whence food is taken up to be processed and consumed in the less fertile suni.[14] But such hints are far from conclusive; while suni people travel more frequently to the temperate zone than vice versa, this is in part because of the greater natural fertility of the lower region, and also because llamas, which have the advantage, as pack animals, of requiring only natural fodder, are kept exclusively in the suni. There is no clearly demarcated surplus product which the suni appropriates from the likina, nor is there evident accumulation in the suni, although population increase there is marginally higher than in the lower tier.

I argued above that direct exchange of use-values should not be translated into monetary terms. It is however worth noting in this context that converting suni–likina exchanges into their cash equivalents does not reveal any consistent bias in favour of one tier.[15] This is interesting particularly in view of the greater distance of the likina from the market. Today cash enters the ethnic economy mainly via the sale of suni products. If the present system continues to operate, it is because it is more convenient for likina producers to maintain economic relations with their suni kin than to incur the burden of transporting their own produce to the nearest market. This remains true in spite of decades, indeed centuries, of fragmentation and twenty years of complete political separation, as the example of the two seceding hamlets demonstrates.

When I discussed with suni people the complaints of exploitation against them by likina people, they responded by pointing to the time and energy they spent in travel. To make the journey with llamas is less costly than travel with Old World pack animals, since they feed exclusively on natural fodder, but it takes far longer, and llamas when fully loaded cannot sustain a great weight.[16] Likina people rely on donkeys and mules whose advantages of speed and greater carrying capacity are offset by the need to buy fodder on the journey. In their complaints about the inequality of exchanges, they do not take travel and transport costs into account; nonetheless the fact that they make the arduous journey to the suni and to the urban markets less frequently than their suni kin travel down suggests that for them too, travel is a cost. For some students of peasant economies, the time involved in travel and transport to meet subsistence needs does not enter into economic calculation. It is unclear how far travel and transport costs are calculated within traditional Andean economies,[17] but the fact is that likina households can more frequently sustain subsistence without moving, and distance from the market reduces the advantage of selling their produce over maintaining the economic links with their suni kin.

5. Forms of labour prestation

Product circulation cannot be understood solely in terms of the objects themselves and the ways they are brought into relationship. Between suni and likina not only products but people themselves circulate and work with kin and exchange partners. The labour bestowed is not calculated closely; it is the gesture of working that underwrites many of the transfers of produce across tiers. To sustain circulation of goods with direct production, or at least the direct prestation of labour, has well-established roots in Andean economic organization.[18]

Labour and produce in an ethnic economy

Helping: labour without direct return

Labour prestation without explicit calculation of return is also a widespread institution in the rural Andes (e.g. Mayer 1974a). Known by the generic term of 'helping' (Aymara: *yanapaña*) it includes both the work done for close kin, and the more formal obligations by which godchildren help their godparents, or a man his wife's parents. The same concept is used for the labour proffered to land-holders by those who borrow parcels from them.[19] Helping is the basis of most collective labour. In agriculture collective work-parties are known as *chuqu*, and both in chuqu, and in the collective work of house building (*utuchaña*) and preparing a feast (*p''ist lur, aña*), labour is given without precise calculation of debts and credits. In all these cases the only remuneration is festive food which all helpers share together, although households respond to solicitations for help on the assumption that when they in turn need it, others will also respond. While people do remember which households have helped them and whom they themselves have assisted, they do not keep strict balance-books in their heads. At least in the conversations I witnessed concerned with organizing or attending a festive work-party, the assumption of obligations was phrased in terms of general social duty on the one hand, and immediate convenience on the other; that is, not in terms of the direct reciprocation of previous labour prestations.

There are two other ways that energy circulates in a comparably general-ized movement (although the concept of helping is not explicitly used). Draught and pack animals (bulls, mules and donkeys) are loaned mostly for no return except fodder for the animal. It might be assumed that house-holds owning draught animals would be less involved in co-operative labour than those with none, given their greater potential autonomy and productive capacity. However the reverse is true: owners of bulls are in fact more often invited to attend a chuqu, and drive their own team. Loans for ploughing can involve extra work for the owner in another way. On one occasion I saw a man whose household owned a yoke of bulls harnessed to his own plough, which was driven by his wife while their daughter came behind planting potatoes. He had lent his bulls to someone else.

The second instance is the use of child labour for herding. Between adults, herding arrangements take a variety of institutional forms, but a hamlet's children are assumed to be generally available. Those who do not have household flocks to mind are expected to herd for other households, and if they refuse they are indignantly criticized as lazy. Here, as with the loan of animals, the beneficiary gives only food in return: in the case of children, a bag of toasted grains to eat during the day, and perhaps a small offering of cooked food when they return from the pastures. Energy circulates in this way also between the two tiers of Laymi territory. Animals – particularly bulls – may be lent for long periods to kin or ritual kin living in the other tier, often to the great inconvenience of the owners, and with no payment other than their immediate upkeep. Children also circulate between the two tiers; for example a child may be sent from the suni to live with childless kin in the likina, where cultivation is not practicable without continuous manuring of the maize fields. Each household must of necessity maintain at minimum a small herd of goats, and the labour of herding is generally assigned to children.

The social relationships along which help is channelled are hard to pinpoint. In the ideology of kinship and ritual kinship, help and loans are freely proffered; but the ideology is self-fulfilling since those involved in a close mutualistic bond will treat each other as close kin, or reinforce the relationship through ties of compadrazgo. Neighbourhood is also important, and for any collective work-party, neighbours (*wisinu*, from the Spanish *vecino*) are recruited along with close kin. In all the labour of preparing a feast, or building a new house (and thus in many cases of instituting a new household), the involvement and interests of the locality are obvious. Feasts are kept primarily by land-holding communities, and the rituals celebrate local deities who guarantee fertility of land and livestock.

In the organization of the agricultural chuqu the involvement of the neighbourhood is not at first sight so obvious, since an individual household sponsors a work-party to cultivate its own fields. The pattern is quite different between ecological tiers. In the highlands, chuqu are held only by households sponsoring a community feast in the coming year, and it is obligatory for them to hold one at least in planting the potato crop. In the likina on the other hand, all stages of maize cultivation by most households are done with chuqu. The reasons for this contrast are not altogether clear, but the fact that in the suni agricultural work-parties are held by the sponsors of community feasts, and that in both tiers they are held only for the cultivation of the major staple,[20] suggests that the difference should be explained not by the technical and ecological requirements of cultivation but by the different social relations in the two tiers. It is striking that there is far more labour co-operation in likina agriculture where land-holding is individualized, and residence scattered, and where members of both moieties and their subdivisions live in each locality. There is in addition a practice in the likina that lends support to the impression of greater communality in agricultural organization. Not every household will hold a chuqu for each stage of the crop cycle. Some households that have insufficient funds to hold their own chuqu will have their fields cultivated without cost. The host household sends the entire work-party on to work the fields of a poorer household after its own have been completed.[21] In addition chuqu in the likina are more festive than in the suni. People wear their best clothes and fronds of molle leaves in their hats; bulls too are decorated with molle. The potentially greater social fragmentation in the lower zone is thus counteracted by a practice which for likina people is clear evidence of their superior generosity and communal spirit.[22]

In co-operative labour that takes the form of helping, mutualistic relationships extend beyond the household to embrace other kin and ritual kin, neighbours and the local land group, and also people living in the other tier. The counterpart of helping is sharing food, and commensality is thus partially extended beyond the household.

'*Ayni*' and '*mink'a*': labour with direct return

The nature of helping relationships is brought into greater relief by contrast with other forms of labour prestation where the returns are more strictly calculated and specific, forms which in Northern Potosí are known by the common terms *ayni* and *mink'a*. Mink'a labour is remunerated by produce while ayni labour is reciprocated by labour, within the same branch of production.[23] Ayni co-operation arises not so much from an absolute shortage, but from a shortage of labour socially defined as proper for one sex only. A widow for example must find a man to plough for her. In one case a *likina* widow arranged on one day to have her ploughing done in return for sowing for the unmarried man on a later occasion. In this way she acquired the necessary male labour, and he the necessary female labour. In another ayni the same widow lent her team of bulls in exchange to the man who ploughed for her. Another common ayni is reciprocal herding arrangements between two women for their sheep, or two men for their llamas.[24] Here the arrangement is conditioned by the fact that herding of different animals is assigned to particular social categories, and when the proper labour is not available within the household, people will look outside the confines of the domestic unit rather than employ different labour. In one ayni for cloth production an unmarried man wove *bayeta* cloth for a widow while she in return spun for him.

In mink'a the worker is repaid in the product to which he or she has contributed. In harvesting, mink'a is repaid with some of the crop gathered on that day. Those who mind flocks on a mink'a basis are given a lamb or kid, as well as having the use of manure, milk and wool. Otherwise payment may be in the form of uncooked food, which is to be distinguished from the commensality that typifies helping arrangements. In other areas mink'a has become a covert form of wage labour (e.g. Mayer 1974a:6; Sánchez, ch. 6 below), but this has not yet developed among the Laymis. Wealthy suni households may recruit labour through mink'a, and in the likina either through mink'a or in the chuqu which account for much of the cultivation process. In either case the resulting yields are used mainly to improve household consumption or increase the livestock base. Differences between households must be understood in the context of an economic system in which accumulation is virtually non-existent and monetization curtailed, and where there is strong resistance to undermining the communal bases of tenure and consumption.

In the distribution of labour, as in the circulation of products, the degree of calculation and balance in returns derives as much from the circumstances in which labour is required, as from the social relationship itself. Helping (*yanapaña*) is proper between close kin, but it is also the mode of recruiting large numbers of workers on the basis of neighbourliness and the mutual dependence of those living in a single locality. Where people co-operate closely, or wish to do so, the relationship can be formalized as ritual kinship. On the other hand, ayni and mink'a where returns are carefully calculated are found between close kin as well as non-kin.

Here again the circulation of labour is founded in flexibility. Labour is organized in a variety of combinations, not based on clearly bounded groups.[25] The ideal of neighbourly behaviour and the institution of compadrazgo cuts across solidary bonds of genealogical kinship, while the traffic between ecological tiers extends the range of co-operation far beyond the arena of the local community.

6. The problem of the production unit

Laymi labour allocation differs from product circulation in being mainly within a single locality, while the latter is founded in ecological specialization and thus relies on social relations maintained across great distances. If we consider the distribution of labour, the locality will assume paramount importance as the unit of analysis; here is the pool of labour which, for reasons of proximity, is regularly drawn on. In addition, an important stimulus to co-operative labour is the preparation of ritual feasts, which are based in a particular locality and reconfirm the right to cultivate and rear livestock. If on the other hand we trace the circulation of produce, our focus of attention will necessarily be broader, to include as a single unit the whole ethnic group, with its widely separate territories. But the circulation of produce between the two tiers cannot be understood without taking into account also the ways that labour – and people – circulate between them.

Clearly the ethnic economy is not self-sufficient. If we further include in our analysis the ways that Laymi produce and labour circulate outside the confines of the ethnic group, concepts of a different order must be invoked. The presence of a major market in the mining centres broadens the range of analysis and at the same time emphasizes the individual household. However, there are mechanisms by which the dissolving effects of money on the Laymi economy are at present restricted. Produce is exchanged directly for other articles of consumption, and the channels by which money enters the ethnic group are limited.

The forms of wage labour preferred by Laymis are a vivid indication of this restriction. In spite of the proximity of a huge casual labour market in the urban mining centres, Laymis avoid working there, whether in mining itself, or as unskilled construction workers or in casual portering. They are to be found working as regular wage labourers only where there is a mine in the immediate vicinity of their homes (for example in Lagunillas, on the road from Uncia to Sucre). For the rest, a tiny scattering find their way to the mines on either a temporary or a permanent basis. It is far more common for people from the suni to avoid the urban conglomeration altogether and to travel right across the altiplano to the Chilean frontier round Llica, a journey that takes three days by truck, or well over a week on foot. There they work in agriculture, mainly clearing the ground for cultivation; they favour this form of wage labour because they are paid in kind, particularly with livestock, or in quinoa. A similar pattern of seasonal labour outside the ethnic group is found among the valley Laymis. The main source of work for the slack season is in the semitropical Chapare region (Department of Cochabamba) where they harvest both for cash and for direct payment in coca and rice. In both tiers Laymis show a preference for work in agriculture rather than mining or industry; they bypass the market by largely avoiding payment in cash, and obtain a form of wage that, overall, reproduces rather than subverts their mixed agrarian economy. Their preference for this kind of wage labour is enhanced in that they work for other Indians (Aymara: *jaqi*). They thus avoid a humiliating subjection to the abuses of non-Indians, and can more easily conciliate wage labour with their self-image as free, proud and independent producers.

For political economy, the exchange of objects precedes the exchange of labour, and takes place at the edges, within the interstices, of the productive community (Marx 1867 ch. 2). Conversely, land and labour are mobile only within the productive community. This perspective has been developed in Meillassoux's analysis of the self-sustaining domestic community (1975; 1978), which asserts a marked discontinuity between production and exchange. The substantivist approach in economic anthropology on the other hand privileges 'exchange' with virtual indifference to whether it is of labour or goods.[26] In both traditions, anthropology has tended to allocate activity into two polarized categories, one *within* a pre-given unit (whether household, lineage, or a larger unit), where circulation is based on pooling and redistribution, and the other *between* units. The former category includes production, and is designated the productive community, or even the mode of production (e.g. Sahlins 1972 chs. 2–3), while the latter is termed exchange.[27] In Meillassoux's analysis the productive community is in part identified through the authority wielded by a particular individual; in Sahlins's later work the domestic unit is characterized by pooling. In both cases there is an assumption of centricity within a single unit, and a predominance of two-way exchanges between units.[28]

In describing the contemporary Laymi economy I have avoided this polarization. Not only does the scale of the ethnic group and the diversity of rights to land preclude defining it as a productive community in the terms of these writers, but also the absence of central authority renders any analysis in terms of pooling or redistribution unsatisfactory. Whether in circulation of produce or the distribution of labour, there is little in the way of central administration. Only in preparing and sponsoring a feast does one household take responsibility for co-ordinating, organizing and stimulating productive effort, and then redistributing the fruits of that labour. This form of what can be called serial or rotating redistribution is an important function of the land group, but it does not re-allocate wealth to the poorer households (since these too must sponsor feasts), nor does festive distribution play much part in circulating goods produced by the specializations of either skilled individuals or ecologically distinct areas.

While there is not a centric principle in the ethnic economy, it would also be wrong to treat it as a series of independent households. Produce and labour circulate within the ethnic group in many ways: the importance of unreciprocated transfers and the absence of strict calculation in many contexts caution against an analysis founded in clear-cut units, or even productive communities. That is to say, while the individual household is a pole of economic activity, its reproduction is mediated through different forms of co-operative links that implicate not only the local land-holding group but ultimately the whole community of Laymis. There is no clear-cut discontinuity between production and exchange at the level of the household or the land group. For the ethnic group as a whole there is a real discontinuity that marks it off from other groups, but within this substantial population there are also many forms of direct, immediate exchange between both individuals and households. The ethnic group cannot then be assigned any absolute status as productive community.

Related to the ambiguous status of the productive community is the conceptual separation made by many writers between labour and its product. Labour when analysed as an object of exchange becomes abstracted. It is only within a productive community or domestic unit that labour is protected from the abstracting quality of exchange. In Laymi economic relations there are some transactions in which the product of labour is distinguished from the work that has created it; such is the direct exchange of use-values in which no further obligations or social relations are involved. In most cases the circulation of produce is embedded in a complex of relationships, involving land-holding and direct labour prestation as a means of guaranteeing the continuance of this circulation.

The forms of co-operation found between Laymis are not simply transfers of labour in general; in ayni exchanges the labour is reciprocated as a particular form, and each form has different social implications. The *sui generis* qualities of labour are even clearer in mink'a, where labour is converted into produce. Often labour and product are transferred within a single branch of production; here labour and its remuneration are conceived in the most concrete way possible, directly through its product.

7. The Laymis and Bolivia

The ethnic economy is clearly not an example of pristine pre-capitalist organization, nor is it in a state of breakdown and imminent dissolution. In part the reasons for this are internal to the organization of the group, or at least local. The Laymi suni is said to have unusually good land for this region; other divisions of the Chayanta Indians, particularly those in the immediate environs of the mining towns, appear to be far more deeply involved in the mining economy (for example the Chullpa, Aymaya and Sikuya). Not all their suni neighbours have retained such substantial territory in the likina zone, having suffered greater depradations from the expansion of private estates.

Apart from the contingency of location, the reproduction of Laymi subsistence must be understood in the light of the highly uneven development of the Bolivian economy overall. The expansion of the internal market has been stunted; while mining developed on an enormous scale Northern Potosí in the late nineteenth century, it did not transform production in the surrounding hinterland. This is partly because the urban centres that developed were company towns, provisioned directly with commercially produced goods from other regions of Bolivia and from outside the country, and large estates had developed little in the area itself (Grieshaber 1977). As a consequence, the staple diet in the mining centres – Uncia, Siglo XX, Catavi, Llallagua – differs strikingly from that of the surrounding countryside. The urban based population consumes primarily rice, wheat-based foods such as bread and noodles, sugar, tea and coffee; meat comes from the vast cattle ranches of Santa Cruz and Beni, which send beef directly to Uncia. Most fibres, cloth and clothing also come from outside the region.

Local produce provides important subsidiary foods for urban consumers (Wennergren and Whitaker 1975), but such commoditization as there has been seems not to have disrupted the subsistence base. There is, in the words of Geertz, no 'clash of cultivations' (1963: 89). The Laymis do not market any goods other than those which they produce for their own subsistence, and for local consumption. The only partial exception to this is the recent export boom in traditional Andean weavings. Laymi cloth, produced for domestic use, can now be bought on the streets of London.

A further reason for the low degree of commoditization is that throughout Northern Potosí there is no market for peasant produce; this is sold mainly on a house-to-house basis, or even requisitioned by the urban administration in times of shortage. The absence of market-places was the result of a conscious policy to keep down the price of locally produced agricultural goods and thus the cost of reproducing the urban work-force.

The separation of the mining towns from the hinterland is further accentuated by the fact that, except in the immediate vicinity of the mines, the local rural population seeks little employment either in mining itself or in related jobs such as construction. Most of the population in the mining centres comes from further afield, particularly from other mines, and from the Cochabamba valley (Harris and Albó 1975). As a result the large mining centres are not linked organically through kinship with the surrounding countryside, and peasants can decide whether, when, and to whom to sell their produce.

Bolivian agriculture has received scant attention from investment programmes of recent decades, and such investment as there has been has gone almost exclusively to the tropical lowlands where production is large-scale and capital-intensive. This, combined with the well-established pattern of supplying the urban markets with imported food and fibres, and a long-standing government policy of maintaining artificially low prices for small-holding produce, has resulted in relative stability, or stagnation some would say, for highland agriculture. However, it is far from clear that a highly capitalized agriculture would be possible in terrain such as that of Northern Potosí. As many have emphasized, the productivity of highland agriculture is maintained by product diversification, and maximum adaptation to slight variations in ecology.[29] Increased commoditization, requiring greater specialization and centralization, would very likely not be feasible. In other parts of the Central Andes the subsistence base has been undermined without thereby producing a trend towards capitalist agriculture (Caballero 1980); in many cases it has led to the abandonment of the land altogether.

This is not to say that the Laymi economy reproduces itself entirely outside the commodity circuit. There is a constant demand for certain commodities, particularly coca-leaf and alcohol, and cheap commercially produced clothing is gradually making inroads into the local system of production. For example, all hats and rubber-tyre sandals are now bought for cash, though some Laymis can remember the time when they made their own hats, and wore sandals made out of the skins of their own llamas. The small extent of this reliance on commercial goods is evidenced by the absence of indebtedness to local traders. They operate mostly on a small scale, in an atmosphere of strong competition; Indians rarely pay any interest on the loans they obtain, and even the sponsorship of feasts has not led to a cycle of debts whereby they are forced to sell ever-increasing amounts of their subsistence crops or their labour. The Laymis have, on their own account, never fallen prey to the *enganche* (= hook) system whereby Indians are enticed into selling their labour by cash advances, formerly in the mines (cf. Flores-Galindo 1973; Harris and Albó 1975), and today in the *zafra* – the cotton harvest in the eastern lowlands.

The Laymis are not dependent on the market to the point where such dependence classically transforms the conditions of production. There are other ways in which peasants have in the past been forced to increase commoditization, particularly through payment of dues to state and church. In the early colonial period the conversion of dues in kind to money payments was used to stimulate the local market (Platt 1978a); however, today, apart from the insignificant land-tax, dues to the state are paid directly in labour on the roads (*prestación vial*) and on school buildings, or in kind to provide partially for the subsistence of rural schoolteachers.[30] In the case of the church, the number of saints' day feasts celebrated has declined considerably, and other dues to the priests who serve them have virtually disappeared.

The ethnic economy has been shaped by circumstances of recent decades, and by the secular organization of Andean agrarian economy. The relaxation of outside pressure in the form of direct surplus extraction may well have reduced the integration of suni and likina; for example it was said that more Laymis practised double cultivation in the past than today. However, this lessening of external pressure has almost certainly been offset by other developments, particularly the slow but steady increase in population over the past century, and increasing labour migration during the slack season, even if this remains small by world standards. While the greater accessibility of markets may in the long term lead to the complete separation of the two ecological tiers, the ethnic economy today owes its continued viability to the flexibility and diversification which ecological complementarity makes possible.

Notes

The original research on which this is based was carried out in 1972–4 with grants from the Social Science Research Council of Great Britain, the Central Research Fund of the University of London, and the Radcliffe-Brown Memorial Fund. An earlier version of this chapter was presented at the XLII International Congress of Americanists in Paris (1976). Among all those who have helped with their comments I would like to thank especially John Murra, Tristan Platt, Barbara Bradby and David Lehmann.

1. See Archivo Nacional de Bolivia, Sucre; Tierras e Indios no. 149 (1592), where the Indians of the *repartimiento* of Chayanta complain about the usurpation of their low-lying valley land. The same document contains the earliest specific reference

to the 'ayllo laime', as forming part of the 'repartimiento de chayanta de la parcialidad de hanansaya'.

2. See for example Sánchez–Albornóz (1978).

3. Various accounts in Alberti and Mayer (1974) show the diversity of possible arrangements in other parts of the Andes. Again, Dow for the Mexican highlands describes an interesting variation whereby highland and temperate regions initiate close economic relations by means of what he calls 'festive pairing' (1977).

4. In Murra's original article the term used to express the discontinuities, and at the same time the gradations, of Andean ecology was the Spanish *piso* (floor or storey). The usual translation into French of this concept is *étage*; in English however the word 'floor' is ambiguous.

5. One particular ethnic group, the Q"äna, whose territory straddles the intermediate zone, are termed by the Laymis 'pure centre' (Aymara: *taypi*). Platt has suggested that even where the territory of the group embraces the intermediate zone, as in the case of Macha, it is conceptually minimized in the interests of duality (1978c); however, he also draws attention to the importance of maize-production in the highlands, thus somewhat undermining the complementary differentiation of highlands and valleys (ch. 2). Only a very few hamlets in the Laymi suni are sheltered enough for maize-production, so that in their case the dual opposition corresponds closely to reality.

6. I have translated the Spanish *parcialidad* as 'division'; Andean social organization has long taken a segmentary form, such that there are no absolute groupings, but rather different levels at which groups are fused, or divided and subdivided (Murra and Wachtel 1978). For the Laymis today, however, the term ethnic group is more appropriate since segmentation is only found within this unit; the Laymis are only in a minimal sense still part of a larger indigenous political grouping.

7. Alongside the indigenous authorities there are also four officers known as *corregidores* in the Laymi suni, elected annually from the total body of adult males. These form an intermediate level of authority between the local jilanqu and the segunda mayor; their status is not related to the structure of land-holding, and in theory they must answer directly to the system of provincial administration.

8. The work of the Agrarian Reform Institute has made little inroad in Northern Potosí. Individual titles were first made over to peasants of this region only in 1975. This tardiness is due not only to the limited finances of the Institute and the inadequacies of the Agrarian Reform Law itself, but also to lack of enthusiasm on the part of the peasants.

9. Known as *uyu*, they are small walled-in fields near the hamlet, and unlike other land they are alienable. See Preston (1974) for the *uyu* system in the Department of Oruro.

10. See for example Fonseca (1973), Bradby (ch. 4 below).

11. See 'The problem of the production unit' in this chapter (Section 6 below).

12. The only partial exception to this is the north-east tip of likina territory, within reach of the small town of Torotoro and thence of the Cochabamba market. Laymis from these hamlets sell some of their maize direct for cash there.

13. This is clear for the Lupaqa (Murra 1972a); and also for the many polities who cultivated in the valley of Cochabamba before its reallocation for state purposes by Wayna Qapaq (Wachtel 1981).

14. However, as I have argued elsewhere (Harris 1978b), Laymi cosmology crosscuts this apparent power relationship. In various dyadic relationships, for example that of wife and husband, the stronger partner is represented as being subordinate to the weaker. Thus while the likina is strong and male, and the suni weaker and

female, the latter exercises a managerial role over the lower zone similar to that of a wife over her husband.

15. For example, a sheepskin which at the time could have been sold in Uncia for $b65.00 (Dec. 1973) was exchanged in the likina for two cooking pots of maize whose price for the kin who bought it would have been only $b24.00. Conversely, in exchanging a block of salt ($5.00 in Uncia) for two cooking pots of maize, the suni partner would be reaping a substantial profit were it translated into cash.

16. According to Thomas, only 20 kg (1976).

17. See Fonseca (1973) and Alberti and Mayer (1974); especially the chapter by Christopher Scott: 'Asignación de recursos y formas de intercambio'.

18. Murra's thesis (1956) emphasized the importance of corvée labour as the chief source of revenue of the Inca state provided by its subject peoples. This tendency to provide the authority's revenues primarily through direct labour, direct production, also underlies his 'vertical archipelago' model (1972a).

19. It is surely significant that labour rent is represented in this way, although it is also treated as a form of mink'a (see below) by which the household or individual receives a loan of land in exchange for labour. Those paying labour rent are treated with great respect, and the sharing of food and coca is emphasized throughout the day.

20. Murra (1960) emphasizes the clustering of rituals around the major staples of the highland and temperate zones.

21. In Aymara the term used for this institution is *ark"ayaña* (= to make to follow).

22. This is not to say that such chuqu are organized by the community as a whole. The composition of each work-party will be different depending on particular kin and ritual kin, factions and competition within a locality. Chuqu can however also be organized by the community as such. In one case I observed, a cabildo in the suni agreed to plough up a new manta collectively, since it was under dispute from a neighbouring ethnic group. Quite separate from these work-parties are the community organized *faenas* which are not festive, but concerned with the upkeep of community buildings, roads and footpaths, irrigation ditches etc.

23. Urbain (1980) emphasizes the *restitution exacte* implicit in the concept of ayni. This is more evident in some contexts than others in Laymi usage. For example, the term is used of revenge killings, between moieties or feuding groups. It is also used of ceremonial exchange between siblings when they sponsor feasts. However, in ceremonial contexts it refers to the lending of ritual objects and utensils for cooking, brewing and storing, between households who in turn must sponsor a feast, and who inevitably do not own all the necessary items. Here I shall only discuss ayni as a form of labour exchange, but evidently its range is far broader. Mink'a also has a wide range of meanings. Perhaps the best translation is 'to work for somebody else', taking into account the ambiguity of the word 'for'. That is, it includes working with somebody else who has instituted the work, and also working instead of another person. It does not for the Laymis have the sense of festive work-party as in Ortiz (1972). It should be noted that a very few suni households also employ wage labour by the day (*jornal*) for ploughing, sowing and weeding.

24. Ownership and inheritance of llamas and sheep is in principle sex-based (see Harris 1978c).

25. It was only after completing this chapter that I obtained Gölte's recent essay (1980). Many of the points made here concerning the flexibility and diversification typical of traditional Andean forms of organization are argued more generally by him.

26. Humphreys (1969) makes this point apropos of Polanyi; it is also true of Sahlins (1965). While Neale (1957 ch. 11) moves beyond this, his account of the Indian

village economy polarizes labour and produce so that the former is associated with reciprocal exchange, the latter with redistribution.

27. Gudeman offers a revealing example of the problem in his perplexity as to whether the exchange of labour belongs in the category of production or exchange (1978: 114). See also the differentiation made by Erasmus between labour for festive food which is called 'co-operation', and labour for labour which is termed 'exchange' (1956).

28. Insofar as Sahlins envisages redistribution at a wider social level, it is premised on the existence again of a higher authority that is able to override the 'centrifugal' tendency of the individual production unit. His theory of the Domestic Mode of Production fits uneasily with his earlier influential article on the Sociology of Primitive Exchange (1965).

29. See Thomas (1976); also Murra (1972a) and Gölte (1980).

30. Few Laymis do military service.

4

'Resistance to capitalism' in the Peruvian Andes

1. Introduction

At a time when the developed capitalist nations of the world appear to have renounced all interest in the Third World other than interest owed to them on money lent and spent long ago, it may seem strange to attribute any force of economic expansion at all to the capitalist system. Curiously enough, the theories of Lenin, Luxemburg and Bukharin seem now to have been an optimistic overestimate of the power of capitalism to transform the world in its own image (Lenin n.d.; Luxemburg 1951; Bukharin 1972). If there is a point, then, in continuing to use the phrase 'resistance to capitalism' in characterizing an area such as the Peruvian Andes, it is not from a belief that there are in existence strong tendencies to capitalize the area which are being resisted, but rather from a wish to start from a position that takes the particular area as *outside* capitalism – as, in important respects, non-capitalist.

Although this chapter concentrates mainly on exchange relations, then, it does so from a framework which does not equate commodity exchange with capitalism. By whatever criterion, whether in terms of forms of property, relations of exploitation, laws of motion, or the protestant ethic, the predominant social relations in the area I wish to talk about are not capitalist ones;[1] and yet relations of exchange, both among the people of the area, and between them and the outside world, are extensive, and have undergone important shifts, it seems, in recent years. But the spread of relations of exchange does not go hand-in-hand with the spread of capitalist relations of production. Indeed, if it did, the capitalist problem of underdevelopment, in the sense of vast areas of unemployment, under-employment, migration and famine, might never have arisen.

If Marx, in analysing capitalism, started from the form of the commodity – the form of exchange most consistent with the capitalist mode of production – this was because the intersection between production and exchange is in many ways crucial to his analysis. It does not mean that all other modes of

97

production can be contrasted with capitalism as being production 'for use' without involving any mode of social distribution of the product. It is one of the more absurd effects of the separation of academic disciplines that while anthropologists (and others) analyse society as forms of exchange, much of Marxist economic history and contemporary analysis finds exchange only in capitalism. Banaji's interesting analysis of feudalism (1977) shows how, both theoretically and historically, there are good reasons for asserting that far from being inimical to exchange, the feudal mode of production thrived on production for the market. Obviously there are many different kinds of exchange, but equally obviously, social production of any kind must involve some form of circulation of the product. Any analysis of a 'mode of production', then, must involve analysis both of production and of circulation, and of how these two processes interact. One of the things I wish to show is that in the case of Andean society, very different forms of social organization can be arrived at according to what form is taken by the circulation of the product.

It would seem that the meeting of two different forms of social organization must take place first of all at the level of circulation, so that it is appropriate to look at this level and see how new forms of circulation affect an old form of interconnection between production and circulation. It is only if we dogmatically concentrate exclusively on relations of production that the problem of the meeting of capitalism and another 'mode' can be theorized as one of 'resistance to capitalism'. I will now try to show this more concretely.

2. The area as a whole

If we were to take an economic cross-section of an imaginary but typical province in the Peruvian Andes we would find examples of virtually every 'mode of production' in the book: modern industrial capitalism in the form of the multi-national mining corporation, large-scale farming for the world market perhaps organized by the same mining capital, traditional *haciendas* presided over by unruly and paternalistic *gamonales*, state capitalism with some form of workers' participation where the Agrarian Reform had taken over one of the two latter forms, petty commodity production around the urban and mining centres, share-cropping and the various forms of pre-capitalist rent, right down to the survival of some communal forms of labour in the Communities. If we start to do the same thing from the point of view of labour in the area, we shall find that not only is it involved in all these forms, but of necessity we must move outside the area in both possible geographical directions: down to the agricultural plantations of the jungle area on the east side of the Andes, and down to the coast on the west, where we will find labour employed both by large- and small-scale

98

capital, and in a welter of petty service and commodity occupations on the margins of the capitalist sector.

Even if we confine our view to the Andean area itself, we find that capitalism is present in the area in many forms. We find wage labour, we find small accumulated funds, we find the products of capitalist mass-production, we find money almost everywhere we go. In what sense are we to say then that the area is 'outside' or 'resisting' capitalism? To show what I mean with an example: if we take Carhuapata, a largely subsistence Community,[2] where a number of the men work in the nearby mines for two or three years of their life, then it would be strange to talk about the Community 'resisting' capitalism. The men may be keen, rather than reluctant, to go and work in the mines. The capitalist firms involved may have no interest in taking over production in the Communities. At the same time, subsistence production itself *is* changed by temporary emigration: not only will changes in the division of labour within the household be necessary, but the possibilities of using the wage for buying in the products of advanced capitalism (fertilizers, improved seed, tools both for agricultural and other uses) mean that the amount of land needed for subsistence may actually be decreased, allowing population increase in the subsistence area. But if the subsistence production differs from some 'pure' model, because of its articulation with capitalism, then so does the capitalist presence; it is not like 'advanced' capitalism, since the wage form is not related to 'necessary labour', nor is it the only way in which the worker and his family can obtain the 'necessaries' of life. The worker's family stays in the Community and often provides him with food while he works in the mine. The wage then becomes 'surplus' from the Community's point of view – a means of access to 'luxury' goods traded in the company store; and from the company's point of view it can be seen in a way similar to that of married women's wages in 'advanced' capitalism – 'pin-money', or 'money for holidays'.

Areas of the Andes such as that surrounding the colonial mercury mine of Huancavelica cannot be described merely as situated anywhere along the line of the 'transition to capitalism'. There is no 'transitional mode of production' which just happens to be taking a very long time in transit. Nor, on the other hand, is there much sense in saying that world imperialism is deliberately 'blocking' the development of the area and extracting huge surpluses by preserving its underdevelopment. The capitalist mining enterprises at present in the area have indeed created enclaves of capitalism, but have no particular interest, negative or positive, in the surrounding agricultural areas. But if they are enclaves from the point of view of capitalist relations of production, the surrounding areas are not thereby untouched by capitalist exchange. On the contrary, more and more capitalist-made goods are penetrating every year, and this trade itself has tendencies both towards conservation and towards destruction of the old modes of production. Yet destruction of the old shows no signs of giving way to creation of a new capitalist order in the countryside. Nor is another capitalist outcome particularly likely – that of total depopulation of the countryside and the absorption of that population in urban industry. The amounts of capital necessary to provide jobs for millions of people at present levels of labour productivity would be quite unthinkable, and certainly totally out of proportion to present rates of capital formation in Peru.

3. Exchange and verticality

The two peasant Communities which today constitute Huayllay Grande and Carhuapata, in the Department of Huancavelica in Central Peru, were originally one – Huayllay Grande. To this day the people of Huayllay insist that Carhuapata is merely an annex of Huayllay, and that it is only since the Agrarian Reform in recent years that the people of Carhuapata have become selfish and separated off. The formal situation was in fact confused prior to the Agrarian Reform. Huayllay Grande had achieved municipal status, with a number of the surrounding highland communities being defined as its annexes, and therefore coming within the jurisdiction of its municipal council and being liable to contribute to municipal works. On the other hand, Carhuapata appears as far back as the 1920s as a separate Community negotiating in law, and finally achieved separate status as a Community in 1951. But the point of view of the Huayllinos is backed up by the fact that the legal title which the Community of Carhuapata has to its lands is nothing but a copy of the eighteenth-century title of the lands of Huayllay Grande with different boundary markers inserted in the text. The existence of settled hamlets in the Carhuapata area only seems to date back about 100 years, that is, hamlets with chapels or churches, of which there are five now. Despite the distance involved nine or more hours' walk for many of the *comuneros* – and the geographical intervention of the 'Spanish' town of Lircay, the capital of the province of Angaraes, the Carhuapatinos still have trading links with Huayllay and, until the comparatively recent split, had participated regularly in the many *fiestas* and *faenas* of Huayllay. Huayllay had been something of a religious centre, and has a locally well-known image in the church as symbol of this; by verbal account, not only Carhuapata but many other of the surrounding highland communities used to participate in the fiestas. With the recent separation off of these communities and the general rush from the thirties through to the fifties to be recognized as independent Communities by the relevant ministry, Huayllay has maintained an almost intolerable burden of fiestas, the expense of which it must now meet alone, in money and other resources – raw materials and labour-time.

Huayllay is an old Spanish *reducción*, a square-plan village with church dating back to 1620, lying at 3600 metres above sea level. Below the village, maize lands stretch down to a river about 600 metres below, some of them irrigated by tributary streams. Around the village lie the wheat, barley, bean and pea fields, while higher up and a few miles along the mountainside lie the several large potato fields rotated communally year by year, where in theory at least every comunero has one plot in each yearly rotation area. In Carhuapata too, the main centre of habitation, containing the largest church, lies at 3600 metres; but in this case it is only a centre in the sense of being a political and religious centre, partly because of its geographical centrality to a community where dwellings are scattered in small groups over an area 20 kilometres long, and 5 or more wide. But although the churches of the two communities are situated at approximately the same altitude, the lands of Carhuapata are concentrated much more in the highland pasture area, where the herds of llamas, used mainly for transport, and alpacas, kept for their wool, feed on the communal pastures. The comuneros of Carhuapata grow potatoes, wheat, barley, beans and other tubers, in the same way as those of Huayllay, and at similar altitudes, there being an overlap in this way even in the middle of the ecological range. However, there are few real maize lands in Carhuapata, although it is cultivated in small quantities even under the difficult conditions at 3600 metres. As Huayllay, therefore, is a community semi-specialized in maize-production, and Carhuapata in meat- and wool-production, we would expect the two communities to exchange maize for meat or wool regularly. This does indeed occur, but as part of a wider interchange between various highland communities lying above and beyond Carhuapata, and the series of villages along the valley in which Huayllay is situated. Transport is nearly always undertaken by the highland traders, who come with trains of 20 or 30 llamas often with an octave of brass bells sounding down the valley. Few villagers of the valley region have llamas, and donkeys cannot survive at high altitudes, although llamas can survive for short periods at the lower levels.

At first sight this kind of interchange seems natural and eternal – one group possesses one kind of lands, the other group another; they therefore specialize and trade. The eternity of this situation seems extremely improbable though, once we take into account the fact that until recently what is now the Community of Carhuapata used to be referred to as 'the highlands of Huayllay' and was presumably under some more direct form of control by the people of Huayllay. We cannot assume, then, that a need to take advantage of the different products of ecological tiers has always taken the form of exchange, as at present.

The fact that the exchange takes place along a vertical axis, that is, between the products of higher and lower altitudes, might very well lead us to explain it by reference to Murra's model of 'verticality' (1975). But we would run up against a basic difficulty in accounting for the recent changes by means of this model. For Murra's model is clearly not at all one of *exchange* between different ecological levels, but rather one of the *direct control* of one level by another. It is explicitly a model of the integration of different regions in production, rather than in exchange. Murra's seminal article was entitled 'The "vertical" control of a maximum of ecological levels'; and in the three cases he describes, this vertical control was achieved by the direct colonization of one level by another. This means that the productive labour of the *ayllu*, kingdom, or empire was spread over various zones. Reintegration of the labour thus divided was ideally achieved by a centralized redistribution of products. In his examples of 'vertical control' Murra finds evidence that the colonists retained rights to land and remained members of their community of origin. This implies that politics too remained centralized, and that the colonies remained in a relationship of political subordination to the centre from which they came. A clear example of this kind of organiz-ation dating from pre-Inca times is the kingdom of the Lupaqa (one of those analysed by Murra), which, while centred on the altiplano of what is now Bolivia, had colonies as much as one week's journey away in the low-lying jungle to the east, and even further away down on the coast to the west. It is abundantly clear in Murra's work that these colonies are not commun-ities of independent ethnic and political affiliation, who have established a trading relationship with the Lupaqa. Whatever the form of circulation actually practised for the products of the colony and the subsistence of the colonists, it is clear that it could not have been one of exchange such as might arise between communities of equal and independent political standing.

So that although the concept of 'vertical control', in its watered-down form of 'verticality', has in recent years been applied to relations of exchange between two Communities on different ecological levels, this would seem to lose any specificity of the concept as a form of social organization, rather than a purely geographical form.[3] In other words, starting with Murra himself, much more stress has been laid on explaining the 'vertical' side of the concept than that of 'control'. It would seem to me crucial here, parti-cularly in cases where permanent residence in the colony becomes establish-ed, to be able to give some answer to the question of *how* control was exerted over the colonized level, and how reunion was established for each new generation. If it is clear that the centralized direction of labour (as under the Inca empire or preceding Andean kingdoms) tended to make the different ecological levels highly interdependent, it is equally clear that there were strong centrifugal tendencies in these social structures, which required enormous military and ideological efforts to contain them, and which aided the Spanish in their conquest of the Inca empire. So, in order to throw some light on the question of social control in the vertical context, I shall look first at some of the material conditions underlying the separation of the two Communities mentioned above, and then see how in their absence a form of vertical control was maintained from Huayllay.

As described above, the tendency nowadays is for each household in both of the communities to have access to levels 2 and 3 in the following schema:

(1) high pastures – llamas, alpacas, sheep, horses and cattle at certain times of the year
(2) potato fields
(3) main residential zone – growing barley, wheat, beans, tubers, and grazing cows, sheep, goats
(4) maize lands

In addition, Carhuapata has lands in level 1, and Huayllay in level 4. The separation of the communities, then, represents a *minimization* rather than a maximization of control of ecological levels. It is true that within this broad framework some families in Carhuapata have houses in two zones, which could be seen as a revival of the old colonization principal. For instance, families well endowed with llamas, alpacas and sheep will have a house at 4000 metres or over, where (usually) some poor relation stays with the flocks, as well as a house in the temperate zone where the majority of crops are grown. But it is also common simply to have a house half-way between these two zones. In Huayllay, where residents still keep to the Spanish pattern, concentrated on one level, a broad enough range of goods can be produced within a minimum of ecological levels for the Community to be relatively independent.

The first and obvious pre-condition for the independence of these two Communities, then, is that a wide enough range of crops can be grown and livestock reared to make subsistence possible within the more limited ecological range. It seems to me extremely important in this connection to bear in mind the technological improvements introduced from Europe in the form of new crops, animals and techniques. Although if we take a very traditional view, we may say, as I stated above, that Carhuapata lacks maize and Huayllay lacks llamas, both of them crucial traditional Andean products; we may also say that the Europeans have introduced substitutes for these and other products. Before the conquest, maize and quinoa were the only grains grown. Quinoa is very laborious to harvest and a high-risk crop, so that some sort of access to maize was essential, whether through direct possession of lands, or through some centralized redistribution system.

But from Europe have come wheat and barley – occasionally one sees oats or rye – as well as the crops that fill in the rotation of these, broad beans and peas. Wheat and barley are obvious substitutes for maize in the diet, and though they do not have the phenomenal powers of multiplication that maize has from seed, they have the great advantage that they can be grown at higher altitudes and with less water. Murra (1975: 45–58) has written about the importance of maize as a crop surrounded by ritual under the Incas; and this is still true today in many Andean Communities. Yet in Carhuapata, where it is not cultivated, although it is much appreciated as food when it is obtained, important Community ritual surrounds the cultivation of barley. When the Community barley lands are ploughed (with foot-ploughs, i.e. dug) for the first time after lying fallow, there is an impressive assembly of people from all over the community. The new Community authorities are elected and a play is enacted by the incoming and outgoing committees. The hillside then becomes suddenly alive with women and children scurrying to and fro, offering and reciprocating different bowls of food to each other, as if acting out some archetypal model of generalized exchange. Similarly, when the Community authorities hold their almost daily councils in the president's house, the first thing they do when they enter the compound, before even greeting those present, is to walk over and kiss a little cross plaited from wheat which hangs on the president's house.

In the same way, it is nowadays possible for the Community of Huayllay Grande to exist in isolation from Carhuapata, where it once pastured llamas and alpacas, because the functions of those animals can be mainly fulfilled through innovations brought from Europe – sheep, goats and donkeys – all of which can live in the temperate zone. Sheep provide wool and meat, goats are kept for making cheese and for their meat, while donkeys are used for transporting loads.

Another crucial pre-condition of the formation of independent highland communities such as Carhuapata was that they should no longer be reliant on maize for making alcohol. It is, as far as I know, an unpublicized feature in Andean ethnography that many highland communities, far from brewing the delicious *chicha de jora*, nowadays lace their festivities with *ron de quemar*, cooking alcohol, locally known as *verdelojo* because of the bright green colouring put in it to stop people drinking it. This is itself a cheap, tax-free and illegal substitute for cane-alcohol of a variable, but superior, quality. At first sight it might seem paradoxical that cane-alcohol and ron de quemar appear to be most widely consumed in the more remote highland areas of the Peruvian sierra, furthest away from the market-places of the valleys and from the jungle and coastal lowlands where cane is grown; but when we see its consumption as facilitating the independence of the highland Communities from the valley maize-producers it is not so paradoxical.

Looking at these technical pre-conditions for the separation of the Communities does not imply a technological determinism, since the new crops, animals, and indeed alcohol, were available in Peru for three or four hundred years before these Communities finally became two, but it does mean that technical conditions no longer made it necessary for there to be a centralizing principle, unifying the diverse ecological zones, and distributing labour among them, in order for a historically given set of needs to be met. It is, to say the least, surprising that so much discussion of the principle of 'verticality' as the survival of pre-hispanic organization has gone on without mentioning, let alone examining, the social effects of these kinds of innovations. Favre (1975) does mention that broad beans were introduced fairly recently (nineteenth century) but does not cite any evidence. I could find no oral evidence from older members of the community of a time when beans had not been grown.

In the case of the separation of Carhuapata from Huayllay Grande we have seen how the introduction of new crops and animals from Europe has in the long term allowed a relaxing of the need to *maximize* direct control of different ecological levels. Exchange of the products of the levels relinquished by the respective new Communities can take place as a supplementary activity (meat for maize). Again in the case of alcohol-production, it is the introduction of a substitute by the Spanish, this time in the form of a commodity on the market, that has enabled the highland people to dispense with maize as a raw material for alcohol.

Apart from these new technical conditions which relax the need to maximize control of ecological levels, the integration of both valley and highland Communities into the wider national market means that cheap substitutes can be obtained for the products of different ecological levels. This in turn implies that the people of the Communities are selling something to get the cash to buy the goods in. In the case of Carhuapata and similar highland Communities, the main sources of cash at present are temporary migration to the mines and the marketing of alpaca wool. Wool seems to have become important at the turn of the century and mining slightly later on, that is, slightly before the Community achieved independence. The people of Huayllay Grande sell some grains, vegetables and new potatoes in Lircay, and a fairly small amount of meat, usually to the mines. Girls pick bunches of pinks or wild quaking-grass on Sundays to sell to people of the highland communities, whom they meet in Lircay, to decorate the ribbons round their hats. The people of Huayllay hardly ever go to work in the mines, but a considerable community comes and goes between there and Lima, and sometimes stays in Lima, where the men work as dustmen or labourers and the women as street-sellers or domestic servants.

This example of the two Communities separating (which has many parallels in the province of Angaraes) shows how, although there are still relationships between highland and valley Communities on a vertical axis, the form of production based on direct vertical control has changed into one where both Communities produce (to some degree) for a series of exchange relationships with each other and with the wider market. Conversely, I think it tells us something about the way control was maintained in the traditional Andean 'vertical' system. This I shall investigate in section 5. But first I wish to say something about political organization and ideologies in the two Communities, as they seem to me to contradict in important ways some commonly accepted ideas of entry into the market and impersonal exchange relations.

4. Community organization and ideology

Carhuapata, far from being a collection of dynamic individuals wanting to free themselves from traditional bonds, actually has one of the strongest community organizations in the area. General assemblies of the Community are held every two weeks, with a system of fines for those who do not attend. In 1975–6, a road was being built with Community labour, again with a system of fines for those who did not do their bit. There was also a lively system of justice in the Community. At one point in 1976 several hundred men and women raided some houses in the highlands of the Community, capturing 17 men known to be involved in the stealing of cattle on the highland pastures, an acute problem in the whole area. The men were then taken down to Lircay and handed over to the national *Guardia Civil*. Five hundred or more people from Carhuapata then hung around in the streets of Lircay for 24 hours, many of them without food, waiting for justice, which of course they did not get but only the prospect of a long and expensive law suit in Lima.

The last feature of community organization in Carhuapata that I wish to bring in here is the *Hermandad*, a Roman Catholic society to which at least half the adult members of the Community belonged (both men and women), and which seemed to involve no more deviant religious belief than a tolerance of the local priest in Lircay and a very regular attendance at Mass in that town. While most other Communities in the area seemed to have quarrelled with the priest and to have as few dealings with him as possible, the people of Carhuapata were his especial favourites, and he would visit them on occasion, using the horse they provided for him. Now the interesting thing about this Hermandad ('siblinghood' is the most accurate translation) is that it was strongly linked with an ideology of progress and, as a collectivity, it expressed many of the same features as were present in the various protestant religions taken up by *individuals* in other Communities. Specifically, it was teetotal, and along with its anti-alcoholism, had strongly rejected what was seen as traditional culture. Music and dancing had been virtually abolished as adult activities, though local song and dance were performed by the children at the primary school's end of year display.

An older member of the Community, all of whose family belonged to the Hermandad, and who himself was a strong supporter of it, explained to me that after serving three successive two-year terms as Community *personero* (president under the pre-1969 structure), he had given up the drink. He just could not take the levels involved any more (and we should remember that what is being drunk is what is used to light a primus stove in Peru). This man and other younger Community leaders spoke often of the need to *salir del atraso* (get out of backwardness); they spoke of 'development', of having been forgotten for so long, of the need to progress, and so on. None of this is remarkable, especially at a time when the government of Velasco Alvarado was trying hard to promote this kind of community ideology. What *is* remarkable is that such a strong and rapid rejection of the old community practices (fiestas, drinking, music, dancing) should go together with a rein-forcing of other community practices, indeed with the forging of a new Community, which could in no way simply be reduced to an attempt on the part of the leaders to impress the revolutionary government of the time.

Huayllay Grande on the other hand showed little interest in the new structure of communities laid down by Velasco's government in 1972. In general assemblies it did little more than meet the legal requirement of two a year. Few local authorities were much in evidence, apart from the president, who was physically beaten up quite badly two or three times while I was there. Huayllay already had a road and running water, as well as an un-completed irrigation project which was a source of much bitterness; so that one could argue that there was no need of co-operation for such basic amenities, which Carhuapata did not have. But this argument was un-convincing especially at a time when a Community like Huayllay, if well organized, might have expected to get, say, a loan from the government to start a co-operative. What is surprising is that the lack of any enthusiasm for modern Community organization went hand-in-hand with a quite remarkable consumption of surplus in traditional religious and cultural activities. Some of the 14 fiestas in the year became fairly privatized among the kin and neighbours of those sponsoring them, but others involved the whole community in spectator events such as the frequent bull-fights in the village square, or lavish displays of fireworks. Most fiestas last from three to five days. The *alcalde* of Huayllay continued to hold a rain-bringing ritual every year in his house, which is well-known from the document on the uprising in Lircay in 1811 (Pease 1974). This consists in ritual drinking, coca-chewing and smoking plus sending out emissaries with presents of alcohol, coca and cigarettes for all the important lakes in the area. This consumption goes on until it has the desired effect in bringing on the rains. It always works. It may take two months of drinking to bring on the rains, though usually it is expected to take about a month.

Quite a common theme of conversation with the visiting anthropologist in Huayllay was the air, water and food of Huayllay, contrasted with those of Lima. There was a quite marked awareness of ecological issues and a nostalgic but genuinely grounded belief that the quality of life was better, in this sense, in Huayllay. Considering that many male emigrants from Huayllay to Lima worked as dustmen, and women as street-sellers or domestics, and that many of them lived on the Cerrito San Pedro[4] in a grotesque parody of their way of life in the sierra, these beliefs are under-standable. What they mean in terms of the differences in ideology between Huayllay and Carhuapata is that the Huayllinos identified much more with a traditional conception of their village, and successful individuals were keen to spend their money earned in Lima on sponsoring fiestas in Huayllay, that is on preserving traditional culture there. Huayllay had become almost a place of tourism for Lima emigrants – somewhere to come and spend a healthy weekend in the country, and an excellent place to retire to. Building houses to retire to in Huayllay was another thing that successful emigrants would spend money on. In Carhuapata, on the other hand, where emigration to Lima was highly exceptional, all nostalgia for the past had been rejected and a new ideology of progress and development substituted. The social extent of the Hermandad and their rejection of alcohol and all forms of traditional surplus consumption, shows, I believe, that this was not simply a minority ideology of the Community leaders, who on the whole were educated, could speak Spanish, and had travelled. The separation of Carhuapata from Huayllay, in itself, was indicative of rejection of a traditional image, since one of the main roles of the annexes to Huayllay was to participate in its fiestas.

Various conclusions emerge from this brief discussion of politics and ideology in the two communities. Firstly, community organization and spirit are directly correlated with an ideology of progress and development. The converse of this is that the village which is ostensibly much more attached to tradition and is more cynical about progress contains far more successful *individuals*. One could almost say that there had been a communal decision in Carhuapata to adopt the protestant ethic. Secondly, one finds that traditional forms of surplus consumption and a nostalgia for a romanticized image of life in the sierra are found in the village that is objectively more developed, more integrated into the cash economy, and in which there is a wider range of internal class differentiation. And conversely, that the urge to progress out of backwardness is found in the community where a much higher degree of self-sufficiency (and consequently of good health) obtains.

Thirdly, although these are attitudes observed some time after the separation of the Communities, I do think they raise difficulties for any simple explanation of separation in terms of the economic interests of dynamic individuals. Samaniego (1978) and Winder (1978), for instance, have both done interesting historical analyses which show how a concept

108

of community was created and sustained by individuals who could benefit from it by privatizing resources obtained in the name of the 'community'. Samaniego gives a particularly relevant account of the secession of a group of highland villages from Chupaca, a lowland district, in the 1890s, and later on in the 1920s, after the previous secession had been annulled, of Yanacancha from Ahuac, the latter having itself in turn split from Chupaca. In these movements, groups of shepherds, formerly controlled by the lowland villages, sought to appropriate and individualize the communal pastures. To do so required fostering the identity of *comunidad indígena* and so acquiring the political protection of the *indigenista* movement at national level and the support of the colonial laws which protected the lands and pastures of the *indígenas* of Peru. But this does not mean that the population actually saw themselves as *indios*, and the legal title of 'comunidad' only became sought after at a time when internal differentiation in the communities was already quite marked (Samaniego 1978: 57). Similarly Winder's analysis of infra-structural projects initiated by the Communities of Sicaya and Matahuasi in the Mantaro valley emphasizes the fact that they 'have in no way altered the unequal distribution of land and economic resources in the village' and argues that projects have been chosen more for the prestige they bring to the leaders who obtain government grants for them, than for any community development aim (1978: 218–19). While not wishing to dispute the validity of these analyses, I do think they are incomplete and exaggerate the power and stability of community elites. In consequence they lead to the very pessimistic kinds of conclusion reached by Winder as to the possibilities of community development in Peru (1978: 236). There is, after all, absolutely no way in which an infra-structural kind of project can ever in itself be redistributive of resource ownership. And it is far from clear that one can devise *productive* projects that would decrease rather than increase existing inequalities, if these projects are undertaken in a basically capitalist market framework. If Community organizations have avoided investing funds in productive enterprises, this is precisely because they would prefer projects which might 'benefit the whole community'. It is hardly the fault of the *Community* organization that productive enterprises demand and create social differentiation in a capitalist economy. As far as projects for Community development go, the experience of the 1970s in the communities I visited was *not* that they were so socially divided as to be unable to take advantage of government offers, but that *even if* they complied with the elaborate form of participatory democracy required by the government, there was in fact nothing at all in the way of development planned for them. The Agrarian Reform did not touch them, as there were no large or even medium-sized landowners within them, neither did they border on any large productive haciendas whose profits might have been redistributed through a SAIS. The Com-

munity of Carhuapata had more success in petitioning the local mining company for aid than it did with the government. In any case, general assemblies
on the whole discussed internal matters, such as the trespassing of animals
on crops, or what to do about the *abigeos*, or whether the visiting anthropologist was a government spy. The only community project being undertaken,
the building of the road, was a purely internal affair, with no outside material
or technical aid, and at the same time was not necessarily going to benefit the
leaders personally who were promoting its construction.

If Samaniego's analysis of the secession of Yanacancha were applicable
to Carhuapata, one would expect the Community to have been created
at the time of Independence, promoted by farmers who were rich in livestock and needed to appropriate the communal pastures, but later on to
have lapsed as an organization. If this is patently not the case in Carhuapata –
the Community appears to have gained strength recently – one might
explain it in two ways. First, this could be a re-application of Samaniego's
principle, after a lapse of time. The original motivation for organizing a
'community' on the part of the rich farmers has been achieved; but a new one
has arisen in the form of possible aid from government agencies towards
Communities which show an active and lively 'traditional' organization.
Alternatively, one might say that over the years, the interests of rich individuals have not diverged that much from those of the Community. This
explanation is actually hinted at in the article by Roberts and Samaniego
on the impact of the SAIS on highland Communities, when they say that
the reason why poorer families do not oppose the richer families in their
pursuit of their economic interests is that '[the poor families] are often linked
by kinship to the richer families and work for them' (1978: 259). If 'richer'
here means 'possessing more lands and livestock', then this statement is
capable of a different interpretation, which is that ownership of resources
is not exclusively determinant of richness or poorness. 'Work' itself is a
redistributive mechanism, particularly in the absence of commercialization
of products. Furthermore, in Carhuapata, productivity is so low that
employing more workers does not mean that the increased product will
compensate for what they must be given in recompense in the way of food.
If this is the case, then it is not surprising that there is a greater communality
of interests, and less internal class struggle within Communities than would
be expected from the distribution of land. This may be true more in the case
of land than with flocks, since land cannot be bought and sold in the Communities at the moment. The cases of individual success in Yanacancha,
described by Samaniego, depend on being able to sell flocks on the market
and then invest the money in education outside the Community.

The association of a strong Community organization with an ideology of progress and a rejection of tradition cannot, I believe, be explained away in the case of Carhuapata as the cynical manipulation of individuals wishing to better their own position. It remains paradoxical only while we look at it from the point of view of individuals and their relations in the market. We must go back and think more about what it means in relation to the Andean system of 'vertical control' in order better to situate this phenomenon of the progressive community.

5. Vertical control as a social relation

If, as we have seen, there was a tendency in the last century for pastoral Communities to split off horizontally from those villages that formerly controlled them on a vertical axis, then we must ask how this horizontality had been controlled in the past. If there is a specifically Andean system of 'vertical control', how did the controllers who were interested in verticalizing social relations succeed in stopping those who were controlled from developing horizontal ones? The question is similar to that posed earlier on: if the ruling class continually tries to *maximize* its control of different ecological levels, then the class whose labour is appropriated through this maximization may see freedom from exploitation through a minimization of the levels they need to work on in order to subsist. Verticality cannot simply be thought of as an ideal, as a maximum pursued by Andean society as a historical subject. If it is, then the whole *class* character of the social systems being talked about, the fact that it is vast kingdoms and an incredibly wealthy empire that captured the European imagination, all this is completely obscured. But this is the consequence of allowing a technical feature, which boils down to living on the side of a mountain, to determine directly a theory of *social* organization in that environment. In other words, if verticality is to be a category wide enough to include social systems as disparate in other ways as the pre-Inca kingdoms, the Inca empire with its *mitmaqkuna*, *aqllakuna* and *yanakuna*, and village organization today, then it must be given content as a social, and not only as a technical, relation.

We might analyse vertical control firstly as a relation of property. One ayllu, kingdom, empire, or present-day village has a relationship of ownership over lands far removed from a central location of residence. These property relationships have been a headache for many colonial attempts to rationalize land-holding patterns, right down to the present-day Agrarian Reform. But the two preceding sections have shown that ownership of land from a distance involves some social system of controlling those who work that land and their product. In this light, vertical control implies a centralized political system with its basis in a way of controlling production on a series of ecological levels; this will enable the centre to appropriate a surplus in order to create and preserve political, ideological and religious power.

We have seen how dependence on the centre can only be maintained so long as there is a real division of labour between the different ecological levels (i.e. so long as there are no successful attempts to horizontalize) and secondly, so long as exchange relationships, which could substitute for a direct dependence are not allowed to develop. Vertical control, then implies both a planned division of labour, and a form of circulation which is inimical to exchange. These conditions were undoubtedly fulfilled on the most spectacular scale by the Incas, who through their hold on circulation managed to centralize the ability to transform tribute production into a form in which it could be accumulated. And one form accumulation could take was the subjugation of new ecological levels, either through incorporation as a colony into a vertical scheme with Cuzco as base, or alternatively through re-colonization by other conquered peoples. In this case vertical control is a social relation in which the surplus appropriated can be accumulated as an expanded set of relations of vertical control. It therefore could be said to be a system with its own 'law of motion'. Many questions could be asked at this point, such as whether it was the most important form of accumulation, either for the Incas, or at other times in Andean history and if so, was it the specifically *vertical* aspect that made it important, or does it perhaps not have more in common with other centrally organized planned states, from Dahomey[5] to the USSR? But the crucial question here is how this way of accumulating social relations of verticality from Cuzco as base interconnected with vertical ownership of lands at a local level. What is the connection between the Incas sending people down to the *ceja de selva* to cultivate coca, or developing a hereditary caste of herdsmen on the highlands to look after the Inca's llamas, and their promotion of self-sufficiency at household and village level, a concept that could include local ownership of lands on different levels? Murra answers this question by pointing to the contradictions involved in the extension of vertical relations by the Incas, their utilization of an ideology of self-sufficiency within the vertical archipelago in order to develop a highly complex division of labour in the production of surplus for the Inca state. He points out that although the maintenance of rights in their community of origin, no matter how distant, constitutes the 'ideological link' between local verticality and Inca state organization, this does not mean that over the years membership of that community became an empty legal form (Murra 1975: 114–15).

There is a danger here in seeing the inordinate *extension* of the system of vertical control as the only source of contradictions in the system. The examples of present-day secession of communities show that, even at a local level, there must be a means of social control over those who live or work on different ecological levels. We cannot assume a consensus within

112

a village, or even within a household spread over different levels, while reserving a conflict theory for looking at the Inca state. In the account of the Inca state given by Garcilaso de la Vega (1960), it is emphatically stated that each household was required to work its own lands before working those of the state or of their local lords. Severe punishments were prescribed for local *kurakas* who abused their subjects by exploiting them, but at the same time, special privileges were granted to local lords in return for allowing the state to appropriate surplus labour from their subjects. So that in the amplification of the scale and meaning of vertical control by the Incas, we find a contradiction not between local subsistence production and the vast organization of surplus production by the Inca state, but rather between centralized and de-centralized appropriation of surplus. If Garcilaso was correct, then the ideology of self-sufficiency could be used by the Inca state against the local lords, as well as possibly vice versa. If the state tried to ensure that each household had sufficient resources in order to live according to some accepted standard, then this would serve to obscure the exploitative aspect of its own organization of the production and circulation of surplus. Production for the state could be portrayed as obeying a higher rationality than production for a local personage.

The present-day example of the secession of Carhuapata is interesting in this context, because it does not just represent the formation of a new, purely pastoral village. On the contrary it is itself already divided into ecological levels, the political centre of Carhuapata being at more or less the same height as Huayllay, the parent community. A school was opened in the uppermost hamlet of Carhuapata during 1976 and there was already a chapel. Were there to be a major conflict of interests between the lower and higher parts of the Community, there could well be new secession movements. Even within households that owned lands on distant levels, it is (as mentioned above) often a poor relation who stays with the flocks in the *puna*. If none can be found, then someone must be hired to do it, under the relationship of *mingado*. Interestingly enough, the word *minga* in this area of the Andes seems to have preserved its colonial sense of a relationship of labour in return for money, dating from the time when an Indian could buy himself off from the obligation to do *mita* labour in the Huancavelica mercury mine. The fine paid in order to be let off the mita duty was equivalent to the difference between the (small) cost of a mita labourer to the mine owner and the cost of hiring a wage labourer on the free market. The hired labourer was termed 'mingado'. This meaning of minga seems to be in marked contrast to the arcadian work parties described by visitors to other areas of the Andes. The explanation given of the word mingado was 'un peón', with an embarrassed smile to indicate the inexplicable hidden meanings.

Even at a very local level, then, I would argue that lands can never be simply 'held' on distant ecological levels. People must also be held in place to work or guard them. At a local level, for instance, as in the case of Huayllay and Carhuapata, the system can only work as long as those in the colony are not allowed to develop relations of equality with other people in other specialized areas by exchanging with them. Huayllay lost its control of the pasture lands of Carhuapata not just because there was a flaw in the traditional system of payment for shepherding, allowing the shepherds themselves to accumulate flocks, as Roberts and Samaniego suggest (1978: 247); but because the shepherds were able to start selling wool on the world market and so appropriate their own product, rather than letting it flow back into Huayllay as surplus. As long as the parent community controlled the means of transforming one product into another (i.e. circulation), then the shepherds did not form an independent community. In this sense, the development of specialization in the division of labour in surplus production under the Incas can be said to be an extension of the social relations of verticality. As long as the specialized labourers, the aqllakuna and yanakuna for instance, who between them produced the final product of *cumbi*, were dependent on the political centre for the transformation of their products, they could not develop horizontal relations of equality.

The ideologies discussed in the last section, which seem paradoxical when looked at solely from the point of view of the market and capitalist relations, become less so when looked at in terms of the break-up of a specifically Andean form of social control, whereby the people of one ecological level control those of another. It is not then surprising that Huayllay, which had controlled Carhuapata (among other annexes) in the past, should cling to tradition, while Carhuapata, having broken out of this vertical control, should strongly reject all those manifestations of traditional culture associated with the consumption of surplus. Interestingly enough, the ceremony in Carhuapata mentioned earlier which marks the election of the community authorities is a celebration of generalized exchange; and on the one occasion when people of Carhuapata still visit Huayllay they now also think of it as solely for the purpose of exchange – the annual fair of Huayllay. In the next section I shall look at various forms of exchange which exist in the area and their implications for this argument about community fragmentation.

6. Forms of exchange

At this point some analysis of what is meant by 'exchange' is necessary. How are we to distinguish analytically between different forms of circulation of the social product? Polanyi (1957), for instance, tried to distinguish various forms of exchange in terms of a kind of social geography, where 'redistribution' stood for goods flowing into a centre and out again, 'reciprocity' for exchanges involving flows from opposite directions, and 'market exchange' for an economy where exchange is everywhere.

Polanyi contrasts the decentralization which characterizes market exchange with the model of the Inca economy where everything is collected and redistributed by a central state apparatus. I want to emphasize a different, and more general, point of contrast, between pre-commodity and commodity forms of circulation of the product, which is in terms of the simultaneity in time brought about by the form of commodity exchange. This is to be contrasted with the concept of pre-commodity circulation developed by Meillassoux (1975) as a system of 'advances and restitutions', that is a chain of gifts, counter-gifts, prestations of labour and other services which balance only over time. Kinship, real and fictive, then becomes a sort of social memory of the state of play. Gifts are often linked to formative events in the kinship system – births, marriages, deaths, and the cementation of all the fictive kin links that go with these events. The very relationships then become the means of remembering these advances over time, with a view to restitution.

It should not be automatically deduced from this that advances and restitutions should be seen in terms of 'reciprocity' with its connotations of equality of exchange. On the contrary, if we analyse circulation as being closely woven in to the system of social relations, then unequal social relations will be reflected in the system of advances and restitutions. In fact, the equality or otherwise of what is circulated over time between members of a family unit, or between the Inca state and its constitutive village, would probably be impossible to estimate, since the objects circulating from different points and at different times are themselves different in kind. Where there is no basis for a common system of measurement (e.g. in terms of labour-time incorporated in the product), then we can only apply a vague concept of interdependence or complementarity, in terms of the use-values being produced and circulated. Without a standard of equality or inequality, then, social relationships must themselves be said to determine the distribution of the social product, and not vice versa.

Once we start to talk about exchange though, and introduce the condition of *simultaneity* in the exchange of products, the picture changes. Exchange starts to take on an abstract quality. The actors and their social relations lose the significance they had when it was necessary to keep up relationships over a long time in order for the two halves of an exchange to be completed. In relation to the Andes, the way in which we could distinguish various forms of exchange analytically is discussed below.

Barter, or 'trueque'

Both these terms are about as generic as 'exchange' itself, and as I understand it, 'trueque' is used to cover generally all non-monetary exchanges of

115

goods, although in practice, local terms are used to talk about how things are actually exchanged in each region. Here I intend to use the word to describe the kind of interchange that takes place between higher and lower ecological levels nowadays. The social side of the exchange has not yet completely disappeared, since one partner usually travels to the home(s) of one or more other partners known in advance, in search of specific products. Even where merchants of a capitalist kind from outside the area penetrate this form of exchange, they tend to form fictive kin-relationships with those they exchange with, accept food from them, be godparent to their children, and so on (Burchard 1974). Trading journeys may be undertaken within a longer-term social fabric of advances and restitutions, within which simultaneity may or may not in fact be achieved. It is common for people who undertake this kind of journey from Carhuapata to go on expeditions to collect debts from previous journeys; so that in practice there is no clear break between truly simultaneous exchange and a system of advances and restitutions. The non-simultaneity of the process is reflected in the fact that in trueque measures tend to be customary, i.e. fixed over time. It is rare to hear of trueque measures changing from pressures internal to the exchanging areas; it is much more common to hear of relative prices of one product in terms of another changing because relative prices on the external market have changed. In the contemporary situation, alternative forms of exchange may in practice be open to the producers. Actually, there was a crisis going on in the trueque system around Lircay during 1976, owing to the very inflexibility over time of the measures used (which were woven woollen sacks of a standard size). As the customary measures could not be changed, the maize-producers were campaigning for the abolition of the traditional measurement system, and the introduction of the Roman balance. In other words the traditional standard of measurement could not be separated, in the minds of the participants, from the quantities being exchanged.

Barter in market places

Like the trading journeys described above, barter may be a way of circulating products of different ecological levels. But many sales in market-places in the Andes take place between complete strangers. On the other hand, there is a continual tendency to build up *casera* relationships, a tie of personal loyalty to a particular seller who in exchange will knock a bit off the price here and there for you, again obscuring the distinction between a simultaneous exchange and one that involves a social relationship over time. In practice, the main advantage to the sellers of this social relationship is unlikely to be in any price differences, since in most markets there is fierce competition between buyers of, for example, wool, and loyalties would be easily overcome if one buyer paid consistently worse prices than others; rather, the advantage that sellers may hope to obtain is that of credit, in the form of advances either of money or of goods. So here again we can link the social bond created through exchange to the non-simultaneity of sale and purchase, in the case of credit the purchase coming before the sale in time. But as compared with the barter undertaken by individual producers who go on trading journeys to known destinations, the market is impersonal. For instance, in the annual fair of Huayllay, potters would arrive from Huancavelica with their wares, which would be sold in exchange for their volume in grain or beans. But though the potters knew in advance what products they wanted to obtain – this being the point of going to Huayllay, which was a grain-producing area – they did not know from whom, nor did they need to know. The whole point of an annual fair is the possibility of simultaneity in a whole series of barter exchanges. According to local accounts, the character of the fair had changed only fairly recently, with the building of the road as far as Huayllay, and earlier, the road to Lircay which brought an inflow of traders from Huanta. (Huanta is the nearest line of access to the jungle region with its important crop of coca-leaf and also tropical fruits.) But prior to the establishment of shops in Lircay, which allowed year-round trading, the annual fair of Huayllay was a main access point for people of the highlands to the jungle products. Similarly, salt is now exchanged the year round for wool in the shops of Lircay, whereas formerly the options were to go on a trading trip, or to buy it in the annual fair of Huayllay. So the market-place provides a different kind of certainty to the would-be exchanger, who knows that she/he can find there a buyer who will have exactly what is needed in exchange. In the case of trading journeys, this kind of certainty can only be achieved by a thorough knowledge of the production of the individuals to be visited. This in turn implies some kind of social bond between them, which the market-place can to a large extent do away with.

Exchange involving money

'Money' is used here in the sense of a general equivalent for all other products. The annual market as a meeting place for barterers has a kind of certainty, when established in custom, so that everybody knows who comes from where with what every year, but there is always the danger that the individual barter exchanges will not balance out. Similarly, on trading journeys, 'social bonds' cannot remove all the uncertainty connected with long distance and poor communications. There is always the danger that the trading partner will not be ready with his/her side of the exchange, through a bad harvest, other economic commitments, or whatever. Money removes the need for simultaneous exchange of commodity for commodity.

By separating out two exchanges in time – commodity for money (C–M) and money for commodity (M–C), but itself lasting over time, it removes the necessity for all former social mechanisms for effecting exchanges over time. It allows the exchange of commodity for commodity (C–C) to be non-simultaneous, in effect by substituting two simultaneous exchanges, C–M and M–C. A general equivalent allows commodity exchange to become generalized, not only in time, but in space as well. Market relations mean that the question with whom the exchange is taking place no longer has any significance, since there is no need for a sustained inter-personal relationship over time. Again, in practice, the possibility of credit in money transactions means that borderlines are not clear-cut. Although money gives the possibility of an impersonal, abstract exchange which does not last over time, credit can open up the time-factor again and create binding personal dependencies. Interest – payment for time – then becomes a way of closing off this factor again, and brings some release from the dependent personal situation of someone who must beg for credit.

I argued above that all forms of exchange are incompatible with the system of vertical control insofar as this was a system of direct control of distant lands. What is confusing nowadays is that so much barter takes place between producers on different ecological levels. But as the population of the highlands in the area around Lircay (in the sense, at any rate, of settled habitation) is relatively recent, it cannot be assumed that barter was the way products were circulated in some older vertical system. In practice, what seems to have happened is that a monetary exchange with capitalism provided most of the material substitutes which released each community from its dependence on the other ecological levels; while such vertical relations as remain evolve into the kind of barter relations described above. Huayllay, for instance, no longer needs prolonged access to pasture lands since it can obtain substitutes for most traditional woollen clothing on the market in Lircay. Some sheep are kept just above the village and some wool is obtained through exchange with the highlands, but the quantities involved are minimal compared with what would be necessary if all clothes, blankets, etc. were home-spun and woven. Although the people of Carhuapata, similarly, do exchange with the valley for maize and wheat, and grow barley on their own lower lands, they are also starting to substitute bought-in flour, sugar, and oats in their diet. This is the case particularly for the pastoralists living in small hamlets in the puna, well beyond the cultivable region.

The town of Lircay is a focus for both circuits of exchange. Many of the shops, especially those at the entrances to the town, deal exclusively in wool, salt and coca-leaf, products of different ecological levels that were redistributed as long ago as the days of the Incas. Other shops act simply as retailers for nationally produced goods, buying little or no produce

118

from the local population, and so acting as intermediaries in a wider, monetary circuit. Through these shops, as well as through similar ones in the mines, capitalism provides a series of use-values that substitute for ones formerly exchanged or obtained by direct links between ecological levels. The progress of capitalism, both in the range of use-values and in their lower price in comparison with the possibilities for production within the pre-capitalist framework, has the effect of reducing the ecological spread of plots necessary to subsistence in the area. So to some extent the monetary type of exchange will tend to supplant the barter forms. There is quite a strict separation of spheres of exchange according to whether money is used or not, even to the extent that a completely different set of prices in *soles antiguos* is used for products which would only be exchanged within Carhuapata.

The possibility of a series of simultaneous exchanges such as can be effected with money implies the breakdown of the old system of vertical control of the circulation of products. There is no longer any reason why those who are being controlled, in this case the highland herdspeople, should be dependent on the lowland grain-producers. But we now have to ask the question why, if money had been present in Peru since the sixteenth century, was it only in the nineteenth and twentieth centuries that these sorts of changes occurred?

7. Money and social forms

Money during the colonial period of Peru served two functions[6] which were not compatible, and the clash between them can serve to illuminate some of the political conflicts leading up to Independence. Although money was first introduced to Peru as a stamp on metals passing into the coffers of the Spanish Crown, and became generalized to the mass of the population as a means for paying tribute, it also very soon spread as a medium of exchange. Each successive layer of society that was responsible for handing over tax-payments to the state fought for the right to exchange that money before handing it over. Thus the Miners' Guild of Huancavelica fought with the central state for their independence as entrepreneurs in order to avoid the dependent status of direct managers of a state-run mine in the late sixteenth and early seventeenth centuries. Later on the *corregidores* intercepted the mita labour destined for the mines, put it to work in spinning, weaving and sugar-processing, and with the proceeds were able to buy out the mita labourers from their duty in the mines. This provoked prolonged conflict with the Miners' Guild in which the state took the side of the miners, eventually going so far as to abolish the office of corregidor altogether, and to substitute for it a more tightly integrated system of regional administration, the *intendencias*. Similarly, we know that many of the noble Indians, who became tax-collectors under the colony, were also able to get rich on their own account, provoking the kinds of specifically Indian revolt against Spanish rule which occurred throughout the eighteenth century, as well as in Lircay in 1811.[7]

Once money is introduced then, there is a conflict between its function as sign of the *vertical* relations in society – as signifier of the surplus rendered upwards in the hierarchy – and its potential for facilitating *horizontal* exchanges across society. The *repartimiento* system[8] as it developed in the eighteenth century is an interesting reconciliation of tax and exchange functions of money, of plan and market ways of producing and circulating goods. This reconciliation was obviously full of potential conflict, eventually resolved in favour of the market and of exchange, and the new Peruvian state after Independence found layers of society other than the Indian population to tax. But even after Independence, and well into the twentieth century, the state continued to control and tax sales to the Indian population of coca and salt, which are the two most essential traded commodities whose production is very much confined to specific areas. So again, state-planned distribution of essentials was used to raise surplus from the mass of the population in a controlled market situation.

The Incas seem to have managed to bypass the problems of the political conflict between centralized redistribution and a market economy by not allowing market exchange to develop on any large scale. Significantly, *mullu*, the token money made from shells mentioned by the chroniclers as having been used in what is now Peru, was actually brought by boat from Ecuador (Murra 1975, ch. 10). This trade was then easily monopolizable by the ruling class, in exactly the same way as the kings of Dahomey were able to control the use of cowrie shells by using not the kind that were found on their own shores, but others produced far away off the east coast of Africa. If the trade in mullu was ruling-class trade, it would not be surprising that the large deposits of them are found in religious sites. All the chroniclers concur, in any case, that the predominant system of accounting used by the Incas themselves was the *quipu*, the system of knots and different coloured strands of cord. If the state controlled the distribution of goods through the quipu system, and if it also monopolized the import of mullu from Ecuador, then it is difficult to see how local rulers could have had the means to transform any surplus they themselves could appropriate into a form in which it could be accumulated. But money and the market allow just this. They allow any surplus to be quickly transformed into a durable form which can be accumulated and used to hire labour through social relations which can yield more surplus. Although the Spanish colony of Peru took over many of the organizational features of the Inca empire, it was not able to maintain effective centralization once money was allowed to develop as a medium of exchange.

'Resistance to capitalism'

At a local level, the tax-collection system worked so as to divide even the Indians against each other during the colonial period. But once they had gained the right not to pay tribute or do mita labour, that is, once they were free of any obligation to do unpaid labour and could therefore expect to *exchange* their labour or its product, then exchange relations with the outside world spread, and led eventually to the secession of many Communities in the area. Nowadays, then, the presence of large amounts of usually very small sums of money in the Communities is indicative of widespread exchange with the wider capitalist economy. There is no particular 'resistance' to this process; on the contrary, most people aspire to it, and it can be seen as socially progressive insofar as it frees people from traditional vertical ties.

This does not, however, mean to say that the presence of money is indicative of capitalist production relations. Though it is quite possible to find money being given in payment for work done in the communities, it is doubtful whether this has anything to do with capitalist relations. Though there are times when land has been bought, sold and rented out in the Communities, there are strict limits to this process, given that most people do not want to alienate land but to pass it on to their kin. In the absence of any real possibility of accumulating large enough quantities of land to introduce any technological improvment over traditional methods of cultivation, paying out wages for labour done on one's land represents merely a deduction from the total product that can be obtained. A man in Huayllay who hired wage labour to help him work his land was considered by his wife to be lazy, not a dynamic innovator. On the other hand, a *mestiza* widow, who owned lands in Huayllay, was unable to do much more than break even on them, because of the large amounts she had to pay, both in money and in kind, to people to work them. Within the Communities, as opposed to between them, there is still a widespread adherence to traditional ways of exchanging products and labour. This is to say that commodity relations have not penetrated *production* in the Communities. Economic power and status within the Communities is therefore based to a large extent on the ability to manipulate or succeed in *exchange* of some kind with the outside, capitalist world.

In conclusion, it is worth pointing out again that at the level of culture and of ideas of the relation to the modern world and the developed economy, there is considerable difference between the two Communities of Huayllay Grande and Carhuapata. If these ideologies seem paradoxical when looked at in relation to the actual economic situation of the two Communities, they make more sense if one sees the two Communities as interdependent ecological levels and if one recalls that Carhuapata has gradually shaken off the political domination of the lower level. This throws light on the theory of verticality in the Andes, since it shows how exchange between

121

levels is related more to the *breakdown* of vertical control than to its maintenance.

Notes

This is a revised version of a paper first given to a conference on 'Resistance to capitalism
in the Andes' in Cambridge in 1977.
1. See Banaji (1977) for a useful discussion of some of the different criteria that have
   been used in the definition of 'mode of production'.
2. In this chapter I use 'Community' to refer to the legal entity (*comunidad indigena*
   prior to 1969 and *comunidad campesina* since then), while 'community' is used in a
   more general sense to refer to a group of people living in the same place.
3. For instance, Burchard (1974) and Custred (1974).
4. The Cerrito San Pedro is a steep hill of sand on the outskirts of Lima. A large shanty-
   town has been established on it, with a format very similar to a village in the sierra
   such as Huayllay. Conditions are horrifically crowded, and there is (or was in 1977)
   no running water to each house nor proper drainage facilities. In the heat of the
   tropical coast this made for appalling living conditions. The parody of the situation
   was that people dressed in their clothes from the sierra would greet each other in
   Quechua as they walked up and down the sandy alleyways.
5. See Polanyi (1966) for the analysis of the eighteenth-century kingdom of Dahomey.
6. I am indebted to Professor Rudi Bloch for the idea of the dual function of money
   built on in this section, although he is in no way responsible for the way I have
   applied it to Peruvian history. Bloch's work on money (1976) has been translated
   but not published in English. The best exposition of the German historical school's
   state theory of money is the work of Knapp (1924) which J. M. Keynes had translated
   into English, but it is highly inaccessible both through its idiosyncratic use of new
   words compounded from Ancient Greek roots and, no doubt as a consequence of
   this, the difficulty of obtaining a copy. However, there is a summary in Weber
   (1965: 373–81).
7. See the document published by Pease (1974).
8. See Golte (1976) for an analysis of the way the *repartimiento* system functioned in
   the eighteenth-century economy.

5

Production and market exchange in peasant economies: the case of the southern highlands in Peru

ADOLFO FIGUEROA

The peasant communities of the Andes constitute a 'reality without a theory'. Despite their undoubted importance in most Andean countries, there are as yet no satisfactory accounts or explanations of their economic functioning and dynamics. In this chapter I shall present an analytic framework to study their process of production and exchange. The peasant community is analysed here in the same terms as one might analyse a national economy, with an internal and external sector, production divided into sectors and technological and trade relations between them. This permits us to describe the production structure and the net result of exchanges between the community and the rest of the economy, showing the relative importance of wage labour, self-consumption and exports in the generation of peasant incomes, and thus their degree of market integration.

I shall apply that framework to the peasant families living in communities in the southern highlands (sierra) of Peru. This is the most 'traditional' and poorest social group in Peru, where conventional views characterize them as 'self-sufficient' economies, 'outside-the-market'. This study shows empirically the degree and mechanisms of market integration of these communities, which constitute the present historical form of the peasant economy in Peru.

1. The analytical framework

Technological and market relations

The peasant community is not only an aggregate of families but a social context which establishes certain economic relationships among its members, in which certain economic decisions are reached collectively and certain economic activities are carried out collectively. It is, indeed, the macroeconomic framework of the peasant family which is the basic economic unit. As such, it comprises three sectors of production: agricultural goods (A), livestock (P), and a wide range of non-agricultural goods such as crafts,

123

Table 5.1. *Inter-sectoral relations in the economy of a peasant community*

		Sectors			Consumption	Investment	Exports		Total
		A	P	Z	C	I	N	M	
Agriculture	A	0	X_{12}	X_{13}	C_1	I_1	N_1	M_1	X_1
Livestock	P	X_{21}	0	X_{23}	C_2	I_2	N_2	M_2	X_2
Z-goods	Z	X_{31}	X_{32}	0	C_3	I_3	N_3	M_3	X_3
Imports in kind	N	X_{n1}	X_{n2}	X_{n3}	C_n	I_n	0	0	X_n
Money imports	M	X_{m1}	X_{m2}	X_{m3}	C_m	I_m	0	0	X_m
Labour	H	X_{h1}	X_{h2}	X_{h3}	C_h	0	N_h	M_h	X_h
Land	T	X_{t1}	X_{t2}	X_{t3}	C_t	0	0	0	X_t
Agriculture	A	S_{11}	S_{12}	S_{13}					S_1
Animals	P	S_{21}	S_{22}	S_{23}					S_2
Tools	Z	S_{31}	S_{32}	S_{33}					S_3

food processing and construction which we shall call 'Z-goods' (Hymer and Resnick 1969). This mix of activities is found in most cases although, to be sure, there are also cases of specialization in potato production, in pastoral activity and in weaving.

In order to undertake production, the community possesses two primary factors – land (T) and labour (H) – and three types of *initial* stocks of products which correspond to the three sectors mentioned above: seed (A), animals (P), and tools (Z). These goods are produced but, since 'one needs commodities to produce commodities', they must be already available as initial stocks if production is to be undertaken. Other inputs enter into the production of A, P, and Z goods as flows, and they either come out of the community's annual production or out of its imports. The community as a whole exchanges with two 'external sectors': the rest of the rural economy (N) (other communities and *haciendas*) and the urban economy (M).

A table of 'inter-sectoral relations' (table 5.1) offers an analytical approach to the relationships between primary factors of production, initial stocks of goods and inputs on the one hand, and the annual product and its allocation on the other. In the table the agricultural production of a particular year is represented by X_1. This product is net in the sense that it excludes the seed used, and it is allocated towards the same year's cattle production and towards the production of Z-goods as inputs (oats, barley, and other animal feeds; produce which is processed into food, such as potatoes for *chuño*, and maize for *chicha*). The remainder of the agricultural production is for consumption (C_1), for the accumulation of further stocks for the subsequent agricultural production cycle (I_1) and for export or sale outside the community (N_1 and M_1).

Production and market exchange

A year's livestock production is represented by X_2. It comprises the number of animals produced, including chickens and guinea-pigs; derivative production, such as milk, eggs, wool and skins; and also dung, which is used as fertilizer. Part of the production from this sector returns to the productive process as inputs: fertilizer for agriculture, and, for Z-goods, milk for cheese, wool for blankets and clothes. Part is consumed as meat, milk, eggs and skins; part becomes investment, as when the stock of animals is increased, and part goes to export.

Z-goods constitute a varied list, of which the main elements are the following:
(a) processed food: chuño, chicha, cheese, and dried meat
(b) textiles: clothes, blankets, ponchos, sweaters, cloaks, sacks, straps, harnesses and lassoos
(c) tools, and repair thereof
(d) construction: houses, public buildings, yards and enclosures, roads, canals, and construction materials such as adobe bricks and roof-tiles
(e) fuel: firewood
(f) trade
(g) transport
(h) other crafts: ceramics, leatherwork, carpentry
Some of these Z-goods contribute to agricultural and cattle production, others to final demand. They contribute to agriculture as sacks and other containers and in the repair of tools; they contribute to cattle production as ropes, harnesses and lassoos; they are consumed as woollen textiles; they are invested in construction; and they are exported as cheese.

Imported products from the rural economy (X_n) go towards production as agricultural inputs, as inputs to livestock production (black salt fed to animals) or as inputs for the production of Z-goods. They also go to consumption, as in the case of maize imported by upper highland communities, and to investment. The same can be said of urban imports: fertilizers, pesticides, medicines for livestock, dyes for handicrafts are intermediate production goods; salt, sugar, kerosene are for consumption; and they go to investment above all as steel implements.

Annual labour, measured in person–days, is used in all three sectors of production, although production may often be in two sectors at once, for example when someone pastures cattle and spins wool at the same time. C_h refers to 'consumption of labour', in rest days or fiestas. N_h and M_h denote exported labour, migrating for seasonal work outside the community.

The stock of land (X_t) is measured by area, and is allocated to agricultural production, to livestock production when sown to alfalfa, and to production of Z-goods when used for building. C_t refers to land set aside for homes, *plazas* or sports fields.

The last three lines represent *stocks* of capital goods which are used in the current year's production – as opposed to the top three lines which represent *flows*, that is quantities produced this year. S_1 represents agricultural stocks required for agricultural production (such as seed, S_{11}). S_2 is the stock of animals used in all three sectors, for example as oxen, as reproducers of more cattle, and as means of transport. Finally, S_3 represents the stock of tools used in the production of goods in all three sectors.

It should be clear that each column of the table represents the combination of factors of production necessary to produce the corresponding good: it is a vector representing a technological process. The four right-hand columns represent vectors of final demand: the composition of goods consumed, accumulated and exchanged. It will also be noticed that the community produces four types of commodities: agricultural goods, livestock, Z-goods, and labour for export to work temporarily elsewhere in town or country.

An empirical estimate of table 5.1 would summarize the technological relations, the productive structure, and exchange relations in peasant communities. It would also show the specific ways by which the peasant economy is connected to the market economy. This estimate is presented in the next section. Before that, the particular geographical setting of peasant communities must be specified, for production structure of any community will be influenced by the characteristics of the ecological levels under its control, micro-climates, and so on.

Ecological levels and micro-climates

It is customary to divide Peru into three major regions: coast, sierra, and jungle (*selva*). This differentiation is based on the high Andean *cordillera* – the sierra – and coast and jungle are merely the regions situated on either side thereof. But some geographers have proposed alternative divisions; in particular Pulgar Vidal (n.d.) insists on the existence of eight ecological levels in Peru. Taking into account the greatest possible number of differentiating factors in the natural environment, Pulgar Vidal distinguishes: coast, *yunga*, *quechua*, *suni*, *puna*, cordillera, upper jungle and lower jungle. In this classification the region usually known as the sierra is divided into five.

The sierra, then, is not homogeneous. The vast range of altitudes contained therein, often in close proximity to one another, exhibit numerous types of soil and climate. As pointed out by Julio C. Tello, 'the climatic conditions of the *sierra* vary from the tropical climates of the valleys and ravines, to the arctic conditions of the high *cordillera*' (quoted in Pulgar Vidal: 13). The clear zonal distinctions made by the inhabitants of the sierra in their immediate environment do in fact correspond to a large extent to the regional classification proposed by Pulgar Vidal.

Table 5.2. *Peru: total and rural population by ecological region, 1972*

Regions	Altitude (metres)	Total population		Rural population	
		thousands	%	thousands	%
Coast	under 500	5929	43.8	1208	17.0
Yunga	500–2000	926	6.9	725	10.2
	(500–1000)	(228)	(1.7)	(122)	(1.7)
	(1000–1500)	(258)	(1.9)	(212)	(3.0)
	(1500–2000)	(440)	(3.3)	(391)	(5.5)
Quechua	2000–3500	4073	30.1	3215	45.3
	(2000–2500)	(892)	(6.6)	(625)	(8.8)
	(2500–3000)	(1171)	(8.7)	(1012)	(14.3)
	(3000–3500)	(2010)	(14.8)	(1578)	(22.2)
Suni	3500–4000	1325	9.8	1101	15.5
Puna	4000–4500	192	1.4	124	1.7
Cordillera	4500 and above	13	0.1	9	0.1
High jungle	500–1000	371	2.7	280	3.9
Low jungle	under 500	709	5.2	444	6.3
		13,538	100.0	7106	100.0

The estimates were reached on the basis of district population figures in the *National Population Census of 1972*. However, they remain approximations because the altitude of each district was assumed to be the same as the altitude of the district capital. The altitudes were obtained from the *Anuario Estadístico del Perú*, vol. 3, Table 2.2.6 (Lima: Oficina Nacional de Estadísticas y Censos, n.d.) and from inquiries at the Instituto Geográfico Militar.

According to Pulgar Vidal the quechua begins at 2300 metres, and the cordillera at 4800. Since the intervals in our sources were 500 metres, a small, but insignificant, part of the area covered by the yunga had to be included in the quechua, while the cordillera was defined as starting at 4500 metres, thus impinging slightly on the puna. However, these errors are marginal.

The five regions mentioned for the sierra define a series of ecological levels. In terms of altitude above sea-level, the *yunga* ranges up to 2300 metres and corresponds to the warm valleys; the *quechua*, the temperate region, ranges from 2300 to 3500 metres; the *suni* is a cold region ranging from 3500 to 4000 metres and the *puna*, the 'treeless zone', rises up to 4800 metres. Thereafter we reach the cordillera where there is practically no agricultural or pastoral activity of any kind.

Table 5.2 shows the distribution of population among the eight ecological levels in 1972. Although the coast contains 44% of the nation's population, 25% of these live in Lima. The next most important region is the quechua, with 30% of the population. Rising from coast to quechua, only 7% of the population is to be found in the yunga because of its harsh environment and very steep terrain. Above the quechua the population again declines until one passes the cordillera and descends the eastern slopes of the Andes to the upper jungle.

Taking the rural population alone – 53% of the nation – the heaviest concentration is found in the quechua (45%), followed by the coast (17%), the suni (16%) and the yunga (10%). Thus the five ecological levels of the sierra comprise 73% of the rural, and 39% of the national population.

Each ecological level evidently exhibits different production possibilities. For each zone Pulgar Vidal lists 'limit products' which cannot be produced at higher altitudes. For the yunga these are sugar cane and certain varieties of fruit (avocado, *lúcumo, chirimoya* (prickly pear), guayava and citrus fruits). As far as the upper limits of the quechua one finds maize, wheat and other fruits (plums, peaches, apples and quinces); and in the suni the 'limit products' are: beans, small tubers (*oca, olluco, mashua*), high-altitude cereals (*quinoa, cañihua*) and vegetables such as *tarhui*. These products of the suni also have a lower limit of cultivation at the border of the suni and quechua. Finally, only potatoes and barley can still be cultivated on the puna, and even then only in some places and with lengthy fallow periods. Barley cannot be cultivated lower than the quechua, but potatoes grow in all the sierra regions.

The ecological levels are also marked by variations in the possibilities of livestock production. For example, camelides (llamas, alpacas and the like) pasture mostly on the puna, while equine and caprine animals are most suited to the lower regions. Given the variation in both flora and fauna, the production possibilities of non-agricultural goods (Z-goods) are also influenced heavily by access to ecological levels. Finally, it should be remembered that even within each ecological level a wide variety of microclimates is to be found, and as a result individual communities possess a wide variety of resources. On the other hand, these resources differ between communities for each has access to different ecological levels and microclimates, which implies that communities have different production possibility sets.

The sample

The remainder of this paper will present the results of research carried out in the southern sierra of Peru, the poorest area of the sierra region in income terms. The peasant families studied are *minifundistas*, possessing for the most part less than five hectares of land; and they are organized in peasant *comunidades*. The family (or household) and the comunidad are therefore the units of analysis throughout the study.

Table 5.3. *The sample communities*

Name	Date of study	Number of families interviewed	Department
Accha–Sihuina	Sept. 1978	41	Cuzco
Ninamarca	Oct. 1978	31	Cuzco
Acobamba–San Marcos	Nov. 1978	40	Huancavelica
Ancobamba	Dec. 1978	40	Apurimac
Ttiomayo	Jan. 1979	36	Cuzco
Huando	Feb. 1979	42	Huancavelica
Culta	March 1979	40	Puno
Jacantaya	April 1979	36	Puno
Total		306	

Eight communities were selected from a sampling frame which contained the most important areas with peasant communities in the southern sierra. The communities vary in their ecological characteristics: Jacantaya, Culta and Ninamarca are typical of the suni zone; Acobamba of the yunga, and the remainder are in the quechua. The only one of the five departments in the area which is not represented is Ayacucho, but this is not of importance since differences between departments are minor.

The data were obtained by uniform questionnaires carried out with peasant families in all the communities. Other informants were also interviewed, in particular persons who occupied or had occupied positions of responsibility in the communities; these provided invaluable information on the social and physical context of the study, which shed further light on the information provided by the families interviewed and also enabled us to detect when the information given by the families was clearly beyond the bounds of local possibilities. The research in these communities was initiated in 1976 with several visits and preliminary data collection (Figueroa 1979). The final stage in data collection, which was initiated in September 1978, lasted two weeks in each community and was carried out by an average of four persons, three of whom worked in all the localities and one of whom was usually a person from the community itself. In cases where the family concerned possessed a faulty command of Spanish the interviews were conducted in Quechua or Aymara. The data collected on flows refer to the previous year ending the week before the interview.

Table 5.3 shows the distribution of the sampled families among the eight communities. It was decided to sample about 40 families in each community, in order to be able to carry out a statistical analysis of the results by communities. All the families interviewed, including replacements, were selected by random sampling. Therefore each sample is representative of its community. On the basis of population data, weights were applied to the sample of families to make it representative of the eight communities and the southern sierra. The reader will find in each table the average values for these two levels of sample expansion as 'sample total' and 'southern sierra' respectively.

2. The unit of production: the peasant family

Size of family and labour force

The family is defined as all those persons who habitually live in the same house. The criterion of residence poses some difficulties on account of permanent and temporary migration, and the rule adopted was to consider as resident any person who lived in the house a total of six months or more in the preceding year.

The average size of family varies between 4.2 and 5 members in the communities (table 5.4). The variation in these average sizes seems to have no particular relation to the community's ecological level. Although the values of the standard deviation of family size within each community are high, the differences between communities seem to be small. These data show that it is difficult to identify a 'typical' peasant family size, at least without taking into account the stage of the household cycle reached by each one.

This study uses two definitions of labour force. The one, designed to take into account the role of children in production and thus to show the family's productive capacity, includes all members of 6 years or more. The other includes persons of 18 years or more and measures the 'adult labour force'; as from 18 years of age, people can carry out adult tasks and they can also obtain identity cards which enable them to move about more easily in the labour market. Neither definition excludes elderly people since there is no formal 'retirement age' and since they, like the children, also participate in production. Table 5.4 also shows that, under the first definition, 'total labour force' varies between 3.4 and 3.9 persons per family, while 'adult labour force' varies between 2.1 and 2.6. Once again, there is a wide dispersal in the measure of total labour force, but this dispersal is reduced for the measure of adult labour force: the vast majority of the families have between 2 and 3 adult members, and this can be said to constitute a typical peasant family.

A further, equally important, observation is that the peasant family is typically a nuclear family. It is extremely rare to find a household with more than one married couple and even in Culta, where 20% of the households had four or more adult members, only a very small proportion of these included two married couples. In the light of these characteristics, one might say that the number of economic units in the countryside is in a sense maximized. Specifically we find that the land is divided into innumerable pro-

Table 5.4. *Size of family and labour force (numbers of persons)*

| | Size of family | | Labour force | | | |
| | | | Total | | Adult | |
	$\bar{X}$	S	$\bar{X}$	S	$\bar{X}$	S
Jacantaya	4.6	(2.6)	3.9	(2.2)	2.6	(1.3)
Culta	4.5	(2.0)	3.6	(1.7)	2.2	(0.7)
Ninamarca	4.7	(1.4)	3.6	(1.3)	2.2	(0.5)
Ancobamba	4.7	(2.5)	3.7	(1.7)	2.1	(0.7)
Ttiomayo	5.0	(2.2)	3.9	(1.6)	2.3	(0.9)
Sihuina	4.3	(1.9)	3.6	(1.5)	2.3	(0.8)
Huando	4.8	(2.6)	3.7	(1.8)	2.1	(0.8)
Acobamba	4.2	(1.7)	3.4	(1.4)	2.1	(0.6)
Sample total	4.6		3.7		2.2	
Southern sierra	4.5		3.6		2.2	

$\bar{X}$ = average; S = standard deviation

ductive units, which would not be the case if nuclear families decided to group together in order to form larger single units.

There are two types of explanation for the nuclear character of families both as production and as consumption units. In economic terms, the cost of establishing themselves separately, especially the cost of housing, is small, at least in comparison to the cost of urban housing: a survey in Lima in 1969 showed that the average household comprised 6.5 persons (Figueroa 1974), the size of the household reflecting the high cost of housing. As a unit of production, this small family size and the rate of household partition reflect the absence of significant economies of scale which might justify the grouping of families and their resources.

A further explanation is to be found in inheritance patterns and in criteria of social status. It is usual for parents to provide their newly married children with the resources necessary for economic independence. To have married children living in one's house indicates that one is unable to provide them with these resources.

Of course, reciprocity and exchange relations between families reduce the self-sufficiency of the household, but in no way do they detract from its importance as the locus of control and allocation of resources.

Land use and fragmentation of holdings

Whereas pasture land can only be used for one purpose, cultivable land offers a choice: it can be planted to crops, it can be sown to pasture, or it

131

Table 5.5. *Distribution of cultivable parcels between cultivated and fallow land (number of parcels per family)*

Community	Type of tenure	Cultivated	Fallow	Total
Jacantaya	private	19.5	15.1	34.6
Culta	private	11.3	0.6	11.9
	laymi	27.6	44.9	72.5
	Total	38.9	45.5	84.4
Ninamarca	private	2.3	1.4	3.7
	laymi	4.7	3.8	8.5
	Total	7.0	5.2	12.2
Ancobamba	private	6.5	0.9	7.4
	laymi	1.8	nd	nd
	Total	8.3	nd	nd
Ttiomayo	private	2.9	0	2.9
	laymi	3.1	2.7	5.8
	Total	6.0	2.7	8.7
Sihuina	private	nd	nd	nd
	laymi	nd	nd	nd
Huando	private	8.5	1.0	9.5
Acobamba	private	2.5	0.3	2.8
	laymi	1.6	4.1	5.7
	Total	4.1	4.4	8.5

can be left uncultivated. If it is uncultivated, it can still serve as natural pasture. The system of arable land tenure varies from community to community; in some it is completely privately owned, and each family uses it according to its own interests, whereas in others part of the arable land is subject to collective decisions. Pasture land on the other hand is always collectively utilized for the private benefit of individual families, all of whom have free access to it.

Table 5.5 shows the distribution of arable land between pasture and crops. The unit of measurement is the number of plots rather than hectares, because the imprecision of replies to questions concerning the size of plots and the enormous number of plots belonging to each family made the estimation of their aggregate size impossible. The estimate in terms of number of plots is an adequate approximation because the use of the plots is independent of their size. The proportion of land assigned to agriculture, rather than pasture, varies among the communities between 46% and 90%.

In six of the eight communities there is a system of collective decision over the rotation of land, known as *laymi*. Jacantaya does not possess this system because it is located on the shores of Lake Titicaca and its land is cultivated in terraces. The terraces are small and possess clear boundaries, so that a family can leave a plot fallow and use it for pasture even while the neighbouring parcel is being cultivated. When plots are larger and do not show clear boundaries, the laymi system is an effective way of separating pasture from cropped land, which explains why a collective decision is needed in such cases. The other community which does not have a laymi system is Huando. This community did have such a system until some twenty years ago, and its disappearance is mainly due to the introduction of modern inputs, mainly fertilizers, which have raised the productivity of the land.

Table 5.5 shows the importance of the laymi system in the other communities; between 21% and 71% of the land cultivated during the years of our research was under this system. Its qualitative importance is further underlined by the observation that it was in these lands that basic food products such as potatoes were sown. The table also shows the extreme degree of fragmentation of cultivable holdings, with a range varying from 9 to 84 holdings per family. In the extreme cases of Culta and Jacantaya parcels are measured in furrows, which are at most 20 metres long. One frequently hears a person saying that he has 'one plot of four furrows, another of six furrows', and so on.

This fragmentation can be explained in part by the desire of producers to avoid erosion when the land is on a slope. But the existence of fragmentation on flat land shows that there is also a demographic and economic explanation. We have already seen how households acquire land upon their formation by inter-generational transfer, and these families must also gain access to land on different ecological levels if they are to produce a range of products (see Platt, ch. 2 above). Although this would seem to reflect a strategy aiming at a certain degree of family self-sufficiency, such a hypothesis does not take into account the wide variations in microclimates, even within the same ecological level, which create variations in yields as a result of frost, hail and floods. Thus the spread of parcels would seem to be a form of risk-averting economic behaviour, which would certainly be consistent with the low level of the producers' incomes.

The number of crops sown and parcels cultivated by each family is shown in table 5.6. The crops involved are: potatoes, barley, oca, olluco, mashua, quinoa, cañihua, tarhui, broad beans, wheat, peas and kidney beans. The average number of parcels per family varies between communities from 4 to 39, and in all the communities families have more parcels than crops, implying that they grow one crop in more than one parcel. Thus in Jacantaya

133

Table 5.6. *Number of parcels cultivated per family by number of crops*

Number of crops	Jac	Cul	Nin	Anc	Tti	Sih	Hua	Aco
0							7.1	2.6
1				5.0			0	0
2			3.2	0			2.4	7.7
3			9.7	2.5	27.8		2.4	28.2
4	2.4	5.1	9.7	10.0	36.1		7.1	25.6
5	2.8	7.7	19.4	12.5	5.6		11.9	20.5
6	13.9	12.8	29.0	22.5	11.1		26.2	2.6
7	22.2	17.9	19.4	12.5	5.6		16.7	7.7
8	16.7	20.5	9.7	20.0			19.0	2.6
9	11.1	20.5		15.0			2.4	0
10	13.9	10.3		2.5				
11	13.9	5.1		0			2.4	
12	2.8			2.5				
Total (%)	100	100	100	100	100	nd	100	100
Average	8.22	7.69	5.58	6.63	4.31	nd	5.98	4.21
Standard dev.	1.97	1.81	1.57	2.30	1.17	nd	2.41	1.84
Average no. of parcels	19.5	38.9	7.1	8.2	6.1	nd	8.5	4.1

8 crops are sown on an average of 20 parcels. Only in Acobamba is there near-equality between the average number of parcels and the average number of crops. The diversification of crop-location is even greater than this indicates, since there is much inter-cropping. This offers further support to the risk-aversion hypothesis.

Capital goods

The capital stock of the peasant economy consists of three types of goods which are used in the production process: agricultural goods (mainly seed), animals and tools. The stock of seed required varies with the amount of cultivated land, which is fixed in each community. This section will deal with the other two types of production goods.

Animals can be divided into three types, depending on their place in the production process. One type is used for consumption of its product, in the form of meat, wool, milk and eggs. This includes sheep, pigs, goats and domestic animals such as chickens and guinea-pigs. The second type is of

Table 5.7. *Animal stocks: number of animals per family*

	Jac	Cul	Nin	Anc	Tti	Sih	Hua	Aco	Sample total
Sheep	6.39	13.08	12.32	4.85	6.97	5.56	3.74	4.03	6.95
Pigs	0.44	1.74	2.42	1.35	1.92	0.61	0.71	0.67	1.09
Goats	0	0	0	1.85	0	0.10	0.91	0.15	
Alpaca	0	2.67	0	0	0	0	0	0	
Chickens	1.64	2.92	1.94	1.78	2.67	2.93	2.17	3.85	2.51
Guinea-pigs	0.89	0.59	5.45	5.95	8.62	4.22	2.95	3.36	3.94
Horses	0.14	1.40	1.13	2.68	0.45	1.71	1.05	0.63	1.17
Llamas	0	0.05	0	0	0	0	0	0	
Oxen	0.14	0.75	0.94	0.53	1.03	0.54	0.57	0.10	0.56
Total cattle	1.33	2.08	3.03	3.65	3.47	2.39	1.00	1.59	2.29

animals such as horses and llamas, used in productive services. Cattle constitute a third type for they provide both consumption and productive services. Each family's mix of these types will obviously impinge on the overall structure of its activities.

It will be seen from table 5.7 that on average the peasant family has very few animals: the average family possesses 7 sheep, 1 pig, 3 chickens, 4 guinea-pigs and 2 head of cattle. These figures appear as weighted averages in the last column of the table. However, the composition of the stock varies substantially between communities, largely on account of ecological differences. Goats are not found in the higher communities, nor llamas or alpacas in the lower ones. But there remain other differences even in those animals which can be kept at all these altitudes, and these have an economic explanation. The communities with most cattle and sheep are Ancobamba, Culta, Ttiomayo and Ninamarca, and those with the least are Huando and Acobamba. In Acobamba the land slopes steeply and there is therefore the constant risk of falls, while in Huando there is an economic explanation as well as an ecological one – the community has no high pasture lands, and therefore does not control enough ecological levels to practise both agriculture and cattle-raising at the same time.

Variation in the endowment of horses is largely explained by distance from a road. The use of oxen in ploughing is limited when deeper ploughing is required than they can do, and when land is too steep or cultivated in terraces. It is for these reasons that there are few oxen in Jacantaya and Acobamba. But in general it can be seen that animal draught power is limited and that to a significant degree the peasant economy depends on human energy. This brings us to its implements. These are of two types: those used in

Table 5.8. *Stocks of implements per family*

	Jac	Cul	Nin	Anc	Tti	Sih	Hua	Aco	Sample total
Foot-ploughs	2.71	0.87	1.13	1.90	1.14	1.56	1.95	1.53	1.57
Hoes	2.83	4.08	1.71	2.63	1.94	2.44	3.71	3.85	3.12
Sewing-machines	0.31	0.41	0.14	0.08	0.17	0.12	0.55	0.10	0.28
Picks and shovels	2.29	2.39	2.19	2.19	3.06	1.86	1.44	3.22	2.40

agriculture, such as ox-ploughs, foot-ploughs (*chakitajlla*), hoes and spades, and those used in the production of non-agricultural goods (Z-goods) especially in construction such as picks and shovels, and sewing-machines.

Table 5.8 shows that the typical peasant family uses a very small range of tools requiring human energy: between one and two foot-ploughs, three hoes and two picks. The variation in the number of foot-ploughs per family as between different communities is largely explained by differences in the quality of land: in Jacantaya oxen cannot be used because of terrace cultivation, and in Ancobamba the poor quality of the soil requires deeper ploughing than can be obtained with oxen. The variations in hoes and spades seem to be related to differences between families of varying wealth, while sewing-machines are a preliminary indication of the wealth of a community, and above all of its modernization. Huando thus appears as the most modern of these communities, followed by the two communities in the Department of Puno: Culta and Jacantaya.

The exposition hitherto has shown that the peasant economy is both small in scale and differentiated in its productive structure. Typically the unit of production (the family) has an adult labour force of about two persons; two or three hectares of cultivable land divided into a large number of parcels (between 9 and 84) and access to a variable amount of pasture land under collective control; its animal stock consists of two head of cattle, one horse, two or three chickens, and four guinea-pigs, and its stock of tools consists of one or two foot-ploughs, three hoes and two picks. This stock of capital goods is used in agricultural and livestock production and in the production of non-agricultural Z-goods. Temporary migration, of course, means that these do not account for all the activities of the family labour force.

Apart from the adult labour force, resource endowment, especially land, varies between communities. The land endowment of the community depends on its access to different ecological levels and on the topography of its land. Ecology defines production possibilities, and topography is an important determinant of the technology used, as we have seen in the limitations on the use of ox-ploughs in Acobamba.

The next section describes the use of labour, land and these capital goods in the production of goods and services for self-consumption and for exchange. This will enable us to estimate the extent of the links between the peasant economy and the market economy in Peru.

3. Production and market exchange

Table 5.9 shows the inter-sectoral flows in six of the eight communities studied. That is, it replaces the symbols of table 5.1 with empirical data, with one modification: the production of each separate sector of intermediate goods – the first three columns of table 5.1 – has been consolidated into one column. This has been done for the sake of simplicity and also because it is often difficult to separate the production of intermediate goods by sector. The N column refers to non-monetary barter transactions, and the M column to monetary transactions. The former measures principally transactions with other communities, the latter transactions with the rest of the economy, above all the urban economy. Two of the communities – Ttiomayo and Sihuina – have been omitted on account of the incompleteness of the data, but the other six are sufficiently well distributed among ecological levels for the representativity of the sample not to be affected. Of course, whenever only these six communities have been used in tabulations, the weights of the sampled families have been changed accordingly to get the expanded values for 'sample total' and 'southern sierra'.

The reader will note that table 5.9 contains certain identities. The figure at the bottom of column 1 is the same as that opposite $A + P + Z$ in the last column. The former represents the value of production viewed from the cost of production side whereas the latter is the value of production by destination, and both must be equal. Because of this identity, self-employment (row 20) was estimated by difference. The transactions in kind have been transformed into monetary values by applying average market prices observed in the monetary transactions. Obviously the valuation of imports to the community must be equal to the valuation of exports when exchange is in kind. This explains the equality between the value at the bottom of column 4 (exports in kind) and at the end of row 13 (imports in kind). For the monetary exchange the difference of total value of exports and total value of imports is due to net transfers that families in the community receive from relatives living in the city. Therefore the last two figures at the bottom of column 5 (exports in money) must be equal to the figure at the end of row 14 (imports in money).

The entries in table 5.9 are all monetary values, *soles* per year, and per family. Therefore, the values for all communities are comparable since

137

Table 5.9. *Inter-sectoral relations in peasant communities (soles per year, per family)*

	A + P + Z Inter-mediate goods	C Consumption	I Invest-ment	N Exports in kind	M Exports in money	Total
JACANTAYA						
A (Agriculture)	3 700	14 896		2 854	5 401	26 851
P_1 (Derived products)	990	1 680		0	107	2 777
P_2 (Consumption)	0	1 151		7	325	1 483
P_3 (Services)	0	0		0	0	0
P_4 (Cattle)	0	594		0	5 603	6 197
P_5 (Other)	0	0		0	0	0
P (Livestock)	990	3 425		7	6 035	10 457
Z_1 (Manuf.)	0	3 825		0	482	4 307
Z_2 (Trade)	0	0		0	3 213	3 213
Z_3 (Other)	0	5 685		0	9 682	15 367
Z (Z-goods)	0	9 510		0	13 377	22 887
A + P + Z	4 690	27 831		2 861	24 813	60 195
N (Imports in kind)	1 000	1 861	0			2 861
M (Imports in money)	4 836	36 638	2 584			44 058
N + M + A + P + Z	10 526	66 330	2 584			
Wages—N	41			0	0	
Wages—M	4 644			0	12 772	
Rents—N	0					
Rents—M	72					
Self-employment	44 914					
Total	60 195			2 861	37 585	
Net transfer				0	6 473	
CULTA						
A	4 966	19 866		287	429	25 548
P_1	2 145	3 066		0	1 502	6 713
P_2	0	3 291		0	2 541	5 832
P_3	0	0		0	316	316
P_4	0	594		25	20 100	20 719
P_5	0	0		0	408	408
P	2 145	6 951		25	24 867	33 988
Z_1	0	4 358		0	0	4 358

Table 5.9. *(continued)*

	A+P+Z	C	I	N	M	Total
Z_2	0	0		0	3 357	3 357
Z_3	0	0		0	1 715	1 715
Z	0	4 358		0	5 072	9 430
A + P + Z	7 111	31 175		312	30 368	68 966
N	44	243	25			312
M	2 707	33 812	4 867			41 386
N+M+A+P+Z	9 862	65 230	4 892			
W–N	1 000			0	0	
W–M	2 052			0	9 403	
R–N	19					
R–M	298					
Self-employment	55 735					
Total	68 966			312	39 771	
Net transfer					1 615	

NINAMARCA

	A+P+Z	C	I	N	M	Total
A	2 345	9 380		837	12 685	25 247
P_1	1 980	2 100		13	0	4 093
P_2	0	9 644		77	2 594	12 315
P_3	0	0		0	0	0
P_4	0	2 560		742	3 000	6 302
P_5	0	0		0	680	680
P	1 980	14 304		832	6 274	23 390
Z_1	0	2 900		116	448	3 464
Z_2	0	0		0	1 232	1 232
Z_3	0	0		0	32	32
Z	0	2 900		116	1 712	4 728
A + P + Z	4 325	26 584		1 785	20 671	53 365
N	125	601	1 059			1 785
M	1 755	17 597	1 461			20 813
N+M+A+P+Z	6 205	44 782	2 520			
W–N	137			0	0	
W–M	908			0	142	
R–N	0					
R–M	0					
Self-employment	46 115					
Total	53 365			1 785	20 813	
Net transfer					0	

Table 5.9. *(continued)*

	A+P+Z	C	I	N	M	Total
ANCOBAMBA						
A	8 777	35 046		351	356	44 530
P_1	825	1 869		0	0	2 694
P_2	0	2 202		98	186	2 486
P_3	0	0		0	925	925
P_4	0	863		0	5 324	6 187
P_5	0	0		5	360	365
P	825	4 934		103	6 795	12 657
Z_1	0	531		5	209	745
Z_2	0	0		0	1 843	1 843
Z_3	0	0		5	84	89
Z	0	531		10	2 136	2 677
A+P+Z	9 602	40 511	0	464	9 287	59 864
N	188	63	213			464
M	1 038	17 619	910			19 567
N+M+A+P+Z	10 828	58 193	1 123			
W–N	60			0	0	
W–M	1 162			0	8 458	
R–N	60					
R–M	17					
Self-employment	47 737					
Total	59 864			464	17 745	
Net transfer					1 822	
HUANDO						
A	7 821	32 210		134	10 050	50 215
P_1	2 000	3 000		0	293	5 293
P_2	0	2 710		73	2 898	5 681
P_3	0	0		0	352	352
P_4	0	1 000		0	3 642	4 642
P_5	0	0		0	0	0
P	2 000	6 710		73	7 185	15 968
Z_1	0	0		0	0	0
Z_2	0	0		21	15 646	15 667
Z_3	0	0		0	9 083	9 083
Z	0	0		21	24 729	24 750
A+P+Z	9 821	38 920		228	41 964	90 933

Table 5.9. *(continued)*

	A+P+Z	C	I	N	M	Total
N	0	201	27			228
M	4 114	46 421	2 536			53 071
N+M+A+P+Z	13 935	85 542	2 563			
W–N	177			0	0	
W–M	8 506			0	4 520	
R–N	1 122					
R–M	371					
Self-employment	66 822					
Total	90 933			228	46 484	
Net transfer				0	6 587	
ACOBAMBA						
A	6 222	24 888		362	4 557	36 029
P_1	2 000	6 000		0	0	8 000
P_2	0	2 240		161	1 048	3 449
P_3	0	0		0	0	0
P_4	0	1 000		0	1 538	2 538
P_5	0	0		0	92	92
P	2 000	9 240		161	2 678	14 079
Z_1	0	117		0	5	122
Z_2	0	0		0	15 282	15 282
Z_3	0	0		0	410	410
Z	0	117		0	15 697	15 814
A + P + Z	8 222	34 245		523	22 932	65 922
N	400	105	18			523
M	1 138	24 868	1 331			27 337
N+M+A+P+Z	9 760	59 218	1 349			
W–N	715			0	0	
W–M	10 335			0	3 841	
R–N	425					
R–M	0					
Self-employment	44 687					
Total	65 922			523	26 773	
Net transfer				0	564	

differences in population have been eliminated. To be sure, the total annual values of a community can be found by multiplying the entries in table 5.9 by the number of families in the community shown in table 5.3, and hence table 5.9 shows the production and exchange structure of the communities.

Intermediate goods

There are three sources of intermediate goods in the communities: domestic goods, derived from each family's own production; goods imported from other communities; and goods imported from the rest of the economy. The table shows that between 45% and 90% of intermediate goods are produced by families themselves, and almost all the remainder are imported from the urban economy. Within the category of domestically produced intermediate goods, agricultural goods figure most prominently and among them the principal item is animal feed. The main intermediate product derived from animals is sheep's wool, while the Z sector produces hardly any intermediate goods. The production of animal feed by the agricultural sector and of wool for textiles by the animal sector constitute the main technological relationships between the three sectors A, P and Z.

Intermediate goods imported from other communities are few. The table estimates a monetary value for wool, salt, wood, straw and pasture. Wood and straw are used mostly for the construction of houses, and there are a few cases of families renting pasture or stubble for animal feed in neighbouring communities. Salt is also fed to animals.

Tables 5.9 and 5.10 show that intermediate goods imported from the urban economy consist almost entirely of agricultural inputs: fertilizer and pesticides. Table 5.10 also shows that there are wide variations in the communities' use of modern inputs. Leaving aside seeds, which are hardly ever improved varieties, and vaccine for animals, which is an insignificant item in terms of cost, we see that communities such as Ancobamba, Ttiomayo and Sihuina hardly use any fertilizer or pesticides at all. Even in those communities where expenditure on these is relatively high (such as Jacantaya, Culta and Huando, which, we shall see, are the least poor of all the communities sampled), this is accounted for by a small number of families only. Of course, the expenditure data do not take into account deficiencies in the method of application of these inputs, which is carried out without any technical assistance. These quantitative and qualitative indications, when combined with the data on capital stocks presented earlier, illustrate the overwhelmingly traditional character of the technology employed in all the communities.

Final demand

The production of the A, P, Z sectors goes to consumption (self-consumption)

Table 5.10. *Average annual expenditure on modern inputs (in brackets: percentage of families purchasing modern inputs) (soles per year per family)*

Community	Fertilizer	Pesticides	Seed	Animal vaccine	Total
Jacantaya	930	622	546	57	2,155
	(75)	(64)	(42)	(81)	
Culta	601	505	839	90	2,035
	(51)	(58)	(53)	(90)	
Ninamarca	404	832	358	40	1,634
	(23)	(93)		(13)	
Ancobamba	0	30	119	40	189
	(0)	(2)	(15)	(7)	
Ttiomayo	184	0	124	6	314
	(14)	(0)		(10)	
Sihuina	15	81	179	9	284
	(2)	(34)		(15)	
Huando	2,440	946	161	73	3,620
	(54)	(28)	(17)	(15)	
Acobamba	364	154	475	8	1,001
	(8)	(5)	(23)	(15)	

and export, since accumulation is almost non-existent (table 5.9, column 3). In no case does investment exceed 8% of final demand and it goes as low as 2%, with an overall total of 4%. Clearly these communities constitute stagnant economies. They are unable to generate any investment from their own resources and the little investment that they do carry out is done with imported goods (column 3, lines 13 (N) and 14 (M)). The main capital goods imported are cattle, sheep, chickens, and tools. The peasant economy does not appear to have sufficient productive capacity to generate its own surplus in livestock and although the interviews contained no direct question concerning changes in the family's stock of animals, it was generally agreed that the communities' stock was not increasing. On the contrary, it appeared to be declining, due to disease, accidents and thefts. Purchases of livestock, therefore, resemble a replacement of stock rather than its increase. Tools are imported largely because there is no domestic industry for the production of these capital goods. In some cases one finds small workshops in local towns which both carry out repairs and 'manufacture' tools with discarded iron from the cities.

Exports are mainly monetary transactions, and only a small fraction is accounted for by transactions with other communities (columns 4 and 5). The distribution of production between self-consumption and export is almost half-and-half except in Ancobamba, which is the furthest from a road and where self-consumption is four times as large as exports. Goods exported are exchanged for intermediate goods, for consumer goods, and for capital goods (lines 13 (N) and 14 (M)).

Self-consumption (column 2, line 12 (A + P + Z)) derives mostly from agricultural goods, followed by animals and their derivatives, with only a small proportion provided by Z-goods. The table also shows that a higher proportion of agricultural production goes to self-consumption than of animal production or of Z-goods. Agricultural production is, indeed, mainly for self-consumption; the same can be said of animal derivatives (milk and eggs), sheep and pigs and domestic animals such as guinea-pigs and chickens and, among Z-goods, woollens and clothes.

The two activities which are clearly undertaken for the purpose of export are cattle-rearing and trade. Cattle are a luxury at these income levels, and peasant producers prefer to sell their cattle and use the money to buy other consumer goods, rather than consume them directly. The rare occasions when they are consumed arise through commitments imposed at the time of community fiestas.

Trade (line 9) is mainly carried out between the community and outside, which is why trade is mainly connected with imports and exports. In fact it is best interpreted as an export of services, selling produce such as cattle outside and bringing in products from the cities or from nearby communities. This last is carried out mainly by people attending the weekly markets in a community; these include both traders who take community production to the cities and peasants from neighbouring communities. Of the eight communities studied, only Sihuina, Huando and Acobamba have weekly markets of their own.

The external sector: monetary exchange

The analysis of monetary imports and exports can draw on data for all eight communities, since data on this subject were collected in the communities excluded from table 5.9. Table 5.11 shows the structure of exports, with trade presented separately from Z-goods, so that exports of goods are distinguished from exports of services, and with income from temporary migrations added, as export of labour.

(a) Exports

The first point to emerge from the table is the diversified character of the communities' exports: in no community does one item account for more than 63% of total export income, and in four of them one item accounts for 50% or more: cattle in Culta (63%), agricultural products in Ninamarca (61%), trade in Acobamba (59%) and temporary migration in Ancobamba (48%). Of export income, 80% is accounted for by two items in three of the

144

Table 5.11. *Structure of monetary exports (percentages).*

Community	Agriculture	Livestock	Z-goods	Trade	Labour	Total
Jacantaya	14.3	16.1	27.1	8.5	34.0	100.0
Culta	1.1	62.5	4.3	8.4	23.7	100.0
Ninamarca	60.9	30.1	2.1	6.1	0.8	100.0
Ancobamba	2.0	38.3	1.6	10.4	47.7	100.0
Ttiomayo	33.0	27.4	0.4	0	39.2	100.0
Sihuina	11.4	27.7	21.0	32.3	7.6	100.0
Huando	21.6	15.5	19.5	33.7	9.7	100.0
Acobamba	17.0	10.0	0.1	58.6	14.3	100.0
Sample total	13.5	29.2	37.4		19.9	100.0
Southern sierra	14.5	25.2	41.1		19.2	100.0

communities, by three items in four of them, and by four items in one of them. Given that each item itself constitutes a range of products, the diversified character of their exports becomes clear.

Exports vary widely both within and between communities. If one looks at those sources which account for 33% or more of each community's exports, one finds that agriculture is important in Ninamarca and Ttiomayo, livestock in Culta and Ancobamba, and temporary migration in Jacantaya, Ancobamba and Ttiomayo. Only Z-goods do not reach this proportion in any community, although they account for 27% in Jacantaya, 21% in Sihuina and 20% in Huando.

The specific features of exports vary from community to community. Jacantaya exports almost all the goods and services which arise in the study. In agriculture, due to a favourable micro-climate, it exports mostly green vegetables which are sold at market in a nearby town (Huancane) and are also exchanged directly with neighbouring puna communities. Income from animal exports consists mainly of cattle. Z-goods exported are mostly fish (mainly the *hispi*) from Lake Titicaca sold in Huancane. Trading income is also derived from dealing in green vegetables.

In Culta, where agriculture is mostly for self-consumption, the main exports are animals, above all cattle. Apart from raising their own, many families buy cattle for fattening and sell them after a few months, financing this activity with their own funds and with loans, which usually amount to about 20 000 soles, from the Banco Agrario. The most common pattern is for people to buy bulls in September and October and to sell them in April or May. In this way they take advantage of the time when pasture is most abundant and also use the bulls for ploughing, since at the same time the land is being prepared for sowing. The bank loans are for a year, and this activity brings a substantial profit. Trading income in this community also derived from cattle, and the income from fattening was divided equally between trade (Z_2) and income from animals (P_4).

Ninamarca exports a range of products: potatoes, barley for consumption, barley for beer and oats. Sales of barley to the beer factory in Cuzco, or to intermediaries who then sell to the factory, are slightly more important than other exported products. Animal sales include sheep as well as cattle. Ancobamba exports cattle above all. The community possesses quite a lot of pasture land and cattle are their main animal product, reared for export. In Ttiomayo, maize accounts for almost three-quarters of agricultural exports, while pigs and cattle account for most animal exports.

Sihuina, in contrast, exports the entire range of its agricultural products, while cattle predominate among its animal exports. It also exports Z-goods in the form of food, principally bread sold at its weekly market. The community earns income from trade by taking valley products – maize, wheat and coca – to the puna where they are exchanged for sheep's meat and wool, which in their turn are sold in community markets both in Sihuina and elsewhere.

Huando also exports all its agricultural products in equal proportions, as well as both cattle and sheep. Its mills and trucks provide Z-exports and cater to the surrounding area and, to a lesser extent, to Huando itself. Trading income is derived from the community's own weekly market.

Finally, in Acobamba, 80% of agricultural exports consist of beans, and cattle and sheep are also sold. The community is located at the end of a road and is therefore a commercial centre, and its market is a source of trading income for the members of the community.

This list illustrates the diversity of export products both within and between communities. The one exception to this variation is cattle, which clearly constitutes a cash product reared specifically for export in all the communities. Even so, the relative importance of cattle rearing also varies, thus further underlining the differences between the communities.

(b) Imports

In contrast, the structure of imports does not exhibit much variation as between communities. Table 5.12 shows that food and drink account for between 37% and 49% of imports. Expenditure of coca, alcohol and cigarettes, which is included under food, is associated with productive activity, since such commodities are used as wage payments in kind, and these are generally considered to be the community's most important expenditures. Table 5.12 shows that these products account for between 3% and 17% of total imports.

A long way behind food and drink, the next most important imports are clothes and footwear, varying between 11% and 29% of the total. Consumer items as a whole account for between 82% and 92% of total imports. Modern

Table 5.12. *Structure of monetary imports (per cent)*

Items	Jac	Cul	Nin	Communities Anc	Tti	Sih	Hua	Aco	Total sample	Southern sierra
Food (coca, alcoholic drinks, cigarettes)	41.9	38.1	42.3	36.9	40.0	45.8	46.1	49.0	43.6	44.8
	(2.9)	(4.3)	(14.5)	(11.6)	(17.1)	(13.1)	(2.7)	(10.2)		
Fuel	3.9	1.9	1.9	2.8	3.2	3.7	4.6	2.4		
Durable goods	0.5	1.1	1.2	0.8	1.5	2.2	0.7	0.7		
Non-durable goods	5.8	4.3	11.2	4.1	9.6	11.0	5.8	7.6		
Clothes	13.9	16.9	14.1	28.7	24.7	15.4	14.2	11.0	15.6	15.1
Education	6.7	5.7	0.5	3.4	1.6	3.7	3.8	2.7		
Fares	7.9	8.1	5.4	3.7	4.1	4.1	3.0	2.7		
Fiestas	0.7	3.0	7.6	8.4	2.2	4.6	0.5	8.9		
Medicines	2.5	2.5	0.3	1.2	2.4	1.5	6.6	0.7		
Others	1.1	0.1	0.1	0.1	0.1	0.1	2.3	5.3		
Sub-total	84.8	81.7	84.5	90.0	89.3	92.0	87.7	91.0	86.8	87.7
Inputs	9.2	6.5	8.4	5.3	4.8	3.5	7.6	4.1		
Investment	6.0	11.8	7.0	4.7	5.9	4.5	4.7	4.9		
Total	100.0	100.0	100.0	100.0	100.0	100.0	100.0	100.0	100.0	100.0

inputs to production are of little significance, varying between 4% and 9% of imports. Capital goods are somewhat more important, varying between 5% and 12%, but remain a small item.

This homogeneity of imports compared to the heterogeneity of exports in the communities is explained by the greater homogeneity of their needs, which are restricted to certain types of food, fuel and clothes, and also by their low and fairly uniform levels of income, to which we turn in section 4 below.

Exchange with other communities

Although there is some monetary exchange between communities, it is mostly carried out in kind, likewise most exchange in kind is accounted for by exchanges with other communities. The estimates of non-monetary exchange can therefore be seen as a measure, albeit an approximate one, of exchange between communities. According to table 5.9, these exchanges in kind account for a very small proportion of both total production (5% at most, as in the case of Jacantaya) and total exports (7% at most, again in Jacantaya). However, the two communities which are not represented in that table show higher proportions: in Sihuina 11% of external exchange is accounted for

Table 5.13. *Ratio of non-monetary exchange in peasant communities (soles per year per family and percentages)*

	Value of exports			In kind share (%)
	Monetary	In kind	Total	
Jacantaya	37 584	2 861	40 445	7.1
Culta	39 771	312	40 083	0.8
Ninamarca	20 813	1 785	22 598	7.9
Ancobamba	17 745	464	18 209	2.5
Ttiomayo	12 530	3 762	16 292	23.1
Sihuina	19 023	2 593	22 616	11.5
Huando	46 484	228	46 712	0.5
Acobamba	26 773	523	27 296	1.9
Sample total				5.6
Southern sierra				5.7

by transactions with other communities, and in Ttiomayo 23%, as shown in table 5.13. Thus one might conclude that exchange with other communities varies substantially, having an average value of 6% of total external exchange.

Our method of accounting for trading activities may have led, however, to an underestimate of this figure. In communities such as Sihuina, Huando and Acobamba, which have their own weekly markets, much of the trading income which has been classified as 'exports of services' in fact derives from exchange with people from other communities; if one were to include such exchanges, the proportion of production exchanged with other communities would rise, but not significantly. Moreover, this modification would apply only to communities which have their own markets.

4. Level and structure of peasant income

This section presents estimates of the level of *total peasant income*, that is monetary and non-monetary income of peasant families. These estimates will enable us to evaluate the degree of poverty in these families. In addition, the composition of that income will also be presented, which will show the sources of income of the peasant economy in its present historical form in Peru.

Levels of total peasant incomes

One method of calculating incomes would be to sum the value, at market prices, of all goods consumed and invested. We have seen that net production (that is, production minus the part set aside as intermediate goods and as replacement of stocks for the next cycle) is divided between self-consumption and exchange. Income, therefore, could be defined as the sum of all consumption plus investment, minus the net balance in external exchange. However, since the value of imports has by definition been equated with the value of exports plus transfers, one might wish to choose a second method, which would calculate income by summing the value of self-consumption, the value of exports of A, P, and Z-goods and the value of income earned from temporary migration. From this one would then have to deduct the value of imported intermediate goods (column 1, lines 13 (N) and 14 (M) in table 5.9) used in the production of $A + P + Z$.

A third method of calculating income is through an estimation of value added. The estimates of total production of $A + P + Z$ and of inputs (domestically produced and imported) enable us to do this, since value added is equal to the difference between these two magnitudes. Furthermore, the interviews provide a direct estimate of income from wages and rents, so that income from self-employment was estimated as the difference between these and total value added. To the income thus obtained by $A + P + Z$ production – the value added – we must add income from temporary migrations (column 5, line 17 (Wages–M)) and thus reach the *total peasant income*. This result equals those calculated as final demand, and the three results are presented in tables 5.14–16.

This method omits one item: self-consumption of services, such as the preparation of food, the provision of fuel, and building repairs. It includes all income from production and temporary migration, the allocation of resources for production, and income-earning services, whether that income be in money or in kind.

The levels of peasant income obtained vary between 47 000 and 82 100 soles per annum per family. On a per capita basis this would yield an income of 12 000–20 000 soles. In dollar terms, at the then prevailing rate of exchange of about 200 soles per US dollar, this would be equivalent to an annual household income of 250–400 dollars, and a per capita income of 60–90 dollars. It should also be compared with the then prevailing minimum wage in Lima, which stood at about 100 000 soles a year, while the average wage in industry was about 500 000 soles a year, and professional people were earning at least a million soles.

The structure of incomes of peasant communities

(a) Self-consumption and exchange

Table 5.14 shows that on average self-consumption accounts for nearly 50% of total income; this proportion varies between 45% and 70% in the six communities. This result shows the very high degree of integration between the peasant economy and the national economy, and leaves no reason for describing the former as a 'self-sufficient economy', or the latter

Table 5.14. *Structure of income of peasant communities: self-consumption and exchange (soles per annum per family; percentages in parentheses)*

Community	Total income	Self-consumption	Exchange A, P, Z	Temporary migration	Imported inputs
Jacantaya	62 441	27 831 (44.6)	27 674 (55.4)	12 772	− 5 836
Culta	68 507	31 175 (45.5)	30 680 (55.5)	9 403	− 2 751
Ninamarca	47,302	26 584 (56.2)	22 456 (43.8)	142	− 1 880
Ancobamba	57 494	40 511 (70.5)	9 751 (29.5)	8 458	− 1 226
Huando	81 518	38 920 (47.7)	42 192 (52.3)	4 520	− 4 114
Acobamba	60 003	34 245 (57.1)	23 455 (42.9)	3 841	− 1 538
Sample total	67 700	34 406 (50.8)	33 294 (49.2)		
Southern sierra	69 071	36 597 (53.0)	32 474 (47.0)		

as a 'dual economy'. To pursue further our analogy between the economy of the community and that of the nation as a whole, we may compare these results with the use of the term 'open economy', which is generally applied to economies in which exports consist of at most 20–25% of the GNP. How, then, can one describe the peasant economy as 'closed' or as a 'self-sufficient economy' when it exports about half its net product?

The main explanation of this openness is the development of highways. The extreme case, with the lowest degree of market integration, is Ancobamba, where exports account for only 30% of net income; but Ancobamba is situated some five or six hours' walk from the nearest road, so the remarkable fact is, that, despite its distance from the highway, the community still exchanges such a high proportion of its net income.

Ancobamba apart, in the remaining five communities we observe an inverse relationship between level of income and the proportion of self-consumption within it: Jacantaya, Culta and Huando, where self-consumption is between 45% and 48% of income, have higher incomes than the others, where self-consumption is between 57% and 58%. However, these are not very strong relationships due to other factors which also influence the degree of self-consumption, such as the diversity of their resources and seasonal variations in the agricultural cycle.

Production and market exchange

Table 5.15. *Productive structure of the communities (percentages)*

Community	A	P	Z	Temporary migration	Total
Jacantaya	38.6	14.3	36.6	20.5	100.0
Culta	26.5	47.1	13.7	13.7	100.0
Ninanarca	44.9	44.6	10.2	0.3	100.0
Ancobamba	59.0	21.0	5.3	14.7	100.0
Huando	46.3	17.1	31.1	5.5	100.0
Acobamba	46.7	20.0	26.9	6.4	100.0
Sample total	43.5	24.5	20.8	11.2	100.0
Southern sierra	46.3	21.9	22.3	9.5	100.0

(b) Productive structure

A different estimate of peasant incomes on the basis of the information contained in table 5.9 derives income from each one of the A, P, and Z sectors plus temporary migration. This is shown in table 5.15, which also constitutes an approximation to the productive structure of the communities.

Agricultural and animal production represent the most important sources of income, but this importance varies between 43% and 90% of the total. (Since imported inputs are used above all for agricultural activities, the value of all imported inputs was subtracted only from agricultural income.) One extreme case is Jacantaya, where Z-goods account for a high proportion of incomes, together with temporary migration. The other extreme is Ninamarca, a community which devotes its resources almost exclusively to agriculture, and where Z-goods account for only 10% of production and migration has scarcely any importance.

The structure of incomes of peasant communities: by wages, rents and self-employment

We now come to consider the social organization of production within the communities, whereas hitherto we have concentrated on their external relations. The unit of control and allocation of resources within the community is the family: it uses the resources available to it, and allocates the labour force to A, P, and Z activities, and to seasonal migration. However, it does not function in isolation; its relations with other families are an essential feature of the productive process. When, as frequently occurs, a family has a surplus or a deficit of a particular good, or of labour, three possible mechanisms of exchange are available to it within the community: reciprocity, barter, and monetary exchange.

151

Reciprocity can be conceived as a special case of interest-free lending: if one receives three man–days in labour one must return three man–days; if one borrows a pair of oxen for two days, one must subsequently repay that person by making a pair of oxen available to him for two days. This form of exchange is clearly a means of achieving the most efficient combination of factors. The most common form of reciprocity is the exchange of labour, known as *ayni* or *minka*: minka occasionally involves social activities as well, in which case the pursuit of economic efficiency is combined with, or even overtaken by, consumption objectives. In this case the criterion of efficiency only fixes the lower limit of factor proportions, consumption being inseparable from the productive process. For these reasons one cannot count reciprocity as a source of income for the households involved.

Barter of goods or services arises when families dispose of different goods or services in excess demand or supply at the same time, unlike reciprocity where the goods or services in surplus or deficit must be exactly the same, though at different times. It follows that where there are no, or few, differences in ownership of resources reciprocity will predominate, rather than barter. Many families obtain an income from the exchange of draught animals, tools and labour, and also from credit. These productive services are paid in a variety of ways, occasionally in produce, occasionally with other types of productive service; but clearly an income is only generated if the exchange yields the return of a product which can be directly consumed or invested, that is, a component of final demand.

Finally, productive services can be exchanged (sold) for money. This mechanism is obviously necessary given the restrictive conditions enabling barter to take place, mentioned above; that is, the requirement that the parties must have different but complementary surpluses and deficits of products and services. In all the communities studied we found a market for productive services, with transparent monetary prices and also with defined terms of trade between goods and services, even though these latter were defined with somewhat less transparency.

From all this we can conclude that there are three types of income in the communities, represented in lines 16–20 of column 1, table 5.9: rental income (from the hiring out of productive services), wage income and income from self-employment. Of these the most important is the last, as is shown in table 5.16, which is directly derived from table 5.9. The proportion of income generated by self-employment varies between 72% and 98%, which shows that, despite its openness to the market, the peasant household still depends predominantly on its own resources in land, animals and labour for its income. For the rest, rents (rental of land, hiring out of animals and tools) are of hardly any significance at all, while wages account for between 4% and 28% of income. If we discount Ninamarca, where almost all income

Table 5.16. *Structure of income of peasant communities: wages, rents and self-employment (soles per annum per family; percentages in parentheses)*

Community	Total income	Local wage employment	Rents	Self-employment	Temporary migrations
Jacantaya	62 441	4 685	72	44 912	12 772
	(100.0)	(7.5)	(0.1)	(71.9)	(20.5)
Culta	68 507	3 052	317	55 735	9 403
	(100.0)	(4.5)	(0.5)	(81.3)	(13.7)
Ninamarca	47 302	1 045	0	46 115	142
	(100.0)	(2.2)	(0.0)	(97.5)	(0.3)
Ancobamba	57 494	1 222	77	47 737	8 458
	(100.0)	(2.1)	(0.1)	(83.0)	(14.7)
Huando	81 518	8 683	1 493	66 822	4 520
	(100.0)	(10.7)	(1.8)	(82.0)	(5.5)
Acobamba	60 003	11 050	425	44 687	3 841
	(100.0)	(18.4)	(0.7)	(74.5)	(6.4)
Total sample	100.0	7.8	0.8	80.2	11.2
Southern sierra	100.0	8.8	1.0	80.7	9.5

derives from self-employment, the proportion is seen to vary between 17% and 28%. In three of the five communities wage income is derived principally from external markets, that is, temporary migration, whereas in two of them the local market is the more important source. Employers in the local labour market include mainly medium-size farmers who coexist with peasant families in the communities. Some peasant families, the relatively rich, also hire labour for wages. This expenditure will appear on the expenditure side of the family budget, which is not shown here.

Structure of monetary income of the peasant family

The structure of total income presented in the foregoing refers to the *peasant community*. Having shown that half of total income in the communities is monetary income, we now turn to the structure of monetary income of the typical *peasant family*. Table 5.17 shows the sources of monetary income of peasant families by communities.

The first conclusion is that monetary income is acquired from a variety of sources. The peasant family deals with several markets at the same time in order to get monetary income. Secondly, the income structure varies significantly between communities. These two conclusions lead to a third one: all sources of monetary income are important for the peasant family. This can be seen in the last column of table 5.17, which is an expansion of the sample to represent the typical family of the southern sierra.

Table 5.17. *Structure of monetary income of peasant families (percentages)*

	Communities								Sample total	Southern sierra
	Jac	Cul	Nin	Anc	Tti	Sih	Hua	Aco		
A	11.8	0.6	58.8	1.5	21.2	13.9	12.8	10.9	10.9	11.1
P	11.7	36.7	23.7	29.2	15.1	21.9	10.7	5.5	20.7	18.7
Z	17.8	15.2	2.7	7.2	0.1	34.2	21.0	15.9	18.5	18.9
W_1	9.0	6.0	5.4	10.3	40.1	10.6	19.3	44.3	15.2	18.3
W_2	21.5	19.7	0.3	22.8	15.1	8.6	9.3	11.6	14.5	13.7
R	0.1	0.3	0.0	0.3	5.0	0.1	0.6	0.0	0.6	0.6
T	17.7	10.0	1.5	16.8	0.7	5.3	10.9	3.4	9.6	8.9
O	10.4	11.5	7.6	11.9	2.7	5.4	15.4	8.4	10.0	9.8
Total	100.0	100.0	100.0	100.0	100.0	100.0	100.0	100.0	100.0	100.0

Symbols: R = rents; T = transfers; O = 'others' (loans, dis-savings)

If income from economic activity alone is considered, that is if transfers and other financial income (loans, dis-accumulation) are eliminated, the structure for the typical family of the southern sierra of Peru is the following: 14% comes from sales of agricultural products, 23% from livestock, 23% from Z activities (which includes trading), 23% from wages in local labour markets and 17% from wages in external labour markets. Thus 40% comes from selling labour power. To this extent a peasant family is also a proletarian family.

5. Money transfers

The last item in table 5.9 consists of transfers. Transfers can be classified in two ways: internal versus external transfers and transfers in kind versus transfers in money. Transfers between households can therefore take any one of four forms. Direct transfers from the state or from other organizations such as the church have not been taken into account, nor are they of any importance at community level.

Transfers in kind take place between families within the community, and include A, P, and Z-goods as well as productive services, especially labour. Monetary transfers take place on special occasions such as fiestas and weddings. These transfers are not represented in table 5.9, but external monetary transfers are included; external non-monetary transfers were not estimated because of the vagueness of the quantities and quality involved, but it was clear that these movements in kind are very frequent both to and from the

Table 5.18. *Money transfers (soles per annum per family)*

	Received	Sent out	Net	Percentage of total income	Percentage of export income
Jacantaya	7 345	871	6 474	10.4	17.2
Culta	3 715	2 100	1 615	2.4	4.1
Ninamarca	0	0	0	0	0
Ancobamba	2 239	417	1 822	3.2	10.3
Ttiomayo	267	0	267	n.d.	2.1
Sihuina	755	0	755	n.d.	4.0
Huando	7 037	450	6 587	8.1	14.2
Acobamba	564	0	564	1.0	2.1
Sample total					8.0
Southern sierra					7.6

community. In communities situated close to a road, parcels are constantly being sent in and out on buses and lorries.

The estimates of transfers show the communities to be net receivers, although, as shown in table 5.18, the magnitudes involved vary substantially. Transfers to the communities come mostly from sons and daughters living in the city, but we also found cases in which the male head of the household was working away and was sending transfers to his family. Transfers out were mainly being sent to children studying in the city.

Table 5.18 also shows the share of transfers in total income and in export income. As a proportion of total income, it is highest in Jacantaya and Huando, and very low in the other communities. Compared to export income, these transfers represent an addition of 17% to purchasing power in Jacantaya, 14% in Huando and 10% in Ancobamba, but an almost insignificant addition in the others. If we expand these results to the southern sierra as a whole, they would yield 8% of total export income.

6. Some conclusions

This study is based on data collected on production and exchange from a sample of peasant families in the southern highlands (sierra) of Peru. The results shown here indicate that the peasant family, the basic unit of production and consumption, allocates its labour force to self-employment to produce three types of goods: agriculture, livestock and Z-goods (non-agricultural activities which include trading), and to wage earnings. Since part of the goods produced are exchanged in the market-place, the peasant family is integrated to the market economy through markets of goods and services and through labour markets. Peasant families exchange direct labour as well as indirect labour, incorporated in commodities.

The quantitative results indicate that for the typical family half of total income is monetary income and the other half is self-consumption. Barter exchange has small significance. This result certainly challenges the usual view that the peasant economy is outside the market system, as a self-sufficient economy. Forty per cent of monetary income for the typical family comes from labour markets and the rest from exchanging agricultural, livestock, and Z-goods in the market. The peasant family is then partially a proletarian family. These are the characteristics of the present historical form of the peasant economy in Peru.

One clear implication of these empirical results is that the poverty of the peasant families cannot be understood in isolation from the rest of the economy. The peasantry is well integrated to the market economy and therefore there exists the logical possibility that its poverty is connected to the development in the rest of the economic system. Moreover, since market prices and wages change as a consequence, among other things, of changes in economic policies and international prices, it is clear that the peasant economy is also connected to the international economy.

Finally, what are the dynamics of the peasant economy? As capitalism expands in the national economy the structure of the peasant economy certainly changes. Rural industry (Z-goods) is being destroyed by modern industrial expansion; agriculture and livestock production are also challenged by technological progress in larger farms within the country and abroad. As a consequence, labour markets become over time the most significant mechanism of integration of the peasant economy to the market system.

Note

I wish to thank the ECIEL Program for the financial and intellectual support given to this research. The study could never have been done without the help and understanding of the peasant families in the communities studied. Many people helped me in this project, too many to mention, but the people more closely related to the material presented here include Daniel Cotlear, Augusto Cáceres, Gabriela Vega and Edgar Norton. I also thank David Lehmann for his help in preparing this version, not only with the English translation but also with valuable comments and suggestions.

6

The Andean economic system and capitalism

RODRIGO SÁNCHEZ

1. Introduction

The central assertion in this chapter is that peasant economic relationships in some areas of the Peruvian Andes, at least at present, cannot be considered as a specific economic system, distinct from the capitalist mode of production. The assumption upon which this argument rests is that the so-called Andean peasant economy lacks the means of its own reproduction and, instead, peasant activities obey more the laws and logic of the wider capitalist system with which they are integrated.

Anthropological studies have argued that the notions and practices of *reciprocity*, among others, constitute the regulating mechanism of Andean economic relationships. This belief has led specialists to suggest the persistence of a qualitatively distinct system which interacts with an alien and dominant system, that is, capitalism. In attempting a critical examination of this approach we will discuss the regulative role of this principle. It will be argued that the persistence of some practices which accord with such a principle is not associated with the existence of a specific economy; rather, it is the product of the determining effects of economic and political forces pertaining to the rules and development of the capitalist system. The principles of Andean culture, as subordinated ideological concepts, merely fulfil the role of legitimizing such relationships.

Specifically, the central mechanisms governing the peasant economy are those concerned with (a) monopolization of land ownership; (b) the maintenance of reserves of cheap and temporary labour; (c) the encouragement of commodity production; and, as a result (d) the differentiation of peasants. All of these are necessary conditions for capitalist accumulation through the appropriation of peasants' surplus product.

These governing mechanisms make the persistence of traditional cultural elements possible by creating economic scarcity among peasants. Thus, shortage and deprivation constrain them not only to develop mutual help co-operative activities, but mainly to accept paternalistic or patron–client ties with those in power. The notion of reciprocity in these relationships, therefore, plays a legitimizing role. However, it is neither the only nor the most important form of legitimization and perpetuation. Frequently linked to it and fulfilling an even more effective function are the political and legal normative systems of the wider society.

In order to develop this argument, then, I will examine the model of reciprocity developed by anthropologists, especially by those working in the Andean area.

2. The conceptual principles of reciprocity

The concept of reciprocity has been regarded as the basic normative framework in the economic behaviour of 'primitive' and peasant societies. The theoretical development of this concept started with Mauss (1951) and Polanyi (1957) who were followed by Dalton (1961) and Sahlins (1972). These authors influenced the approach of a number of anthropologists focusing on the Andean region.

As understood in the literature produced by this school, known as the 'substantivists' (Leclair and Schneider 1968), *reciprocity* is a social relationship which links a person with others, as individuals or groups, as well as linking groups and communities with each other. This social relationship contains a complex set of exchanges which includes not only goods and services, but also forms of behaviour according to shared institutional and ideological frameworks, termed 'institutional processes' by Polanyi (1957). According to this view, economic activities cannot be understood independently of the social structure in which they are embedded. Starting from this theoretical assumption, and referring to the exchange of labour between Andean peasants, Mayer says:

comuneros (members of peasant communities) must take care to maintain close social relationships with their workers. The use of reciprocity implies cultivating the kinship network, providing assistance and hospitality, feasts, and generous contribution to the necessities of kin in order to preserve good relationships with them throughout the agricultural cycle (1974b: 84).

The emphasis on social relationships in this type of exchange, however, does not exclude the existence of economic interest among the parties. There is always the element of economic maximization which makes it almost impossible to identify a purely equal exchange. Thus, reciprocity contains an intrinsic element of competition similar to that which exists in monetary market exchange, although this is not to say that the two cannot be distinguished from each other. Transactions are related to competition for social prestige and social acceptance, while those of the market type are more related to competition for material profit. It is for this reason that, in the latter, the exchange takes place in an atmosphere of haggling between the parties, whereas reciprocity prohibits open display of haggling because it takes place between pre-established social groups within such frameworks as kinship, friendship and neighbourhood.

Some of the main expressions of these principles in the Andean area have been analysed by anthropologists. They identify two levels of exchange for contemporary peasant communities: the first being between individuals and households taking the forms of *ayni, minka* and *trueque*; and the second between households and the central local authority representing the *comunidad*, taking the form of *faena* or *servicios comunales*. We will look here only at the first two forms: ayni and minka.

The institution of ayni consists of an exchange in which a granted service is returned at some future opportunity. It can have as the objects of the exchange a range of items such as labour, ceremonial services and also matters of everyday life such as money loans, animals and so on. For each ayni exchange to take place it has to be requested by one of the parties who is in need of the good or service. This action sometimes takes on a ceremonial connotation. The person to whom the request is made usually defines the conditions of the exchange although he would find it difficult to refuse. Once the required object has been granted or completed, the beneficiary bears the obligation to return it when the requirement or opportunity arises.

A similar type of exchange happens under the form of minka. Its specific differences from ayni are that it usually takes place in the form of exchange of labour for goods. The labour offered by one party is not returned in labour but with payment in goods or other specific services such as portions of crops, animal draught power, fertilizers, etc. Minka is usually practised between one person and several others. The one receives labour from the others and for this he is obliged to provide food and drink during the time of work apart from the payment he gives in return. Usually the event of minka is followed by a social occasion when a great deal of food, drink and coca is consumed. The exchange ends when every one of the labourers has been rewarded; normally no further obligation is expected from either of the parties.

It is generally understood, although not explicitly, that reciprocal exchanges are conceived as fundamentally normative statements and are expressions of an ideal type of social structure, which cannot be identified in pure and objective terms in fact. Reciprocity in strict terms is not more than a set of 'rules of the game' (*ibid.*: 37); the existence of these rules does not imply an exact correspondence to the game itself, nor does it exclude the presence and use of other sets of rules. Furthermore, the rules and the content of reciprocity are not the same through space and time; rather they vary according to specific local and historical conditions.

However, a great deal of the literature postulates an objective correspondence between the norm and practice. For example, Mayer notes:

> reciprocity as a *concept* and *praxis*, represents a fundamental element of a communitarian mode of production which originated in pre-Inca times, and, although it has lost purity and undergone alterations as it has entered into contact with other modes of production, still persists at present (*ibid.*: 14).

The correspondence between *concept* and *praxis* would imply the existence of egalitarian or even communitarian economic relationships. This is unlikely to be true. Contrary to this, what Mayer seems to suggest is that the norm of reciprocity can be found as concept and practice, although the actual relationships are unequal. Elsewhere in the same volume Mayer argues that reciprocity takes place in two ways: symmetrically and asymmetrically. The first, it is said, contains equal benefits for the two parties involved, and the second does not do so. According to this, the ayni system is identified with the first type and the minka system with the second.

The literature contains a large amount of description on the workings of these systems in rural communities, in the past and during the contemporary period. The data derive from intensive field work and the reports seem to give a large number of cases supporting the idea of the existence of a coherent economic system based on the principles of reciprocity. An example is the following statement:

> access to land, to the additional labour force and the resources of other households, are part of a complicated system of reciprocal relationships between families and the community; these relationships take place to such an extent that it is possible to speak of a system of agricultural production in the community of Tangor, which is not precisely incorporated into the monetary market but is predominantly based on reciprocal exchange. In this system, factors such as ecology, demography, technology, politics and religion play an important role, but reciprocal relationships constitute the nexus which articulates all these factors to make up a coherent and ordered system (*ibid.*: 65).

It is quite clear that the economic system to which the author is referring implies three basic elements: it is a non-monetary system where the productive and distributive processes rest basically on the subsistence needs of individuals and are regulated by the ideological principle of reciprocity. In this way it can be contrasted with the Western capitalist economy which is based on monetary exchange, marketing purposes and a rationality oriented to profit accumulation.

Here it is important to emphasize that such a definition of what is understood by an economic system takes as its starting point three interrelated aspects: the *means of exchange* (monetary or non-monetary), the *individual purposes* (subsistence or marketing) and the *ideological system* (reciprocity or wealth accumulation).

It can also be noticed that a system like this could function only under close and isolated conditions. However, the same author argues that such an economy has to be seen in relation to the national society, and that peasants are involved in both the non-monetary and market economies:

Half of the community's population live outside the village, mainly in Lima, earning their living within economic systems in which reciprocity does not exist, at least at the level of production. However, even in such conditions, the social links based on reciprocity are still important for migrants from Tangor to find markets, jobs, accommodation and other kinds of support within an urban context which is alien to them (*ibid.*).

Thus the two economic systems are found not only in rural areas, but also in the urban industrial sector. In this argument what the author seems to suggest is a form of dualism. While the industrial market economy tries to integrate the subsistence sector and destroy it for the sake of monetary expansion, the native Andean economy defends, or modifies, itself, and also tries to incorporate market elements into its own normative system. The history of Andean society, then, can be understood in terms of the contradiction and the 'battle' between these two opposed economies.

The current approach to the Andean economy, although it focuses on the peasant sector in close relationships with the wider society, presents a number of crucial limitations. For example, it contains a methodological bias insofar as it defines the economic system by superficial indicators such as non-monetary exchange and individual needs. Secondly, it seems to fall into a new dualistic view which would appear to derive the socio-economic process from the interaction of two structural entities, rather than from the class struggle. Both of these implications rest on the assumption that the central element around which the Andean economy functions is the principle of reciprocity. In order to overcome these limitations it is of primary importance to analyse this last assumption and to attempt an alternative approach. With this purpose we will look next at the material from the district of Andarapa in the province of Andahuaylas, southern highlands of Peru.

3. The contemporary economic process in Andarapa

Three principal processes have been taking place in the area during the past two decades; firstly, there has been a proletarianization of a large sector of peasants whereby they have been incorporated into the capitalist system as wage labourers. Secondly, and in contrast to the former, there has been a reinforcement and intensification of production based on the nuclear family. This process consists of the increase in the amount of privately (as opposed to communally) controlled land and in the control of labour by the household unit. The third process is the differentiation among peasants which involves the widening of the gaps between rich and poor sectors.

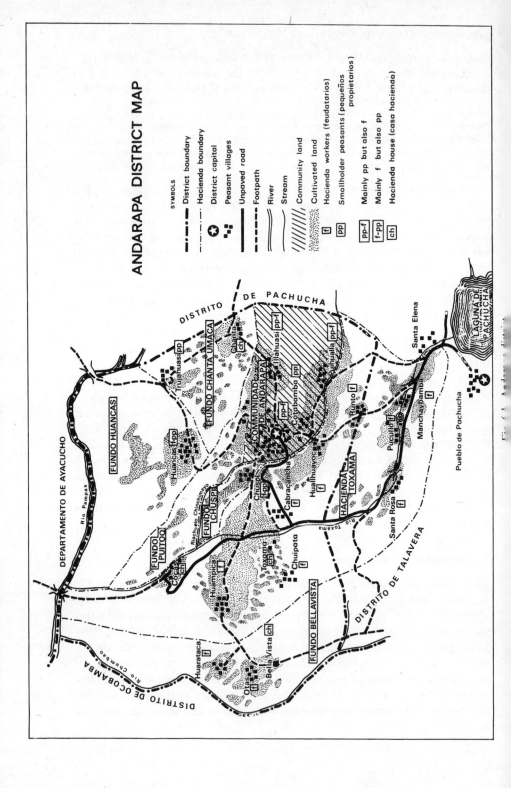

Fig. 6.1 Andarapa district.

Table 6.1. *Distribution of households according to their access to arable land in Andarapa*

10 or more hectares		4 to 9.9 hectares		1 to 3.9 hectares		Less than 1 heactare		Total no. of households	
No.	%	No.	%	No.	%	No.	%	No.	%
50	3.2	87	5.5	589	37.4	847	53.8	1573	99.9

Source: Censo Nacional Agropecuario 1972 and additional municipal and communal records.

These processes were the result of a crisis in the hacienda system, which could not maintain its control of the land and maintain peasants as rent-paying producers. The Land Reform legislation of 1969 was intended to solve this crisis by changes in land-holding systems, creating co-operatives in the place of the old haciendas and *fundos*. However, these co-operatives could be organized only by investing foreign capital and recruiting peasant labour on wage contracts. In this way, despite government rhetoric about the 'transfer of land and power to the hands of peasants', the bulk of the peasantry were to be converted into proletarians. However, the co-operative organization and peasant proletarianization met a number of difficulties after the passing of the law. As the Land Reform project was delayed in the area and the control of the large properties become loose and inconsistent, peasants took advantage of this situation and expanded their household plots by illegally taking over the demesne area of the haciendas. The collapse of the hacienda system had freed them from labour–rent obligations, and the ineffectiveness of President Velasco's Reform made it possible for them to increase their control of land and develop their own domestic economy. However, the distribution and control of land was unequal as some peasants took more than others. Those peasants who in the past enjoyed greater favour with the *hacendado* were in a position of prestige and power, and consequently found it easier to accumulate land. Although the majority of the remaining peasants received additional plots, the proportion of poor households in terms of access to land remained the same. In 1972, poor households, possessing less than four hectares each, still constituted 91% of the total population. Moreover 53.8% of the families still possessed less than one hectare per household, as we can see in Table 6.1.

Of the three processes mentioned, economic differentiation and the development of domestic household production are definitely the most important, at least during the period 1969–74. During this period the application of the Land Reform project largely failed in the area and peasants

Table 6.2. *Distribution of 32 households among socio-economic groups in Andarapa*

Categories according to local affiliation	Socio-economic level*			
	Rich	Middle	Poor	Total
Independent peasants (*comuneros*)	—	4	7	11
Hacienda workers (*colonos*)	1	2	9	12
Comuneros and colonos combined	2	3	4	9
Total	3	9	20	32

*The categories rich, middle and poor correspond to levels of wealth calculated and shown in table 6.4.

were left relatively free from outside control. This fact raises the question as to how far in a situation where the hacienda system is in collapse and state control is weak, peasants were able successfully to organize their household and village economy? What characteristics were shown by that economy and how far can one say that the process corresponded to the model of peasant economy as described by anthropologists? More precisely, did the principles of the Andean economic system constitute the central reproductive element of the process?

In order to answer these questions we will analyse next the productive and exchange processes among certain sectors of the peasantry in Andarapa. We will examine particularly the precise role played by some practices based on the principle of reciprocity. We will later compare those practices to the alternative forces influencing the peasant economy. The analysis will be concerned mainly with a sample of 32 households whose economic activities and relationships have been recorded in detail during one agricultural cycle. The data refer to land acquisition, comparative levels of wealth, organization of labour and levels of investment. The 32 families, although they cannot be statistically representative of the total population due to their small number, do constitute some examples of the different sectors into which the *andarapinos* have been divided (see table 6.2). They have been selected at random taking into special account the variety of situations and processes in which peasants are involved. The data come from repeated and intensive interviews, both formal and informal, with the household members.

The basic characteristics of each household and their respective household heads are shown in table 6.3. In order to give a closer picture of their access to resources and income, however, we compare their land ownership

Table 6.3. *Basic characteristics of the 32 sample households in Andarapa district*

Household no.	Name of household head	Status*		Linked to hacienda (h) village (v)		Village of residence[†]	No. of years the household has been established
1	Roberto	CF	rich	Chanta	(h)	Illahuasi	22
2	Rosalio	F	rich	Huancas	(h)	Huancas	13
3	Mariano	CF	rich	Chuspi	(h)	Chuspi	25
4	Isaac	CF	middle	Chuspi	(h)	Chuspi	26
5	Isidro	C	middle	Andarapa	(v)	Andarapa	41
6	Fortunato	C	middle	Andarapa	(v)	Andarapa	20
7	Sixto	F	middle	Toxama	(h)	Manchaybamba	8
8	Abraham	CF	middle	Puitoc	(h)	Andarapa	12
9	Virgilio	C	middle	Andarapa	(v)	Andarapa	6
10	Guillermo	C	middle	Andarapa	(v)	Andarapa	16
11	Leonidás	F	middle	Huancas	(h)	Huancas	20
12	Evaristo	CF	middle	Puitoc	(h)	Andarapa	44
13	Julián	CF	poor	Chuspi	(h)	Andarapa	22
14	Eulogio	F	poor	Toxama	(h)	Manchaybamba	4
15	Cirilo	F	poor	Toxama	(h)	Manchaybamba	35
16	Marcelino	C	poor	Andarapa	(v)	Andarapa	14
17	Gerardo	C	poor	Andarapa	(v)	Andarapa	42
18	Germán	F	poor	Toxama	(h)	Manchaybamba	4
19	Patricia	C	poor	Andarapa	(v)	Andarapa	3
20	Juan de Dios	CF	poor	Chuspi	(h)	Andarapa	12
21	Pablo	F	poor	Toxama	(h)	Manchaybamba	50
22	Simón	C	poor	Andarapa	(v)	Andarapa	34
23	Leandro	C	poor	Andarapa	(v)	Andarapa	34
24	Vicente	F	poor	Toxama	(h)	Manchaybamba	2
25	Antonio	F	poor	Chuspi	(h)	Andarapa	2
26	Julio	F	poor	Toxama	(h)	Manchaybamba	10
27	Juana	CF	poor	Chuspi	(h)	Andarapa	28
28	Miguel	CF	poor	Chuspi	(h)	Andarapa	50
29	Dionicio	F	poor	Toxama	(h)	Manchaybamba	8
30	Exaltación	C	poor	Andarapa	(v)	Andarapa	14
31	Claudio	C	poor	Andarapa	(v)	Andarapa	15
32	Máximo	F	poor	Chuspi	(h)	Chuspi	13

*C = *comunero* (village smallholder not linked to hacienda); F = *feudatario* (hacienda worker, with no land in the community); CF = both statuses: *comunero* and *feudatario* at the same time.
Categories of rich, middle and poor, established according to table 6.4.
[†] See map, figure 6.1.

Table 6.4. *The distribution of wealth and annual agricultural production among 32 households in Andarapa district (in £)*

Groups	House-hold no.	Land owner-ship (value in £)[1]	%	Annual agri-cultural production[2]	%	Livestock[3]	%	Other[4]	%	Total (£)
Rich	1	1250	41.9	224	7.5	1517	50.6	—	—	2981
	2	1000	54.3	103	5.6	740	40.2	—	—	1843
	3	473	25.8	72	3.9	1285	70.2	—	—	1830
Middle	4	711	45.6	127	8.2	720	46.2	—	—	1558
	5	780	57.0	118	8.6	470	34.3	—	—	1368
	6	540	43.9	32	2.6	635	51.6	24	1.9	1231
	7	510	42.4	374	31.1	320	26.5	—	—	1204
	8	720	60.1	32	2.7	445	37.2	—	—	1197
	9	870	73.4	22	1.9	264	22.3	29	2.4	1185
	10	695	63.5	115	10.5	240	21.9	44	4.0	1094
	11	790	72.9	145	13.4	140	12.9	9	0.8	1084
	12	380	36.3	45	4.3	622	59.3	1	0.1	1048
Poor	13	260	27.4	32	3.4	640	67.5	16	1.7	948
	14	370	48.9	177	23.4	210	27.7	—	—	757
	15	490	64.8	52	6.9	214	28.3	—	—	756
	16	320	44.2	14	1.9	358	49.4	33	4.5	725
	17	260	41.5	21	3.3	345	55.1	—	—	626
	18	400	67.7	166	28.1	25	4.2	—	—	591
	19	480	82.6	21	3.6	80	13.8	—	—	581
	20	300	53.0	26	4.6	240	42.2	—	—	566
	21	330	59.4	15	2.7	210	37.8	—	—	555
	22	316	60.3	12	2.3	130	24.8	66	12.6	524
	23	430	91.1	39	8.3	—	—	3	0.6	472
	24	255	58.1	132	30.1	25	5.6	27	6.2	439
	25	160	36.5	38	8.7	240	54.8	—	—	438
	26	160	38.6	36	8.7	218	52.7	—	—	414
	27	225	54.5	28	6.8	160	38.7	—	—	413
	28	220	66.5	31	9.4	80	24.2	—	—	331
	29	200	61.9	13	4.0	80	24.8	30	9.3	323
	30	200	68.7	11	3.8	80	27.5	—	—	291
	31	250	90.3	9	3.2	18	6.5	—	—	277
	32	210	95.0	11	5.0	—	—	—	—	221

Calculated values:
1 1 hectare without irrigation = 10 000 soles; 1 hectare with irrigation = 20 000 soles.
2 Amount of production calculated according to the market price in 1974.
3 Market prices in 1974: cattle: 8000 soles = £80; sheep: 600 soles = £6; horse: 3000 soles = £30; goat: 400 soles = £4.
4 *Includes* trade income and salary earnings, *excludes* wage earnings and credit.
Figures calculated in £ sterling at the rate of exchange of 100 Peruvian soles per £ in 1974.

levels with their annual agricultural production, livestock ownership and trade. This is represented in table 6.4, which shows that in many cases, especially among the richest households, livestock holdings are the main sources of their wealth, whereas among the poorest it is their plots and their crops. From table 6.4 we can see that the process of development of the household economy and of economic differentiation among households take place through four different processes: (a) the accumulation of land; (b) the increase of agricultural productivity; (c) the accumulation of animals and (d) in a few cases, the development of trade and migration. In order to understand how each of these tendencies develop, it is necessary to look separately at the control of land and other resources, labour relationships and the practices of exchange and consumption. Elsewhere (Sánchez 1977) I undertake an analysis of each one of these, but here I will analyse only labour relationships. I have chosen this particular area of discussion for it is here that the notion of reciprocity is supposed to influence peasant life most.

4. Labour relationships and the role of reciprocity

Three forms of labour relationship among households can be identified in Andarapa. They are, in order of their frequency: intra-household, wage and reciprocal labour. The first corresponds to labour obtained from the members of the household unit: household head, spouse and children. The second entails labour obtained through cash payment. And the third refers to contracts of exchange of labour/labour and labour/goods; that is ayni and minka respectively. This reciprocal form takes place usually between parents and their married children, between brothers running distinct households, between other close relatives or between neighbours whether linked through ritual kinship relationships or not.

According to these uses of labour we can distinguish two main groups of households among those included in the sample (see table 6.5):

Group I includes households with the greatest access to land and highest annual agricultural production. They have three hectares of land or more with an average of five hectares and an average production of £136. At the same time this group makes the greatest use of wage labour: an average of 34.2% of the total annual labour input. The group includes 13 households, that is 40.6% of the sample. Furthermore, analysis of variance shows that we can distinguish within this sector two sub-groups: sub-group I_1 making use of mainly wage labour and including 7 households (22%); and sub-group I_2 making use of mainly intra-household and reciprocal labour and consisting of 6 households.

Group II corresponds to those 19 households (59.4% of the sample) who have the least access to land (less than 3 hectares and an average of 2.0

Table 6.5. *Land, labour input and agricultural production among 32 households in Andarapa, 1973–74*

Group and Household no.		Cultivated land (hectares)	Household and reciprocal (%)	Wage labour (%)	Annual labour input	Annual agricultural production (£)
I_1	1	9.00	70	30	264	224
	4	5.80	56	44	117	127
	10	4.50	51	49	128	115
	7	3.50	33	67	116	374
	14	3.00	14	86	129	177
	18	3.00	44	56	189	166
	24	1.50	42	58	100	132
I_2	2	6.70	100	—	63	103
	11	6.50	75	25	94	145
	8	6.25	100	—	60	32
	5	5.75	94	6	133	118
	3	4.50	84	16	138	72
	6	4.30	93	7	61	32
Average (I_2 and I_2)		(4.9)	(65.8)	(34.2)	(122.5)	(139.8)
II	12	2.80	98	2	105	45
	19	2.70	100	—	25	21
	17	2.70	98	2	54	21
	21	6.60	92	8	64	15
	15	2.50	100	—	128	52
	22	2.00	91	9	76	12
	23	2.00	94	6	64	39
	16	2.00	83	18	35	14
	20	2.00	100	—	38	26
	31	2.00	100	—	30	9
	9	1.70	86	14	36	22
	29	1.50	100	—	32	13
	28	1.45	100	—	33	31
	32	1.30	100	—	42	11
	13	1.30	100	—	48	32
	26	1.00	94	6	50	36
	27	0.80	31	69	48	28
	25	0.75	88	12	34	38
	30	0.66	100	—	25	11
Average (II)		(2.0)	(92.5)	(7.7)	(48.6)	(25.1)

hectares) and to agricultural production (an average of only £25 a year). This group also makes least use of wage labour (only 7.5% of their total annual labour input). They work the land mainly by making use of intra-household and reciprocal labour. We can distinguish a section of them, almost 50%, who do not hire wage labour at all.

168

A conventional interpretation of these two groups of peasants would classify them as *modern* and *traditional* and their economic behaviour would be explained in terms of subsistence and market-oriented rationalities (see, for example, Ortiz 1972). The first group would be said to have been integrated into the wider society, as they run capitalist forms of enterprises; and the second would be thought of as resisting the capitalist penetration and making efforts to maintain their Andean economic system. The present analysis attempts to show the misleading character of this view and seeks an alternative interpretation.

The first general point to notice in regard to the average figures in both groups I and II is that the higher use of wage labour is also related to high levels of access to land. Thus, the availability of this resource is the basic condition for the type of labour they use. However, this is not all. The existence of a clear distinction between sub-groups I_1 and I_2 and some exceptional cases (such as household 24 which does not have the corresponding level of access to land), mean that the use of labour depends on other factors also. Such factors would be the availability of capital for agricultural investment, which makes it possible to increase the scale of production although the amount of land may be small. The sources of finance for peasants in the area are even scarcer than land. Only a few of them can obtain it, and they must use a variety of channels.

Let us examine each of those households in group I who are mostly involved in the use of wage labour.

Roberto, head of household 1, comunero and feudatario at the same time, is the richest in the sample as the major land and livestock owner. As a relative of one of the six landlords in the district he received almost all the land he owns from the hacienda in the way of inheritance, although he describes himself as being a traditional worker in the hacienda and has the same rights to land as any other feudatario. He uses mainly intra-household and reciprocal labour, but a large proportion is wage labour. He pays the labourers with his earnings, which are large in comparison with the other households in the sample.

Isaac, head of household 4, similarly a comunero/feudatario, has most of his land in the hacienda area and has been favoured by the traditional *patrón* because of his special relationships with him as a *mayordomo*. He combines the three forms of labour but the proportion of hired labour is highest and reaches almost 50%. The cash with which he pays wages and invests in agriculture comes mostly from his large agricultural income and also from his livestock sales.

Guillermo, head of household 10, exclusively comunero, is a local official, being a judge of the district, and spends most of his time attending to public affairs from which he gets a comparatively significant amount of cash. He also does temporary skilled work as a builder. He does not have much land compared with others, but his extra-agricultural income allows him to hire labour to work on his plots.

Sixto and Eulogio, heads of households 7 and 14 respectively, are feudatarios and, not being the richest in land, obtain finance from the bank and are still able to rent extra plots to cultivate. Their migratory experience in developed agricultural areas enabled them to gain a command of techniques and of the Spanish language, both of which facilitate access to helpful urban contacts. The availability of cash and the need for a larger number of workers in the shortest time at peak periods seem to be related to their preference for wage labour.

Germán and Vicente, heads of households 18 and 24, are also feudatarios with not much access to land, but because of their migratory opportunities they managed to save a certain amount of cash and bring it home. They invested most of their money in agriculture, which beside technical migrational experience makes them two of the peasants most anxious to improve their farms. They see wage labour as more economically advantageous and efficient than reciprocal labour.

Thus the availability of finance for investment and technical experience are the determinant factors in peasants' choice of wage labour over other forms. This explains why those households from sub-group I_2, in spite of their access to land, are not able to hire labour and prefer to cultivate their plots through households and reciprocal labour. In this sub-group, household heads 2, 3, 8 and 11 have most of their land in hacienda territory and indeed they have accumulated the largest amounts of land in the sample. Even so, they could not obtain enough produce and cash to make significant investments, neither did they have the technical resources to increase their level of production. Their average annual agricultural production came to only £84 compared to the £188 of sub-group I_1. This might also explain their small use of wage labour. None of them has had a successful enough migratory experience to allow him to accumulate savings nor has any of them been in a position to apply for bank credit. Similarly, household heads 5 and 6, two of the richest comuneros in terms of land ownership, in a similar situation to those mentioned above, have not found any opportunity to increase their investment or their agricultural techniques. Their use of wage labour is small due mainly to their shortage of cash.

Sources of finance and technology are also absent in the case of the whole of group II, among which we have to consider the limited availability of land as the first element determining the lack of wage labour. Consequently in this group the level of agricultural production is the lowest, coming to an average of only £25 a year. The exceptional case of household 27 shows a high proportion of wage labour, due to the particular conditions of having a household head who is a widow, and therefore not able to return any

Table 6.6. *Distribution of 32 households according to types of labour input and amount of cultivated land*

Socio-economic group	Household no.	Cultivated land (hectares)	Household labour %	Reciprocal labour %	Wage labour %
I_1	1	9.00	36.0	34.0	30.0
	4	5.80	36.0	20.0	44.0
	10	4.50	37.5	14.5	49.0
	7	3.50	29.0	4.0	67.0
	14	3.00	14.0	—	86.0
	18	3.00	42.0	2.0	56.0
	24	1.50	41.0	1.0	58.0
Average			33.6	10.7	55.7
I_2	2	6.70	74.0	26.0	—
	11	6.50	65.0	10.0	25.0
	8	6.25	75.0	25.0	—
	5	5.75	77.0	17.0	6.0
	3	4.50	77.0	7.0	16.0
	6	4.30	71.0	22.0	7.0
Average			73.1	17.8	9.0
II	12	2.80	62.0	36.0	2.0
	19	2.70	52.0	48.0	—
	17	2.70	94.0	4.0	2.0
	21	2.60	92.0	—	8.0
	15	2.50	100.0	—	—
	22	2.00	62.0	29.0	9.0
	23	2.00	46.8	46.8	6.4
	16	2.00	68.0	14.0	18.0
	20	2.00	75.0	25.0	—
	31	2.00	77.0	23.0	—
	9	1.70	58.0	28.0	14.0
	29	1.50	66.0	34.0	—
	28	1.45	76.0	24.0	—
	32	1.30	88.0	12.0	—
	13	1.30	84.0	16.0	—
	26	1.00	86.0	8.0	6.0
	27	0.80	31.0	—	69.0
	25	0.75	47.0	41.0	12.0
	30	0.66	88.0	12.0	—
Average			71.1	21.3	7.7
Total average			62.8	18.3	18.9

reciprocal labour; there is no-one among her family or kin who can take charge of her farm.

Let us now distinguish household labour from reciprocal labour in order to find out the economic and social factors influencing both of these types of labour, and especially the reasons why peasants sometimes become involved in reciprocal labour relationships.

Table 6.6 shows the relationships between the size of cultivated land and the three types of labour in use. The first evidence we find here is the overwhelmingly high frequency of the use of household labour, particularly among the poorest 25 cases, and the very limited use of the other two forms. This would mean that the productive process among this category (sub-group I_2 and group II) cannot be seen as resting on labour relationships between one household and others, but rather on intra-household family labour organization.

Moreover, reciprocal labour, as in ayni and minka systems, tends to have a higher frequency than wage labour, as shown by the average percentage. The same happens in both large and small land-holdings. Thus, in general terms, according to what has been said above, a first statement would be that those 25 peasants of sub-group I_2 and group II, as they lack financial sources and techniques to increase their production, cover their need for extra labour by means of reciprocal exchange.

However, it seems that the content of reciprocity is not as simple as this, for we find to some extent the same frequency of reciprocal labour not only at the low levels of land ownership, but also among those rich peasants using mainly wage labour and controlling finance and technology. Furthermore, a comparison of the extra labour required for each household with the use of reciprocity shows the absence of statistical relationships between both dimensions. We can see this in table 6.7, where the first item is defined as the relationship between the size of cultivated land and the number of household members capable of work (productive members). The outcome of the table is negative. That is, the reciprocal labour used has very little to do with the different levels of requirement of extra labour. Thus, it appears clear that in these cases the practice of reciprocity is to be explained by factors other than 'labour shortage'.

If we explore kinship outside the household we find that we cannot assume that because households have close relatives and ritual kin fellows in the village they use reciprocal labour more than other forms. The figures in table 6.8 include in the category 'relatives and ritual relatives': fathers, brothers and brothers-in-law of the household head and his wife; and also the number of *compadres* and *ahijados* of the couple with whom reciprocal exchange usually takes place. The table refers only to those 25 households who do not use wage labour as the main system. From the average percentage

Table 6.7. *Land, working members and extra labour input among 25 households in Andarapa (1973–4), grouped by per capita availability of land*

Household no.	Cultivated land (hectares)	No. of working members	Cultivated land per working member	Reciprocal labour %	Wage and reciprocal labour %
8	6.25	3	2.83	25.0	25.0
3	4.50	2	2.25	7.0	23.0
2	6.70	3	2.23	26.0	26.0
6	4.30	2	2.15	22.0	29.0
Average				20.0	25.7
5	5.75	3	1.91	17.0	23.0
11	6.50	4	1.62	10.0	35.0
12	2.80	2	1.40	36.0	38.0
19	2.70	2	1.35	48.0	48.0
17	2.70	2	1.35	4.0	6.0
21	2.60	2	1.30	—	8.0
16	2.00	2	1.00	14.0	32.0
20	2.00	2	1.00	25.0	25.0
Average				19.3	26.9
9	1.70	2	0.85	28.0	42.0
15	2.50	3	0.83	—	—
29	1.50	2	0.75	34.0	34.0
28	1.45	2	0.72	24.0	24.0
22	2.00	3	0.66	29.0	38.0
32	1.30	2	0.65	12.0	12.0
13	1.30	2	0.65	16.0	16.0
23	2.00	4	0.50	46.8	53.2
31	2.00	4	0.50	23.0	23.0
27	0.80	2	0.40	—	69.0
25	0.75	2	0.37	41.0	53.0
26	1.00	3	0.33	8.0	14.0
30	0.66	3	0.22	12.0	12.0
Average				21.1	30.2

This table excludes 7 households in the sample, group I_1, who are mostly involved in wage labour use.

Table 6.8. *Relatives/ritual kin fellows and reciprocal labour input among 25 poorest households in Andarapa 1973–4*

Household no.	No. relatives and ritual relatives	Reciprocal labour %
26	1	6
3	1	6
22	1	29
5	1	16
2	2	19
11	2	10
29	3	34
		(17.1)
32	4	12
31	4	23
28	4	24
21	4	—
15	4	—
23	7	—
20	7	25
19	7	40
17	7	
8	7	25
13	7	12
		(14.6)
30	8	12
27	8	—
25	8	45
12	8	31
16	10	14
6	13	22
9	15	27
		(21.6)

Figures in brackets denote averages.

of reciprocal labour we can see a slight relationship with the frequency of relatives, but it cannot be regarded as a strong one.

In order to understand the conditions under which reciprocity takes place, we will next examine some of the households in a differentiated way: those who have little access to land and make use of a high proportion of reciprocal labour; those who are also poor peasants but do not make use of reciprocity; and finally, those rich peasants who tend to be involved in reciprocity in spite of their high proportion of wage labour input.

Table 6.9. *Sources and types of labour input (household 12)*

Participant	Relationship with household head	Household labour	Reciprocal labour	Wage labour	Annual man–days (1974)
Evaristo	head	65.0			
Doctora	wife	3.5			
Nicanor	brother		1		
Glicerio	son		12		
Jacinto	son		7		
Abraham	daughter's husband		11		
Juan	son's son		2		
Simón	son's son		2		
Pedro	son's son		2		
Total		68.5	37		105.5

Reciprocity between poor households

The case of *Evaristo*, head of household 12, is one in which the agricultural product cannot cover expenses for hiring labour. Evaristo and his wife, as the only working members of his household, cannot manage to do the annual work of his 2.80 hectares of cultivated land. He and his wife are both aged over 60 and their capacity for work is lower than average. However, it could be said that Evaristo's advantage is that he is one of the villagers with the largest number of close relatives. He has eight close male relatives living nearby and most of them are his married sons and sons-in-law, with whom he exchanges labour and services almost constantly. In terms of agricultural work they give him 36% of his annual labour input (see table 6.9). The important feature of this kin group is the close co-operation which takes place not only between Evaristo and his children, but also between each of the young couples.

On the other hand, *Antonio*, head of household 25, also uses a large amount of reciprocal labour, but this is because of his economic dependence on his relatives. Antonio has the highest proportion of labour done on a reciprocal basis: he owns only 0.75 hectares which he can easily cultivate, being only 21 years old and quite capable physically. Neither has it to do with his large number of close relatives: he has 10 male relatives with whom he can exchange services at any time. Antonio exchanges mostly with his father, as table 6.10 shows. So the reciprocal labour input for Antonio can only be understood in terms of his particular relationship of co-operation with his father. Antonio is the youngest son in his family. His five brothers and sisters are all married and live separately. He normally lives with his

Table 6.10. *Sources and types of labour input: the case of Antonio (household 25)*

Participant	Relationship with household head	Household labour	Reciprocal labour	Wage labour	Annual man–days (1974)
Antonio	head	11			
Alejandrina	wife	5			
Román	father		11		
Sergio	brother		2		
Benedicta	sister		1		
Others	non-relatives			4	
Total		16	14	4	34

parents, and although he got married two years ago, he has not managed to build a new house and still has to depend on his father's favours. He helps him in his farming and also receives similar services, not as a member of the same household but as the head of a new one. In addition, Antonio, as the youngest child and the one living close to his parents and looking after them, expects to inherit his father's house and a large piece of land.

Let us examine now the cases of *Cirilo* and *Juana* who, although they are two of the poorest peasants, do not make use of reciprocity at all. Cirilo, as head of household 15, seems to be quite self-sufficient with his own labour, cultivating his 2.5 hectares with the help of his wife and young children. However, his level of production (£52) does not cover the subsistence of his family and he has to work as a wage labourer for his neighbours and in the provincial town for several weeks a year. Cirilo is 56 years old and has four close relatives in the area, his brothers and his wife's brothers, but his ties with them are very weak. Cirilo does not approach them for reciprocal labour frequently. Most of them live in different villages and they hardly visit each other. The only one living near to Cirilo is Germán, his youngest brother, head of household 18. Even so, they do not easily get involved in labour exchange. The reason seems to lie in the quality of past relationships. Germán has inherited their parents' house without having, according to Cirilo, helped and looked after them for long enough. Cirilo has not received the inheritance he would have expected from his parents and this has created a rift between the brothers which prevents relationships of co-operation from taking place.

Juana, the head of household 27, presents a more dramatic picture. She is a 45-year-old widow and lives alone with her young daughter who helps her to some extent with her farming. The piece of land she owns is one of the smallest in the sample (0.80 hectares altogether) but she could not manage to cultivate it by herself and has to hire wage labour from her neighbours. People who work for her usually do so for a low wage (15 soles, which is half of the normal wage) because, as they say themselves, 'she is a poor lady, she needs help'. In order to pay the wage, she has to work in simple artisanal activities or has to depend on occasional cash gifts from her children who work in the urban centres. She has a total of six close relatives (brothers and sisters-in-law), but none of them gets involved in reciprocal exchange with her. As a woman she could not return the labour services. Consequently, the only type of favours she is able to receive from them are occasional loans of cash or goods, which she has to give back in the same form when she is able to do so. She is usually in debt for long periods.

From the four cases presented we can point out some possible determinants of reciprocity exchanges. First, the case of Juana suggests that reciprocity depends on the degree of practical material benefits a person is able to offer to his counterparts: efficient labour, goods and services. This fact seems to be evident for the cases of Evaristo and Antonio who are very hard workers and reciprocate well the labour of their ayni fellows, although they are poor in respect of goods. But it does not seem to be evident in the case of Cirilo who is also a strong and good worker to the extent that he usually works as a wage labourer. Second, it can also be suggested from the case of Antonio and Evaristo that reciprocal labour exchange is more associated with kinship relationships and particularly with father–child and brother–brother relationships.

This argument would assume that those peasants linked by kinship ties are likely to be involved in reciprocal exchanges with each other. This, however, is not a frequent phenomenon. It often happens in Andarapa that kinship groups are involved in rather distant, if not hostile, relationships. The cases of Cirilo and Juana are clear examples of this fact. They have close relatives living near them but they do not co-operate with them. The incoherence between kinship and co-operation for the whole sample of households is shown in table 6.8, as already indicated.

A more consistent explanation of reciprocal co-operation is offered by the wider material benefits to be obtained from the exchange. This means that a person involved in reciprocity is not only interested in the labour he receives but is principally interested in the significance of that exchange in the context of the past and future benefits or losses for him. The cases of Cirilo and Antonio give grounds for his argument. Cirilo would be happy exchanging labour with his brother Germán were it not for his resentment over the inheritance issue. In fact Cirilo believes that the ayni system is economically much more beneficial because the person works harder and more efficiently than a person working for wages. In the same way, Antonio, although he could earn more cash as a wage labourer somewhere else, works from time to time with his father. He does so because he is interested in obtaining the inheritance which he has to justify by offering help and protection to his parents.

At this stage it is necessary to focus on similar aspects of the kinship groups of Evaristo and Juana. Evaristo, it has been said earlier, has a more closely inter-linked kinship group compared with the others in the sample. In table 6.9 we can see that those with whom he exchanges labour are his two sons (Jacinto, 42 years old and Glicerio, 38), and his son-in-law Abraham (36). All of them have already received their respective inheritance but the father has not yet completed the division of his remaining 2.8 hectares of land. So the three successors have to co-operate with their father, not only because they are all satisfied with the pieces of land already granted to them, but also because they expect to receive more. So they have to justify their right by giving services to their father.

On the other hand, Juana is one of eight brothers and sisters, all of them married and in middle age. She has not received much land in inheritance as her parents were not rich farmers and the small pieces they owned were very much subdivided between the large number of successors. She does not have any special rights to claim from her brothers although most of them live in the area. She has mostly to depend on herself and the eventual support of her two children living in Lima.

It is suggested therefore that reciprocal exchange of labour within the kin-group is related more directly to one of the several forms of access to and transfer of land ownership: the inheritance system. The norms governing inheritance in the area might be influenced to a great extent by the national laws, as one of the tasks of the local judges is to issue documents legalizing this form of transfer. This is the case only for that sector of village land which is privately owned. It could not happen with the plots located in the hacienda territory where the succession to the control of leased-out plots is mostly done in informal ways. It is frequently mentioned in Andarapa that people have a traditional custom by which the youngest child, either male or female, has the right to inherit the house of his parents. They all explain that this is because the last child is the one who tends to stay with his parents and look after them in their old age, while the older children have already got married and have their own households. This rule might apply to the parents' house but there is no such predeterminate consensus for the distribution of land among the siblings. Usually it happens that this distribution is not egalitarian and the criterion used by the testator is the amount of material and personal services he has received during his life from his successors. Sometimes they mention that an additional criterion would be degree of need shown by each of the successors (e.g. a large number of children to feed), but precisely this neediness usually leads to the tendency to offer a higher level of services to justify a special consideration in inheritance. This would be the case especially when alternative economic resources are not available. This means that not all the children rely equally on their inheritance rights. Those who show a major interest in them are usually those who have the least successful economic career of their own.

The kin-group of Evaristo is a good example of this fact. His two sons, Jacinto (42 years old and still unmarried) and Glicerio (38 years old) are living in the area as *colonos* of two of the fundos. They are uneducated and hold small plots of land (barely 1.5 and 3.0 hectares respectively). As he has no children Jacinto has been given a smaller plot in inheritance (only 0.5 hectares). Glicerio, married with five children, has for his part been granted the larger piece (1.5 ha). Because this preference was given to him, Glicerio and his three older sons give frequent help and personal support to Evaristo (see table 6.9). On the other hand, his daughter Lucila also lives in the village and is married to Abraham, to whom Evaristo has offered and already given one of his best and largest plots. Abraham's debt and his obligation to co-operate as closely as possible with his father-in-law are evident. Finally, the last daughter, Benita, 28 years old, migrated ten years ago to Lima and has a permanent job there. She does not expect to come back to the village and, in spite of being the youngest child, she has claimed no inheritance rights, at least up to the present time.

It now seems possible to argue that peasants get involved in reciprocal labour and co-operation principally because this form of exchange constitutes one of the possible means of access to economic resources. In other words, co-operation is a form of response to shortage of land and the absence of alternative ways to obtain it, or the absence of other types of resources. Those individuals practising reciprocal labour exchange tend to combine the inheritance with land obtained by other means such as purchase or labour rent, including political protest movements and so-called 'illegal' appropriation of land in the hacienda areas to increase their limited access to this basic resource. The scarcity of agricultural land and production in Andarapa always had its origin in the monopolization of land ownership by landlords and rich peasants, as well as a persistently low level of the forces of production e.g. technology. It is the maintenance of such monopolistic ownership and the tendencies of the dominant classes to exclude peasants from the control of the land that explains why peasants co-operate among themselves in order to mitigate their poverty.

Reciprocity between rich and poor peasants

Let us see now what happens among those rich peasants who are involved in reciprocal relationships in spite of their major preference for wage labour. Let us look at two such cases: Guillermo and Roberto. *Guillermo*, 37 years old, head of household 10, owns 4.5 hectares of cultivated land and has

179

Table 6.11. *Sources and types of labour input: the case of Guillermo (household 10)*

Participant	Relationship with household head	Household labour	Reciprocal labour	Wage labour	Annual man–days (1974)
Guillermo	head	19			
Celia	wife	10			
Rene	daughter	12			
Emiliano	father		2		
De la Cruz	brother-in-law		2		
Juan	brother-in-law		5		
Rusilio	brother		1		
Armandina	sister-in-law		5		
Virgilio	ahijado		1		
Others (2)	sisters-in-law		2		
Others	neighbours			64	
Total		41	18	64	123

eight people in his family unit, the highest number in the sample, of whom only three are capable of work on the land: himself, his wife and one of the children. He also has numerous relatives and ritual kinsmen living in the village, numbering 16 altogether. Although he has been a school teacher and a successful migrant in Lima in the past and at present enjoys a high level of local prestige, in that he has often been appointed to several official posts in the district, he nevertheless approaches some people for reciprocal labour exchange, mainly his close relatives: father, brother and compadres. At the same time he employs the highest number of wage labourers on his farm. It can be said of Guillermo that he is involved in reciprocal exchange of labour neither because of a shortage of family labour nor because of a lack of cash or goods, but rather because he is interested in maintaining his social relationships with his relatives and compadres. In fact, most of them are poorer in land and cash; Guillermo as a rich person with high prestige feels that he should help and protect them, not only to ensure their support for his social position, but also to have access to cheap and secure labour sources.

In doing so Guillermo combines both ayni and minka systems. He returns the labour of his father and brothers in the same form. In the case of his sisters and brothers-in-law and his ahijados (adopted children) he reciprocates their labour in goods and administrative services as he occupies a public position. However, as shown in table 6.11, Guillermo obtains more reciprocal labour from the second set of relatives through the system of minka.

Table 6.12. *Sources and types of labour input: the case of Roberto (household 1)*

Participant	Relationship with household head	Household labour	Reciprocal labour	Wage labour	Annual man–days (1974)
Roberto	head	80			
Antonia	wife	16			
Jesús	wife's brother		14	2	
Emeterio	wife's brother		2		
Helmo	compadre		4		
Simeón	ahijado		4		
Lucio	ahijado		2	4	
Catalina	compadre		2		
Lucía	compadre		2		
Moisés	compadre		2	2	
Cirilo	ahijado		2		
Nasario	ahijado		2		
Anacleto	wife's cousin		2		
Fortunato	wife's uncle		5		
Rosalio	compadre		5		
Emilio	compadre		5		
José	compadre		5		
Fausto	compadre		5		
Toribio	compadre		5		
Inocencio	compadre		5		
Rosendo	compadre		4		
Genaro	compadre		4		
Pablo	ahijado		4		
Gliserio	compadre		3		
Félix	compadre			4	
Vicente	compadre			2	
Teófilo	ahijado		2	4	
Others	neighbours			60	
Total		96	90	78	264

Roberto, head of household 1, as the richest in the sample combines three types of labour in almost equal proportions; but compared with the other households he uses reciprocal and wage forms more often and household labour not very much. He has the largest number of people involved in his farm (see table 6.12). This fact is associated with his influential position in the community, not only because he is rich in land, but because of his command of the Spanish language, his higher level of education, his successful migration to Lima in the past and his skills in local political administration. As such, although he has a small number of close relatives, he has developed the largest network of ritual kinship, to the extent that people say 'Roberto is compadre of everyone'. The patron–client relationships between him and his compadres and ahijados, then, cover a wide range of activities: he is able to offer political-administrative services as he usually occupies some official post. In return he receives labour services as well as support for his political position, but this also legitimizes his greater control over land which would otherwise be unacceptable. For Roberto to depend exclusively on wage labour – he has enough cash to do that – would not have the same social effect because of the impersonal nature of cash transactions, and also because of the family nature of relationships between people involved in the exchange where labour is by no means conceived as a commodity but rather as a personal and voluntary service to be offered. The type of reciprocity Roberto practices corresponds exclusively to minka where it is clear that the major benefits are channelled to him.

There are several points to take into account in regard to the two last cases described. Both the nature and the purpose of the exchange are based on the system of minka rather than on ayni. Minka involves more concentrated relationships between several people, usually the poorest who offer their labour and a single person, usually rich, who receives the labour and reciprocates it in goods or some form of service. This system implies a certain degree of division of labour between the participants which is determined by the relationships between people and the land. The landowner fulfils a directive role in the labour process and those giving him the labour assume a subordinate position. While in the system of ayni, both parties perform the same role, working together or separately on each other's land, in the case of minka one of the parties usually acts as the labourer; the other, although he can intervene personally in the working team is not obliged to do so as he returns the service in a different way. Moreover, his wife provides food, drink, coca and cigarettes during the working period. The owner of the land acts mostly as the organizer of the labour, determining the specific tasks of each worker although he does not supply the tools.

The purposes of the exchange in the form of minka are more related to its actual objects (labour, crops, draught power, etc.), although the parties could make use of the exchange to obtain further and additional benefits. To be precise, the rich person is primarily interested in obtaining the labour of the poorer people in a way that it is easy and cheap to recruit; but he also seeks social support for his position of power and prestige, which in turn allows him to maintain and expand his wealth. On the other hand, the poorer people are above all interested in obtaining the goods offered to them. This interest is based upon the fact that they themselves do not produce enough crops for their subsistence. For this reason they are also interested in maintaining these relationships in order to have access to the goods as often as possible.

Both of the parties in the exchange try to disguise the materialistic aspects of such transactions by expressing them in terms of kinship relationships and morals. As real kinship ties are usually absent among the people involved, ritual kinship ties are built up to fulfil the same role. In this way, the process of exchange is expressed in a language which is superficial to it. The embedded nature of economic exchange, however, does not necessarily mean that the ritual kinship structure and ideology of reciprocity determine the reproduction and maintenance of the relationships. The basic reason for the poor peasants to engage in exchange is their continuously poor economic condition. They do not have alternative means to improve their access to resources nor to produce enough goods. The fact that some peasants have obtained more land and improved their economy is not counter-evidence to the argument, but rather confirms it. Once the villager has improved his economic condition, he abandons his position of labourer, assuming instead the opposite role and contributing to the impoverishment of others. As opportunities for economic expansion are limited and the forces of production do not offer alternative ways of increasing production, as in Andarapa, poor peasants will be bound to continue practising such forms of exchange; and to realise that the only way to ensure their subsistence is by being linked to rich peasants or other powerful people in kinship-like or patron–client forms of relationships. The process of differentiation which enlarges the gap between poor and rich peasants and their general exclusion from real control of land and of production, and the obstacles to their improving their production, are the forces responsible for the persistence of such forms of exchange and of beliefs in the ideology of kinship and reciprocity.

5. The poor peasantry of a capitalist society

We have argued so far that the production process is not centrally influenced by the conceptual elements of Andean culture. The notion of reciprocity only constitutes an ideological instrument to disguise overtly exploitative economic relationships on the one hand, and to ensure the survival of exploited sectors of the peasantry on the other. As such, it is rather the effect of distinct political and economic processes both internal and external to the peasant society. What we will attempt to show now are the relationships between those determinant processes and the capitalist system as a whole. Our contention here is, firstly, that peasants, although they cultivate their plots other than by a wage labour system, do not have full control either of the land or of what they produce. The mechanisms by which peasants have access to land are mostly determined by local and national political power processes. In the same way their surplus product is appropriated by dominant classes which are directly linked to the overall capitalist system. Secondly, household economic processes and reciprocal exchange constitute only a limited proportion of their economic activities. The bulk of the production they need to sustain a household comes from their involvement in wage labour at local or regional levels. Similarly their income and consumption patterns are largely dependent on outside sources directly concerned with regional trade and capitalist industry.

We have indicated earlier the process of differentiation consisting mostly of land accumulation by a few peasants, leaving the majority of people in continuous scarcity. This process of differentiation does not occur in isolation from the capitalist society. Among other ways it is directly related to it as an expression of the phenomenon of primitive accumulation. It implies the separation of large sections of peasants from the control of land with the consequence that it makes them dependent basically on the sale of their labour. As such it can be seen as part of the general tendency of capitalism to monopolize the means of production and separate the direct producers from its control. This process of separation is obviously not absolute. Poor peasants still own small amounts of land which they work themselves. Nevertheless the size of plots is not sufficient to cover the minimum consumption of each household. So in order to survive, peasants are compelled to offer their labour either for goods or for cash.

Before we discuss this issue further, let us see how far that sector of peasant production which is not involved in wage labour is also appropriated in part by local and outside capitalists. As the product obtained through household and kin labour, it is firstly collected by the producer himself; the appropriation of the surplus product takes place at the moment of exchange. The exchange might happen in monetary or non-monetary forms. Both forms contain an element of unequal exchange which would be the mechanism of appropriation. As in Andarapa both forms of exchange take place according to the market price of the goods, the rate of the unequal exchange may be regarded as similar in both cases. The transactions in Andarapa take place between the peasant producers and the local traders and rich villagers who collect agricultural products to take to the regional market and bring back industrial products to the village.

The relative significance of this particular form of appropriation is limited compared with the instance of labour surplus extraction. Due to low levels of land and labour productivity, the production of crops for the outside market is fairly small. Moreover, those involved in this form of appropriation are the rich and middle peasants who have the highest agricultural production. Thus the rich are as much the victims of capitalist exploitation as the poorest.

Let us see now the appropriation of surplus in the process of production. The first evidence to consider comes from table 6.6, in which we can see that the major proportion of annual labour inputs for the villagers included in the sample is performed in the form of intra-household labour. The

Table 6.13. *Size of households and labour inputs in 1974 among 32 families in Andarapa district*

Household no. (see table 6.3)	Total no. of members (consuming)	Productive members	Labour input, total man–days per year
3	2	2	138
9	2	2	36
12	2	2	52
17	2	2	54
27	2	2	48
5	3	3	133
19	3	2	25
22	3	3	76
25	3	2	20
28	3	2	33
1	4	3	264
16	4	2	35
18	4	2	189
21	4	2	64
23	4	4	64
29	4	2	32
32	4	2	42
6	5	4	61
7	5	2	116
13	5	2	48
14	5	2	129
15	5	3	128
24	5	2	100
8	6	3	60
11	6	4	94
26	6	3	50
30	6	3	25
2	7	3	63
4	7	4	117
10	8	3	128
20	8	2	38
31	8	4	30

other two forms, reciprocal and wage, are indeed limited. Even among those rich households, the wage form of labour comes to only 56%.

Conventionally one could interpret this fact by suggesting that the productive system of Andarapa villagers is largely different from capitalism. Moreover, some followers of Chayanov would prefer to term it a 'peasant mode of production'. It will be argued here that this is a false interpretation. Chayanov's rule of the equilibrium between the intensity of labour and the number of consuming members of the household could not be sustained in Andarapa according to table 6.13, where these two variables are not consistently associated. The productive level of each household would

Table 6.14. *Main expenditure items among 32 households in Andarapa, during 1974, in £*

House-hold no.	Urban-type goods*	Children's education	Housing and household goods	Drink coca and leisure	Agri-cultural inputs	Land purchase	Livestock purchase	Total annual ex-penditure
7	79	—	75	9	110	—	—	273
1	90	—	30	22	130	—	—	270
14	74	—	80	8	120	—	—	282
18	64	—	—	24	35	—	—	126
11	88	5	25	19	12	—	—	149
24	59	—	60	8	49	—	—	176
4	40	20	20	7	10	—	—	97
5	33	5	—	5	17	—	70	130
10	40	80	11	16	12	—	—	159
2	11	12	—	16	9	—	30	78
3	26	—	3	7	10	55	—	101
15	13	8	—	4	6	—	—	31
12	17	5	8	3	6	—	—	39
23	10	5	—	4	5	—	—	24
25	18	—	58	13	4	—	—	93
26	3	3	—	3	5	—	—	14
8	26	15	10	7	5	—	—	63
13	4	6	—	5	3	—	—	18
6	19	12	15	3	7	—	—	56
28	19	—	—	2	3	65	—	89
27	16	7	2	2	15	85	—	125
20	7	5	2	4	3	—	—	21
9	50	—	38	2	9	—	—	99
17	15	9	61	5	8	—	—	98
19	40	—	—	1	2	—	—	43
21	3	6	—	3	5	—	—	17
16	9	—	5	15	6	—	—	35
29	4	—	40	7	4	—	—	55
22	12	—	—	15	6	—	—	33
30	74	15	—	2	2	—	—	93
32	13	—	10	2	3	—	—	28
31	31	12	—	4	4	—	—	51

*'Urban-type goods' refers to food, clothes, health services, which are obtained through the market.

be rather the result of various factors: size of land owned, quality of the soil, availability of agricultural inputs and extra-household labour. Furthermore, the level of production, obtained through the system of intra-household labour, generally falls below the consumption needs of the family. This is directly related to the fact that the amount of annual man–days' labour put into their plots by each household is very limited, especially among the poorest peasants. Table 6.5 shows that the average man–days per year for the last 19 households (62% of the sample) is only 25! This suggests

Table 6.15. *Total surplus product, possible investment and sources to cover the deficit, among 32 households in Andarapa, 1974* (£)

Household no.	Annual cash income	Annual expenditure	Total surplus or deficit product	Possible investment or expenses*	Sources to cover the deficit and extra incomes
7	359.35	273	86.35	A + H	—
1	358.28	270	88.28	A	—
14	312.35	280	32.35	A + Debts	Labour sale
18	159.28	126	33.28	A	Labour sale
11	91.42	149	− 57.58	—	Labour sale and loans
24	87.35	176	− 88.65	—	Labour sale and trade
4	144.49	97	47.49	A	—
5	251.21	130	121.21	A + H	—
10	123.56	159	− 35.44	—	Local officer
2	120.49	78	42.49	A	—
3	174.14	101	73.14	A + H	—
15	16.35	31	− 14.65	—	Labour sale
12	72.14	39	33.14	H	—
23	3.28	24	− 20.72	—	Support of relatives
25	11.21	93	− 81.79	—	Labour sale
26	− 17.58	14	− 31.58	—	Labour sale
8	58.42	63	− 4.58	—	Labour sale
13	− 12.65	18	− 30.65	—	Labour sale
6	− 12.65	56	− 68.65	—	Trade and carpentry
28	95.79	89	6.79	—	Labour sale
27	170.14	125	45.14	Debts	—
20	− 45.44	21	− 66.44	—	Labour sale
9	4.14	99	− 94.86	—	Trade
17	3.14	98	− 94.86	—	Support of relatives
19	− 5.79	43	− 48.79	—	Labour sale
21	− 20.72	17	− 37.72	—	Support of relatives
16	− 21.72	35	− 56.72	—	Labour sale and trade
29	− 22.72	55	− 77.72	—	Trade
22	65.21	33	32.21	Debts	Local employment
30	37.42	93	− 55.58	—	Labour sale
32	− 24.72	28	− 52.72	—	Labour sale
31	− 44.44	51	− 95.44	—	Labour sale

*A: Agriculture
H: Housing

that the labour activities of these peasants are mainly outside their plots; which in turn raises the question of how far the subsistence of these families depends on their own agricultural production. The answer seems to be that it does not go very far. One has also to take into account that the consumption in each household includes not only agricultural goods but also urban industrial goods, child education expenses, housing and household goods, drink, leisure and agricultural inputs and so on. The proportion of expenditure on these items is indicated in table 6.14, which shows that

Table 6.16. *No. of man-days' labour necessary to cover the minimum consumption level of the 20 poorest households in Andarapa*

Household no.	Total annual surplus product	No. man-days' labour (£0.25 per man-day)	No. working members
11	− 57.58	230	4
24	− 88.65	354	2
10	− 35.44	141	3
15	− 14.65	58	3
23	− 20.72	83	4
25	− 81.79	327	2
26	− 31.58	126	3
8	− 4.58	18	3
13	− 30.65	123	2
6	− 68.65	275	4
20	− 66.44	266	2
9	− 94.86	379	2
17	− 94.86	379	2
19	− 48.79	195	2
21	− 37.72	151	2
16	− 56.72	227	2
29	− 77.72	311	2
30	− 55.58	222	3
32	− 52.72	211	2
31	− 95.44	382	4

These figures include only 20 households with insufficient incomes according to table 6.15.

this type of expenditure involves all rich and poor peasants, though in different amounts.

If we compare the expenditure levels with the total cash income obtained from agricultural production and livestock sales (see table 6.15), we find that the deficit in the household budgets is quite high and involves a large number of households – a total of 20.62% of the sample. The same table gives a rough idea not only of the possible use the rich peasants will make of their surplus but also, more importantly, it shows the sources the poorest have available to cover their insufficient production. In a few cases this insufficiency is compensated for by trading activities and by economic support and loans from close relatives, but as a general rule peasants are constrained to sell their labour. Thus, wage labour activities constitute the most important source of complementary incomes for the majority of the households. This is made evident in table 6.16, where we find that the average number of man–days each household has to reach in order to complete its minimum level of consumption is 223 per year! This means that *the household head,* if there are no other working members in the household, *is compelled to labour at least 61% of the days of the year for cash or goods outside the household.*

Table 6.17. *Labour migration among 32 households in Andarapa district*

Household no.	Total length of time of labour migration (in months)	No. of children in labour migration in 1974	No. of brothers/sisters in labour migration in 1974
7	28	—	2
1	124	—	2
14	51	—	3
18	144	—	4
11	36	—	1
24	144	—	3
4	48	—	4
5	6	5	3
10	108	—	9
2	18	—	4
3	—	—	4
15	6	1	3
12	—	1	—
23	—	3	2
25	65	—	2
26	72	—	—
8	72	—	1
13	55	—	—
6	21	1	2
28	—	2	—
27	—	3	2
20	48	—	1
9	60	—	5
17	—	3	—
19	60	1	—
21	—	1	—
16	132	—	6
29	23	—	—
22	72	3	3
30	30	—	6
32	30	—	6
31	24	—	1

There are two questions to examine at this point. These are the form in which peasant labour is employed and the sector to which the employers belong. There are two forms of labour employment: minka and the wage system. At the local level both forms are used by those offering labour and by those recruiting it. As shown in table 6.6, however, the proportion of wage labour used by the richest households is greater than minka labour recruitment at local level, but it is of small significance compared with the number of days poor peasants must work for a wage in order to reach subsistence. Therefore the wage system remains as the more generalized form.

Rodrigo Sánchez

As we have said at the beginning, the rich local households constitute only a small sector of the dominant groups which employ peasants' labour. The others are landlords in nearby areas, urban traders, industrialists, mining centres, or capitalist coffee planters in the *ceja de selva* and humid lowland. According to table 6.17, the number of household heads who have had no labour migration experience at all, or whose children or close relatives have had none, is very small.

Thus it appears clear that the image of peasant subsistence producers as rural cultivators with little or no involvement in the capitalist economy is largely a fiction.

7

Property and ideology: a regional oligarchy in the Central Andes in the nineteenth century

FIONA WILSON

1. Introduction

This chapter will focus on a group of families who constituted the oligarchy of Tarma, a province in the Peruvian Central Andes, during the nineteenth century. It explores the relationship between these families and their *haciendas* in a period when links with the wider economy and society were being re-established after the chaotic years which followed the end of Spanish rule. The argument will suggest that it was impossible in practice for these families to institute an easy or thorough transition from the regional socio-economic system that had become entrenched under early republican conditions to one permitting a sustained expansion in the production of goods for an external market. As a result of this inability to inaugurate change, the economic position of the established oligarchy was weakened. I hope to throw some light on how and why a regional oligarchy became so vulnerable and lost the control it had previously exercised over particular resources in the province. This was the first stage of a process taking place in an increasingly dependent economy in which the most important cash-earning resources were acquired directly by foreign capital.

I will begin by outlining the historical background, physical environment, population distribution, agrarian structure and composition of the Tarma oligarchy. After this introduction, the precise problem tackled in the chapter will be defined and analysed under three headings: relationships between oligarchic families and their property, the dramatic rise in the market demand for one specific *tarmeño* product – cane alcohol or *aguardiente* – during the 1860s, and the response by Tarma property-owners to opportunities for earning cash through commodity production.

Historical background

During the 1820s the liberation armies succeeded in bringing an end to Spanish rule in Peru. But in the early years the newly independent country

191

could hardly be described as a nation state, for it was close to disintegration. In the absence of a centralized political apparatus, many armed bands roamed the country under *criollo* or *mestizo* chieftains (*caudillos*), competing for wealth and power. Under these anarchic conditions, Andean regions became largely autonomous, with local political power passing into the hands of oligarchies composed of property-owners whose activities were no longer circumscribed by representatives of the state, as had been the case throughout the Spanish colony. Associated with political disruption was economic recession: in comparison with the late colonial period, the early nineteenth century saw declining levels of trade and the money economy became much more restricted.

This political and economic hiatus did not endure for long. With the guano bonanza of the 1840s, and subsequent expansion of commodity production (especially cotton and sugar) on the Peruvian coast, the country began to participate increasingly in the world capitalist system (Yepes 1972; Bonilla 1974; Macera and Hunt 1977). The development of large-scale commodity production on the coast led to an expansion of the domestic market and had repercussions in certain Andean provinces, as will be demonstrated. The provinces also responded to the new trading opportunities by producing a greater range and volume of export goods; incomes generated by these sales could then be spent on consumption and investment goods imported into the provinces. Thus, during the century, several Andean provinces were drawn back into the wider economy: the southern sierra through the export of wool (Flores-Galindo 1977), Cerro de Pasco through mining (Herndon 1853; Gerstäcker 1862) and the Mantaro valley through food-production for the internal market (Samaniego 1974).

Economic developments went hand-in-hand with the slow, hesitant regeneration of the Peruvian state. The first tentative moves to form a more effective government were made by the Civilista party under its leader, Manuel Pardo, during the 1870s. But the process was brought to an abrupt halt by the War of the Pacific, 1879–83. Only at the end of the 1880s did a president emerge (Andrés Cáceres) who was capable of re-establishing a measure of state authority (Bonilla 1978). Up until the turn of the century, provinces continued to enjoy considerable political autonomy. This independence was reinforced by a Law of Municipalities passed by the Pardo government in 1873 which gave provincial councils wide powers to levy taxes and take decisions on local investment. Only in the early twentieth century were the Lima authorities able to start imposing state rule over the country.

Environment, distribution of population and agrarian structure

The province of Tarma straddles the eastern slopes of the Andean cordillera. In the second half of the nineteenth century the region constituted a small rectangular territory of about one hundred kilometres from north to south and two hundred from east to west. It is a vertical world with altitudinal change reflected in environment and resources. Three zones can be clearly distinguished: the high mountains and plateaux of some 4000 metres to the west with rich deposits of silver, copper, some coal and salt as well as extensive natural pasture; a temperate sierra valley zone of highly productive agriculture situated at about 3000 metres; and to the east, the upper Amazon basin known as the *montaña* at altitudes below 1200 metres where a wide range of subtropical crops can be grown. Tarma has existed as a distinct regional entity from pre-Inca times despite incorporation into two successive empires. Throughout this long period, the regional political centre has been located in the principal sierra valley.

In the period under review, about half the provincial population (21 000) lived in the river valleys of the temperate heartland and the rural population density was some 70 persons per square kilometre (Perú, Ministerio de Gobierno, 1878). In contrast, in the highlands to the north and west and in the recently recolonized montaña to the east, the population density fell sharply. Densities ranged from some six persons per square kilometre in the northern highland districts of Junín and Carhuamayo down to two persons in the western districts of Yauli and Marcapomacocha. The montaña was a true frontier. These subtropical lands had been the domain of Amazon tribes from the time of the Juan Santos Atahualpa rebellion of 1742–55 until 1847 when President Ramón Castilla authorized a military expedition to reconquer the main Chanchamayo valley. From the fort of San Ramón, the troops killed members of the indigenous tribes or expelled them from a belt of surrounding land which formed the nucleus for white settlement. Though colonization was well under way by the 1860s, the number of settlers remained small.

The agrarian structure of Tarma at the regional level showed a remarkable degree of spatial regularity. Three concentric zones centring on the provincial capital of Tarma can be discerned – each associated with a different type or mix of land-holding institution. Virtually all the land of the inner ring of the temperate valleys surrounding the town had been awarded by the Spanish Crown to Indian communities. In the uplands, immediately above the valleys, haciendas predominated. Most of these estates were small in terms both of area and size of resident population which, according to the 1876 population census, ranged from a total of 6 to 90 persons.

The third concentric zone cannot be so neatly defined, for it contained a wide variety of environments from the mountains down to the montaña and a mixture of hacienda and Indian land. From the perspective of the provincial capital the zone was remote and its particular characteristics stemmed from its isolation. By the latter half of the nineteenth century, the largest and wealthiest haciendas of the province were found in this zone.

193

They clustered in a few strategic areas, principally along the east–west route leading up from the coast and continuing east to the frontier of the new montaña colonization.

Taking the province as a whole, the hacienda was still a relatively insignificant component of the agrarian landscape. Only 14% of the rural population (a figure which excludes only the population of Tarma town) was reported by the 1876 census as living on estate properties. But in certain highland and montaña districts the situation was changing very rapidly. In Marcapomacocha, 69% of the district population lived on the huge livestock haciendas, and on the opposite side of the province some 55% of the population in the montaña colonization zone were resident on the embryonic plantations.

In the outer concentric zone there were also extensive Indian lands and the most independent communities. Communities had managed to survive with comparatively little outside interference, especially along the eastern Andean slopes. In contrast, communities lying within or adjacent to the belt of expanding estates (both in the sierra and montaña) exhibited a very different form of independence. They were engaged in a bitter fight, which was to continue for decades, over access to land.

Composition of the Tarma oligarchy

During the nineteenth century the regional oligarchy was composed of nine families of European extraction. The pre-eminence of these families can be shown in three ways. First, between them they had accumulated most of the haciendas in the province. Second, they controlled the political institutions and positions of authority and third, they were dominant in all social relations with Indian or mestizo inhabitants, keeping alive certain tributary relationships of colonial origin. Some of the families had originally settled in Tarma during the colonial period and had acquired extensive properties. In other cases the founders of the dynasties had arrived at Independence; a group including Argentinian mule traders and Spanish officers who elected to remain in Peru. They had married women from established land-owning families and had accumulated a number of estates during the years of political and economic chaos. (For a detailed discussion of the origins of the oligarchic families, see Wilson (1978).)

Although intermarriage between the leading families had been frequent in the late colony and early republic, the pattern no longer persisted by the mid nineteenth century. The families resided chiefly in Tarma town and urban society had become deeply divided. Visitors to the town lamented the violent feuding and plotting which rival family groups indulged in (Valle 1876). The most outstanding cleavage lay not between old colonial families and those who might be considered 'nouveau riche', but rather between people of similar backgrounds; colonial families led the fighting in the 1870s, and by the 1890s their place had been taken by more recent arrivals. Factionalism was characteristic of regional oligarchies throughout the Andean zone in the period. Favre (1965) has noted the feuding behaviour in Huancavelica, and Jacobsen (1978) the divisions among the landed families of Azangaro, in Puno.

As property-owners, the families of the oligarchy had responded to the Andean environment by amassing congeries of separate holdings located in a variety of resource zones. These included mines and large livestock haciendas in the highlands; mixed arable and livestock estates on the valley slopes above Tarma town; and some small irrigated plots on the valley floor near Tarma, which were acquired mostly in the nineteenth century after Indian communities had been deprived of all state protection. In addition, the families of the oligarchy who had assisted with goods or cash in the re-conquest of the montaña in 1847 were rewarded with land concessions. Though the Castilla government had given vague recommendations that the indigenous people should be allowed to remain on reservations, in reality the whole early re-settlement zone was carved up into large properties.

On the pastoral and agricultural haciendas of the sierra and on the montaña estates up to the 1860s, labour relations were based on the payment of rent. Indian families lived permanently on the properties and they paid rent in the form of labour and/or product in return for the right to use portions of the hacienda property on which to produce subsistence. This resident labour could be relied on to produce some surplus product for the owners every year and, as a result, owners could live as rentiers taking little or no part in the management and having no need to invest in the property. But in a system where the bulk of the land area and means of production were in the hands of the resident workers, two major disadvantages were readily apparent. Productivity was extremely low and, as a result of customary rights and obligations between the owners and the resident workers, there was strong resistance to change.

The other important sphere of activity for male members of the regional oligarchy was public service. In return for support given to a candidate for the presidency, many were rewarded with appointments in the network of political authorities and held the posts of prefect or sub-prefect in Tarma or elsewhere. A few were given responsible jobs in the Lima government and many served sporadically as officers in the army or Guardia Nacional. Though all these posts carried some remuneration, none lasted longer than a particular president's tenure of office. None was therefore sufficient to provide economic security for the space of a lifetime and therefore they had to be combined with property ownership. In addition, the copious records of the Tarma provincial council, especially after the political decentralization law of 1873, amply demonstrate that many chose to devote their energies to local civic affairs. Some were evidently sincere in their attempts to improve the public good and take an active part in the trans-formation of Peru, but public office was also highly attractive because of the opportunities it brought for peculation and self-advancement.

The research problem

The specific research question to be discussed stems from the following empirical observations. In the mid-1860s the families of the oligarchy found that they could earn extremely high cash returns from the sale of one commodity – aguardiente – which they produced on their montaña properties. This opportunity was an unexpected windfall. It was not the first time that the families had sold goods for cash, nor was it the first time that goods had been sold outside the zone of production. The novelty lay in the magnitude of the returns. The Tarma owners responded rapidly and for a time were able to transform themselves from rentiers into entre-preneurs eager to manage and invest in their properties and turn them into commercial enterprises geared to commodity production. But despite this initial success, the Tarma owners were unable to sustain their position as aguardiente producers. One by one the families lost their montaña properties to 'outsiders': immigrants who had recently arrived in Peru and who had no kin or social connections with the Tarma oligarchy.

This brief summary sets the context for the question to be examined. Why did the oligarchic families lose the control they had previously establi-shed over properties where the highest cash returns were forthcoming? It may be suggested at the outset that the answer can be sought along two paths of analysis. One path would involve concentrating on the newcomers in order to present the argument that these recent immigrants to the province possessed particular qualities or advantages which made them superior to their *tarmeño* rivals. These might include easier access to capital, or informa-tion, or a business mentality that allowed them to think in terms of rate of profit rather than of gross cash returns.

The alternative approach is to focus attention on the structure of the oligarchy's socio-economic system and explore this in the context of family relationships. This latter path is far more intriguing as a research problem for the following reason. Having labelled a social group an oligarchy and defined this oligarchy in terms of its economic, political and social dominance in a region, it is necessary to suggest how and why 'outsiders' could have begun to threaten the position of such a powerful established elite. It may be hypothesized that the oligarchy's loss of property and therefore its loss of access to cash must have represented some later stage in a much more lengthy and complex process. The changes taking place during the nineteenth century must have placed this section of regional society in an increasingly vulnerable position.

2. Relationships between families of the oligarchy and property

The relationship between owners and property will be examined at two levels beginning with the single estate property owned by a branch of an extended family group. The inheritance custom adopted in republican Peru meant that after the death of an owner the property was divided among his immediate family. Almost always the widow received a half share while the remaining half was divided in equal portions among all the children, both male and female. The Departmental Property Register reveals conclusively that it was incumbent upon one of the male heirs – either a son or a son-in-law – to reunite the ownership of the hacienda during his lifetime and so become the sole owner of the property by the time of his death. It could take more than twenty years for this 'heir apparent' to reunite the property. He inherited a share following the death of the widow, but in the main had to gain the consent of his brothers and sisters in order that they sell their shares of the parental estate for some cash payment, or resort to trickery and deceit to appropriate the portions inherited by others. Obviously the temporary division of ownership made little difference to the way in which the property functioned as a unit of production. Resident workers continued to pay rent regardless of ownership division.

This inheritance pattern appears to have represented a compromise between conflicting needs. On the one hand, the system ensured that each member of the family could look to the property to provide status, security and a means of survival until some alternative source of income or another estate were found. On the other hand, from the point of view of the continuity and power of each property-owning family in the longer run, it was important that haciendas remain intact as economic enterprises. Ownership rights might periodically be divided, but the viability of the estate was not to be threatened on account of a permanent physical division of the property among competing heirs.

A necessary pre-condition for the successful functioning of this type of inheritance system in the early republic lay in the possibilities for the outward expansion of the estate sector. The evidence from the property register suggests that male family members who relinquished their shares of the parental estate to the 'heir apparent' did have the opportunity of acquiring or forming other estates in the province, most notably in the recently recolonized montaña. Though notarial archives reveal that there were occasional disputes and squabbles among heirs over property, the large majority of the Tarma estates passed through division and consolidation of ownership two or three times in the course of the century.

197

It is possible to link this inheritance pattern with the explosive relationships that pertained among families of the oligarchy noted above. It can be argued that by the middle of the century each family group felt bound to maintain a separate identity from rival families living in the same town in order to ensure its own survival. This strategy affected marriage patterns. Marriage between children from rival family groups of the oligarchy was considered taboo. To the present day, parents instil in their children a deep mistrust towards members of particular families, even after migration has taken place to Lima. And as adults, they cannot give any rational explanation for their attitudes. The behaviour in the mid nineteenth century was possibly motivated by the fear that if intermarriage were allowed to occur freely, then it would be possible for a son belonging to one family group to take on the role of 'heir apparent' over his wife's family's property. He could then reunite the ownership of this latter property in his name and thus dispossess the original land-owning family of part of its patrimony.

Daughters were prevented from marrying into a rival family group at all costs. Instead, they were used primarily as lures by which a Tarma family might attract European immigrants who could be expected to contribute skills, connections, money or prestige to enhance the position of the family group. Several German, Italian and French immigrants to the sierra were co-opted in this manner and after their marriage adopted the class interests of the oligarchy. During the 1870s a split had become apparent among the foreign immigrants in Tarma town. During this decade, most newcomers refused to ally themselves through marriage to oligarchic families and, in response to the growing commercial opportunities in the province, became part of an emerging middle class that was increasingly conscious of the profound class difference separating it from the oligarchy. Thus the mere fact of European birth need not have indicated membership of the local oligarchy. If no suitable European immigrant was found, then daughters were often married to close kin such as patrilateral cousins in order to keep the property within the same family group which, as we shall see, comprised several branches.

Though the inheritance law adopted in republican Peru made no distinction between the property rights of males and females, in practice women were being effectively deprived of decision-making power over the estates they had inherited. The women of the Tarma oligarchy were, in general, the vehicles through which property passed to males. Possibly this represented a continuation of inheritance customs established back in the colonial period. But the property register suggests that the pattern was changing over time: in the early decades of the century, significantly more women were represented among the estate-owners than in the later decades when opportunities for earning cash from several different types of property were expanding.

From a discussion of the relationship between owners and property at the level of the individual estate, the following general conclusion emerges. The definition of rights to property within a particular branch of an oligarchic family group was, to a certain extent, indeterminate, because members held overlapping claims. This fundamental ambiguity was expressed in a variety of ways. First, though siblings might sell their inheritance shares to a brother who was reuniting the ownership of an estate, this did not lead automatically to a deprivation of rights to the product of that property. Notarial archives suggest that some distribution of product might continue to take place. Second, there was considerable uncertainty over the rights to property of illegitimate children. Notarial archives contain several examples of successful lawsuits waged by illegitimate offspring against legitimate heirs for cash payment in lieu of a portion of the father's (or, very occasionally, the mother's) estate. Third, in the case of women, there were no recognized rules governing how, in practice, rights to property were to be divided between female heirs and their husbands.

Each of the nine oligarchic family groups was composed of several separate branches, the numbers of branches varying between three and seven. In general, every branch owned at least one estate in Tarma province as well as urban property in Tarma town. If the focus is shifted to the family group as a whole, then it appears that they each accumulated congeries of properties with estates located in many different resource or ecological zones. Although each property was independent as a legal entity, this did not mean that they were economically entirely separate. As most family members lived in Tarma town, it was easy for one branch with, say, a surplus of maize to exchange with another branch which had produced an excess of livestock products. Thus there was a tendency for each kin-group to set up its own circulation system through which subsistence goods could be redistributed.

It is important to view this behaviour in the context of the general economic conditions prevailing in the Andes during the early republic. With the decline of trade, urban citizens depended for their consumption on goods produced on their own properties. Furthermore, though Indian communities were still required to pay tribute (under its republican guise of *contribución de indígenas*), this was collected wholly in cash by the central government and not in the mixture of cash and kind for both provincial and national levels of administration, which had prevailed under the colony. The end of colonial rule and the post-Independence changes meant that regional oligarchies became more dependent than previously on their own resources. But by virtue of the land accumulation policy and internal distribution system, the families of the Tarma oligarchy were able to achieve a relatively high level of self-sufficiency in the necessities of life.

Despite this down-turn in the money economy in the early nineteenth century, property owners could not dispense with cash altogether. Some earned a little money by selling wool to the export market, meat to the mining settlements and a few tropical products (especially brown sugar cake, or *chancaca*, and coffee) to sierran towns. But by far the most important source of cash was the family silver mines. Each family owned at least one mining property in the district of Yauli or in Cerro de Pasco, the adjacent province to the north. The mines were all located in high, bleak, inhospitable zones at a distance from the major labour reserves and areas of productive agriculture. To engage in silver production even on a relatively small scale, miners needed to find labour, food supplies and a wide range of inputs. Given the smelting technology employed at the time (described, for example, in Herndon 1853), virtually all the requirements, with the exception of mercury, could be furnished by Tarma province.

Property records suggest that, in the colonial period, the need to service silver enterprises had frequently acted as a powerful incentive leading to the accumulation of complementary properties; that is, properties located in more favourable environments to supply labour, food and inputs. By the mid nineteenth century, complementary properties that supported the mining activity had been inherited by different branches of the kin-group. And the circulation system in which goods were transferred between members could also be used to channel labour and goods to the family member who managed the silver enterprise. Though mine-owning members of regional oligarchies, such as Tarma, probably had less access to loans for investment than immigrant rivals based in Lima (who had been accumulating mining properties in the central sierra since the 1840s), they did possess the crucial advantage of access to privileged sources of labour and goods from estates owned by kinsmen. For them, mining was a more or less seasonal activity drawing upon labour during the Andean agricultural slack season. Clearly, the local mine-owners also employed labour directly from the peasant sector and bought in additional goods. But it is impossible to determine from the records what proportion of the labour and goods used in mining came from family property compared with external sources, or the manner in which family members were reimbursed for the supplies. In the type of family economy being described, it would have been very difficult to pin fixed monetary values on labour or goods from haciendas, because value could not be expressed in monetary terms. However, there is little doubt that owners of mines were obliged to offer some cash return after the silver had been sold to those family members who had made the enterprise viable.

The conclusion that emerges is that by the mid nineteenth century the Tarma estate economy was characterized by a two-fold division. The majority of the property-owners were rentiers but a few can be appropriately defined as entrepreneurs. There was a corresponding division between properties: haciendas producing small surpluses of goods under a system of rent in labour and in kind, and other properties, especially silver mines, whose main function was to earn cash. Labour relations on these latter enterprises tended to be more complex. There were some tied workers and their families, but in addition a significant number of male labourers were recruited among the peasantry and employed on short contracts.

At a superficial glance the two sectors might look as though they belonged to quite different types of socio-economic system: a pre-capitalist subsistence economy and a capitalist commodity-producing one. But as I have attempted to demonstrate, such a distinction would be totally misleading, for it both ignores the intricate linkages binding one sector to the other, and also implies that commodity production was a recent development reflecting the changing trading relations of Peru in the nineteenth century. On the contrary, the evidence suggests that such a division had characterized the Andean economy over a much longer period and that its origins lay far back in colonial times. There had always been tensions between the two parts of the system and these generated its dynamic. However, once external conditions began to alter dramatically after Independence, with Peru's incorporation into the capitalist world, the division could lead to debilitating discord and, in the end, to intense contradictions.

In nineteenth-century Tarma the division was discernible at the level of each extended family group and gave rise to further ambiguities in the class's ideology concerning property. Given that silver mining was the principal source of cash for the oligarchic families, they had gradually come to consider mining enterprises as a collective resource providing sufficient cash with which to buy the relatively limited range of luxury goods available from outside the Tarma region. The fundamental question that arose with regard to ideology was whether the silver mine was considered to belong to the family group as a whole or to the individual member whose name appeared in the title as its legal owner. While the family group looked to the revenue as a means of buying consumer goods, the mine-owner felt a growing need to allocate a larger proportion of the cash earned to investment, especially at a time when the mining economy of the central sierra, in general, was beginning to recover. In this situation of conflicting claims, who in the last resort could take the decision on the distribution of cash between the immediate needs of consumption and the longer term need to increase investment as a way of expanding future output? The interests of the family had diverged from the interests of the member who owned and managed the mining property.

3. The dramatic rise in demand for alcohol

During the early republic the two most important goods sold for cash throughout the sierra were alcohol and coca. The consumption pattern of both these goods had a long and complicated history and by the mid-nineteenth century demand came from two main sources. They were acquired by the elite of property-owners, priests and urban authorities primarily for distribution to Indians in lieu of payment and they were also bought directly by the peasantry. In the latter case, the effective level of demand obviously depended upon access to money, with the result that consumption had become closely linked with the prosperity of the mining sector. The recovery of mining was responsible for the growth of wage employment in the mines and also generated employment in the related activities of transport and petty trading. Given the relatively limited usefulness of cash in the regional economy of the 1850s and 1860s, much of the cash paid out was spent on alcohol.

Two types of alcohol were sold in the central sierra: *chicha* made from maize, brewed by the peasantry of the temperate valley zone and aguardiente distilled from cane on large estates in the provinces of Pisco and Ica on the Peruvian coast. The production of chicha could not keep pace with the rapid increase in demand, for this maize land was primarily needed for producing food and fodder crops which also supplied the expanding mining economy. By the time that W.L. Herndon, a traveller from the United States, recorded his observations in 1851, aguardiente from the coast had become far more important than chicha. Herndon was dismayed by the amount of drunkenness he witnessed on his travels. Even the smallest Andean settlement contained a 'grog' shop – the only retail establishment in existence – and he noted that 'drinking seems a very general vice amongst the inhabitants of these wet, cold and highly elevated plains'.

Not long after Herndon's visit the supply of alcohol from coastal estates began to fall seriously short of sierra demand. In 1855 a *botija* of aguardiente had cost 12 pesos, but by 1869 the same quantity was being sold for 16 pesos (V. Peloso 1976 – personal communication). In the light of later inflation rates this increase looks very modest, but it worried the government sufficiently for reports to be issued lamenting the situation. Various reasons can be adduced to account for the increase in the price of alcohol. Demand in the central sierra was clearly rising fast, but it can be suggested that at the same time there was a fall in the volume of aguardiente available for sale to the sierra. With the incorporation of the Peruvian coastal economy into the international trading system, the estates of this region increased their output of export goods, cotton and sugar. Expansion of exports was particularly marked during the 1860s when the world price for cotton rose sharply, due to the American Civil War which cut exports of cotton from the plantations of the south. In response, estate-owners on the Peruvian coast substituted cotton for sugar cane and vines (both of which could be used as the basis for aguardiente).

For the province of Tarma, events on the coast set in motion a process of regional import substitution. The recolonization of the montaña had reached a sufficiently advanced stage for there to be a rapid increase in the production of alcohol. Since 1847 owners of montaña land grants had experimented with a wide range of tropical crops and they had already discovered that sugar cane flourished exceedingly well on the raised terraces bordering the main rivers. They had also made some initial investment in primitive processing equipment to transform the sugar cane first into chancaca and later into aguardiente. By 1855, when Antonio Raimondi, the Italian naturalist, visited the San Ramón zone, the bulk of the cane harvested was being distilled into alcohol.

4. The aguardiente bonanza and the response of tarmeño owners

The exploitation of Tarma's montaña colony had depended very largely on resources brought down from sierra properties. Though settlers had made an effort to capture the Amazon tribesmen for use as slaves, it had proved impossible to instil a work discipline or prevent them from escaping back into the bush. Workers had to be found, therefore, in the highlands, to undertake the arduous tasks of clearing the dense tropical vegetation and planting crops. From the early days, tarmeño owners of montaña property organized colonization and production along very similar lines to their kinsmen who owned mining enterprises. Both these zones of commercial production were geographically and environmentally marginal and both therefore relied on the labour and goods from the temperate heartland. Thus, until the 1870s, Tarma owners who could look to their kinsmen to help provide resources were more successful than other landowners (mostly men who had first come to the region as soldiers to man the San Ramón fort). Dependence on the sierra for food tended to continue over time, for the estate could then aim to produce the maximum volume of aguardiente by devoting all of the cleared cultivable land and all the scarce labour reserves to its production. Notarial archives reveal that formal, legally binding agreements were sometimes arranged among family members to send labour from the sierra properties to the montaña estates. Furthermore, tarmeño owners in the montaña could expect kinsmen resident in Tarma town to provide another source of servile labour. Municipal records of the 1860s contain several revealing references to a resurgence of colonial systems of forced labour in which the urban authorities compelled Indians to work in the montaña.

Tarmeño aguardiente producers needed access to capital for investment: labour and goods were not sufficient to establish an aguardiente enterprise. In the early years alcohol could be produced through the use of relatively inexpensive equipment. Cane was crushed in wooden presses constructed on the spot from local wood, powered at first by oxen and later by waterwheels. The juice was then boiled in metal vats purchased outside the region, but the fuel – crushed cane – was a by-product of the estate. An *alambique*, or still, was needed to distil the alcohol, and this item probably represented the largest cash outlay. Aguardiente was then stored in large locally-made wooden casks and transported in goatskins from the sierra to its destination. Notarial archives suggest that tarmeño settlers borrowed the necessary capital from family members, especially from foreigners co-opted through marriage. These financial arrangements were recorded only rarely when disputes arose later over repayment, and then usually only when non-family members were involved. The evidence does allow the tentative conclusion to be drawn that tarmeños were able to enter aguardiente production by drawing not only on family labour and goods but also on the cash savings of certain members.

By the early 1870s, some 120 000 *arrobas* of 25 pounds each of aguardiente was exported to the sierra from the San Ramón estates. According to figures prepared by the Tarma provincial council, out of this total some 60 000 arrobas was being sent to the Mantaro valley, 40 000 to the villages of the Tarma sierra and 20 000 to the mining camps of Cerro de Pasco and Huarochirí. Once cash returns started flowing into the hands of tarmeño producers, they could contemplate investing a larger share of the proceeds in more productive equipment and also use cash to recruit larger and more secure supplies of labour. In sum, they could hope to take the necessary steps to transform their estates into plantations.

The statements made in the last paragraph were phrased with care, for it is over the consolidation of the estates into plantations that tarmeño aguardiente producers confronted a deep dilemma. At the same time that the entrepreneur needed to allocate a larger amount of cash to investment, kinsmen in the sierra felt a growing need for cash to spend on consumption. The crisis within the family hinged on who could take the decisions on the distribution between investment and consumption, and this was intricately linked both with the power structure within the family and with the attitudes of family members towards rights to property. The crisis was exacerbated by two direct repercussions of the aguardiente bonanza and also by the operation of a third factor that arose independently as a result of long-term structural changes taking place in the Tarma economy.

The first repercussion of the bonanza was a commercial transformation of Tarma town. The pattern of response had been set in Lima in the 1840s when imported goods flooded the capital to capture incomes earned by the export of guano (Bonilla 1974), and later in Cerro de Pasco during the 1850s when high revenues from mining brought the first major influx of foreign merchants and artisans to the central sierra after Independence (Gerstäcker, 1862). In Tarma, a host of foreign and Peruvian traders with merchandise imported from Europe and artisans with a much wider range of skills than had been available previously arrived in the province. The goods could only be purchased with cash. By the early 1870s, a number of emporia had been opened in Tarma town stocked with luxury articles: wines and spirits, tobacco, clothes and shoes, china and glass, furniture including billiard tables and grand pianos. All of these goods had been manhandled over the high Andean passes, for the Central Railway was only completed as far as Chicla, on the Lima side of the cordillera, in 1875. Once this process of commercialization was underway, the families of the Tarma oligarchy came to associate status in urban society with the rapid adoption of European life styles.

The second direct repercussion of the aguardiente bonanza was the arrival of large numbers of immigrant adventurers who had been wandering through the sierra in search of profitable investments. News of the fortunes to be made by alcohol production travelled fast and attracted the attention of many would-be pioneers. Because the montaña was a frontier zone, involvement of 'outsiders' in the aguardiente sector was relatively easy. No longer were immigrants forced to follow the example of their predecessors and marry daughters of the Tarma oligarchy in order to get land; instead, they could now apply to the government for titles to this 'vacant' state-owned land.

Though the independent immigrants settling in the Tarma montaña in the 1870s had no access to properties in the adjacent sierra to furnish labour or goods, they could possess other advantages. Most brought some capital with them and a few, labour. For example, former contractors employed in the construction of the Central Railway brought squads of workers with them down to the montaña, and immigrants from the coast brought some Chinese coolies. In general the prospects for immigrant entrepreneurs were improving over time as the Tarma peasant economy came to respond to the opportunities of servicing the needs of the montaña. Prominent peasants who held command over land, men and mules could act as crucial intermediaries, recruiting labour as *enganchadores*, transporting supplies of food and distributing the aguardiente to very great numbers of small consumption points. Immigrant entrepreneurs appear to have faced fewer social barriers in establishing alliances with members of the peasantry than the Tarma oligarchy did.

Once an immigrant aguardiente producer had overcome initial difficulties and had begun to establish a wide network of alliances with peasant agents, he was able to invest in his property. By the mid 1870s, some immigrant owners had imported small steam engines to power the cane crushers and therefore could dispense with water-wheels and riverside sites. A few had improved the internal transport system of their estates by installing small railways or aerial ropeways to take cane cut on lower fields up to a central mill. The reports of observant travellers, such as Giordano (1875) and Valle (1876), reveal that investment had reached a high level even before the outbreak of the War of the Pacific in 1879 despite the isolation of the Tarma montaña. The geographical marginality of the area had not appreciably held up the rate of technical advance.

The third factor affecting relations within oligarchic families was a diminution in the stock of available estates that members could acquire. During the first half of the century, after the flight of many colonial land-owners, the Tarma oligarchy had been slowly expanding its domain and zone of influence outwards towards the margins of the province. But regional oligarchies from the surrounding towns of Jauja to the south, Lima to the west and Huánuco to the north had been following a similar strategy, with the result that continued outward expansion became more difficult. In addition, immigrant entrepreneurs resident in Lima had gained control over mines and certain livestock haciendas, especially those of Marcapo-macocha. Further expansion into the montaña was halted by the growing numbers of immigrant aguardiente producers and, after 1873, by a govern-ment-sponsored Italian colony of smallholders. The growing stability of estate ownership and lack of opportunities to acquire new properties served to compound the pressures exerted by members of oligarchic families for access to revenues from the montaña estates.

Tarma families could press home monetary demands upon kinsmen in the montaña in two ways. Within a family, they could demand repayment of previous loans and higher payments for labour, food and other inputs sent down to the montaña from sierra property. Tensions already latent within the extended family group over the definition of rights to property and the organization of the internal circulation system could reach breaking point. But the evidence suggests that the conflict of interests came to a head in broader arena: the provincial council. One of the Tarma council's first actions after the political decentralization of 1873 was to levy a high tax on aguardiente as it left the montaña. Tarma collected revenue on behalf of all the districts of the province and also for the adjacent province of Jauja where consumption was highest, despite the Jauja council's complaint that this was illegal. Some of the resulting revenue was spent on grandiose public works but at least a proportion of the income was shared out among the office-holders.

The imposition of this tax sparked off an extremely hostile response in the montaña. Suddenly pressures building up within oligarchic families found an outlet and tarmeño producers became the ringleaders of a violent revolt against the provincial council. Regardless of origin and, in the case of the tarmeños, regardless of the factions into which the oligarchy had been divided in the sierra, estate-owners recognized that they shared a common identity as Amazon pioneers and that their interests were opposed to those of sierra property-owners represented by the provincial council. The aguardiente producers refused to pay the tax and mounted a campaign in Lima arguing that the Tarma provincial council had no right to impose such taxes on a commodity. The conflict over the incidence of taxation arose not simply on account of a divergence of interests, but also because it represented a clash between two opposing ideologies. Up to this date, virtually all local taxes were levied on consumption and trade and had acted as a deterrent to the development of commodity production and exchange. Now the aguardiente producers were demanding freedom from taxation on the grounds that an 'infant industry' needed to be stimulated. If a tax were collected at all, then the revenue should benefit the producers not the consumers.

The struggle between aguardiente producers and the provincial council continued for several years with each side trying to convince the Pardo government of the legitimacy of its position, and the government vacillating between the two groups. Finally, on the eve of the War of the Pacific, a decree was issued awarding the tax revenues to the producers on condition that the money be spent on improving the track between the sierra and montaña. This was a resounding victory for the producers which deeply shocked the Tarma council. The oligarchy had assumed that since Tarma was the provincial capital and held a higher rank in the administrative hierarchy than the montaña, a mere district, they would ultimately win government approval. Members of the oligarchy had been accustomed to having the ear of the president and holding powerful posts in Lima; government support of the rebels in the montaña was totally incomprehensible. What the oligarchy had failed to realize was that the nature of the Peruvian state had been undergoing a transition. New and powerful political groups were emerging – producers of export goods, merchants and a growing number of mining and industrial entrepreneurs. The arguments put forward by aguardiente producers, who were developing Peru by opening up the Amazon jungle, appealed far more to these groups than the arrogant stance taken by a reactionary provincial council.

Immediately after the montaña's victory the country was immersed in war. Chilean forces occupied the Tarma sierra from 1881 to 1883 and caused considerable destruction. But while immigrants, as neutrals, were free to proceed unmolested, Peruvian nationals were obliged to fight and pay large cash sums to both Chilean and Peruvian armies. After the war, the evidence on montaña property-ownership and transfers in the 1890s suggests that the level of tarmeño participation had diminished markedly. Not only were 'outsiders' now more numerous, but most Tarma families had sold their aguardiente estates. During the 1860s and 1870s each of the nine families of the oligarchy had owned at least one montaña property, but by the end of the century only two families survived as producers and even they now owned fewer estates there.

The loss of the montaña estates by tarmeños can be discussed at two levels. Certain generalizations can be made as to why individual families parted with their property but it is also important to explore, at a deeper level, the more fundamental reasons for the increasing vulnerability of the oligarchy as a social class, which made members less able to overcome setbacks in family fortunes. One conclusion to emerge from an examination of the land transfers is that only very rarely do tarmeños appear to have been willing vendors. In general, if they did sell, it was because they were forced to do so in order to repay loans borrowed from non-family members on the security of the property. The estate was forcibly put up for public auction, then purchased by an immigrant. A variety of financial pressures occasioned the sales: legal disputes with rival families or with other branches of the same family that ended unfavourably for the montaña member; the need to meet large unexpected demands for money; or simply a long slow slide into debt. Yet in the aguardiente economy of the period when all producers were endeavouring to invest, immigrants as well as tarmeños contracted sizeable debts. However, the evidence makes plain that tarmeños were far more liable to lose their property than immigrants because the money-lenders tended to foreclose more readily on them. The reason for this bias is not hard to discover. By the 1890s, Italian merchants based in Tarma town, who had come to dominate the trade in imported luxury goods, had also taken on the role of chief money-lenders in the regional economy. After the War of the Pacific these merchants became increasingly involved in the aguardiente sector, but only in an indirect manner. They entered into informal partnerships with other immigrants (usually also Italians) whom they financed and supported and for whom they procured property on which a certain level of investment had already taken place.

The second conclusion that can be drawn from the land transfer evidence is that the majority of the estates were lost by tarmeños after the death of the original owner when a woman (usually the widow) had inherited the bulk of the property. Two factors can be put forward to explain why tarmeño women were more vulnerable than men in the face of financial pressure. First, there is no doubt that money-lenders pressed widows extremely hard for repayment of debts incurred throughout the lifetime of their husbands. There was usually insufficient cash left in the wills to meet the repayment and widows were forced to sell family assets. The second factor is a corollary of a comment made above on the position of women as property-owners. Women from oligarchic families were not expected to play an active part in the administration of their property. In this respect their social role differed significantly from that of women of the peasant sector, who commonly took control over property especially when men in their family worked in the mines or as transporters and traders, or of women from the developing immigrant society in the montaña, several of whom became highly successful managers of large properties.

Property and ideology

The women of the Tarma oligarchy had been socialized into believing that they could not manage an estate. If they found themselves in charge through accident of inheritance, they avoided the responsibility by seeking the help of male relatives, or by renting it out or selling it, on the grounds that as poor helpless women they had no alternative. Neither male relatives (because of their other commitments) not tenants were reliable managers of a widow's property. The widening sexual division in decision-making over property and therefore in rights to that property had suited oligarchic families in one respect: families had been able to expand in size and thus preserve and expand their control over sets of complementary estate properties through the marriage strategy adopted. But at the same time the policy carried with it serious disadvantages for the family group once it began to specialize in commodity production. Participation in the aguardiente sector in the long run demanded that provision be made for continuity in estate management, if a property was not to be lost to rival entrepreneurs. But through the inheritance practices adopted and by socializing women to see themselves as uninvolved in the management of property, oligarchic families had tended to increase their vulnerability at specific moments of their life-cycles.

The fundamental reasons why the Tarma oligarchy became increasingly vulnerable were intimately connected with its ideology of property. The way of thinking had developed under socio-economic conditions prevailing in the colony and in the early years of the republic. In the final analysis property was seen to belong to the family groups, with two results. First, decision-making at the level of the congeries of properties owned by a family depended on the distribution of power within the family group; and second, the system worked because of the indeterminacy and ambiguity surrounding the specific rights held by individual members to the property and its product.

To respond fully to the opportunities presented by the aguardiente bonanza, the members of the Tarma oligarchy, intent on becoming entrepreneurs, needed to change the prevailing ideology of their class of origin. It became necessary for land to be seen as *private* property; a commodity belonging solely to the legal owner named in the property title. Thus, the crucial prerequisite for the transformation of a property-owning oligarchy into a class of capitalist entrepreneurs was that property should be recognized not as a common or collective resource, but as a resource in which rights were owned by an individual. In reality, little change in ideology was possible; a conclusion that would have come as no surprise to the tarmeño aguardiente producers. They were painfully aware of the obstacles they faced in trying to change their kinsmen's perception of property. The power structure within the family group precluded any easy transition to a different ideology, for inevitably this would have had the effect of altering the distribution of that power. Therefore, although at the beginning of the aguardiente boom tarmeño producers had been able to respond to the opportunities opened up by the sudden increase in the demand for alcohol, they had been unable to sustain their position in the longer run. For it proved impossible to escape from the pressures exerted by the family group and therefore impossible to compete against the powerful combination of immigrants and money-lenders.

Sources

The evidence on which this article is based was collected in Tarma province during two periods of field work using archival sources and also family histories to build up a picture of past and present attitudes to property held by landowners. The most important archives consulted were the municipal records of Tarma, containing the correspondence of the Tarma mayors and the *Actas* (Minutes) of the provincial council from the 1860s, electoral registers and tax lists; the Departmental Property Register from which material on some 97 Tarma estates was found; notarial archives of the nineteenth century; local newspapers published sporadically from the 1870s and annual reports submitted to Lima by the prefect of Junín or sub-prefect of Tarma.

I have drawn on the following nineteenth-century published sources: Gerstäcker (1862), Giordano (1875), Herndon (1853), Ministerio de Gobierno, Perú (1878), Raimondi (1855) and Valle (1876). For more recent published sources, see References.

8

Multi-levelled Andean society and market exchange: the case of Yucay (Peru)

ANTOINETTE FIORAVANTI-MOLINIÉ

1. Introduction

In seeking to define the specific characteristics of Andean society and economy J.V. Murra has developed the concept of a system of vertical production (Murra 1972a). In this region the desert coasts, interrupted occasionally by oases, contrast strikingly with the *quechua* region and its fertile valleys (at 3000–3500 metres), with the high plateaux and their *puna* vegetation (above 4000 metres), and with the subtropical forest of the Amazonian side of the mountains.

Murra shows how a nucleus of settlement controlled resources on several 'floors' or 'niches' through the establishment of colonies at varying distances. Settlers in peripheral colonies kept their houses and all their rights in their communities of origin. The colonies could be shared with other ethnic groups from other nuclei who were establishing outposts on the same pattern.

In his analysis of this vertical economic system, Murra draws on numerous examples taken for the most part from a detailed analysis of the *visitas*, inquiries carried out on the spot by the Spanish colonial administration whose wealth of information is revealed by Murra's work. Thus the central nucleus of the 'archipelago' of Chupaychu people in the region of Huánuco was about one day's walk away from both corn fields situated at a lower altitude and potato fields higher up. Above the centre of Chaupiwaranqa, the salt mines of Yanacachi and the pasture lands of Chinchaycocha (4000 metres), were groups coming from other nuclear settlements. Lower down, at various altitudes, the Chupaychu could grow – starting from the top – cotton, coca, and forest products such as wood and honey. Here again members of different ethnic groups are found together in the same cultivated areas. These areas are never further than four days' walk away from the centre and every settler kept his house and his right to land in Chaupiwaranqa (Murra 1972a).

This network of islands situated in a variety of environments thus constituted a 'vertical archipelago'. The general model outlined here could sometimes vary, depending in particular on the distance between nuclear and peripheral settlements: for example, outlying settlers might engage in specialized production, and might themselves live in villages, transforming the ties of reciprocity with their community of origin into ties of dependence. Murra suggests that the institution of the *mitmaq* during the Inca empire can be explained by the transposition of this local geographical model to a structural model at the level of the state: the vertical archipelago is replaced by another archipelago, independent of ecological factors, yet bearing certain features in common with the 'vertical archipelago'.

One may ask to what extent contemporary Andean societies still control multiple ecological floors. To quote Murra again: 'the functions of the vertical islands in the archipelago and the status of settlers have undergone political, economic and social changes which deserve detailed study' (*ibid.* and Molinié 1980).

There is no description in contemporary anthropological studies of societies formed of a nuclear settlement and permanent outlying colonies in continuous relationship with each other. Nevertheless, since the appearance of Murra's work, anthropologists working in the Andes have looked for contemporary manifestations of an 'ideal of vertical control'. We can group such manifestations under two headings; some societies control production on different floors through possession of a territory which covers them all. Tristan Platt shows how Macha society (Northern Potosí, Bolivia) is divided into two moieties (upper and lower) each with a share in the upper and lower floor, thus forming a four-part structure (Platt 1978c; see also this volume). Stephen Webster shows how the Qeros of Cuzco possess a vast archipelago of lands stretching from the high llama and vicuña pastures at 4500 metres to the tropics at 1500 metres. Temporary shelters are dispersed throughout these different floors (Webster 1971). Other societies, in contrast, exercise vertical control through a network of exchanges of a type not accounted for in Murra's model. Carlos Fonseca describes the particularly interesting case of the contemporary inhabitants of the Chupachu region studied by Murra in the visita referred to above (Fonseca 1972). We find numerous further examples of exchange in the papers edited by Alberti and Mayer (1974).

Without trying to find 'survivals' of Murra's model, we can therefore look in contemporary Andean society for manifestations of an 'Andean ideal' of self-sufficiency based on the various forms of control of multiple ecological floors, and in particular for changes in the traditional system brought about by the market economy. We shall do this in a study of the valley of Yucay, as it was before the application of the 1968 Land Reform Law. Unlike the other societies where research has been done on the vertical system, society in the valley is highly integrated with the money economy,

212

exhibits marked differences of wealth between social categories, and shows very little concern for traditional Andean belief systems. Nevertheless the society has devised a subtle strategy to achieve the 'vertical ideal', which combines the two patterns we have distinguished: direct control of land on levels other than that of the valley itself, and the continuous practice of exchange, in particular in the form of barter.

2. A vertical environment: the islands of the archipelago

From the Sacred Valley of Yucay, some 50 kilometres north of Cuzco, one can see the three typical landscapes of the quechua region: the river Urubamba runs at a height of 2850 metres through green fields, between the high snow-capped mountains of the north and the dry plateau of Maras–Chinchero to the south. At this point the Urubamba is called Vilcanota; rising in the Raya range of mountains on the borders of the Peruvian and Bolivian altiplano, it flows through Yucay and down to the canyon of Machu-Picchu on the semi-tropical floor of the *ceja de montaña*, merging with the Apurimac river in the Amazonian forest, where its name changes again to Ucayali.

The Sacred Valley

Some six hundred metres deep, and on average one kilometre wide, the valley has a notably symmetrical profile. The village of Yucay stands on a lateral river which flows down from the northern range into the valley. The surrounding cultivated area with its luxuriant vegetation is spread over magnificent terraces constructed under the Inca empire. The soil, composed essentially of alluvial matter, is fertile. On account of its latitude (13° south) Yucay has a high-altitude tropical climate; the year is divided between a rainy season which goes from October to March and a dry, colder, season from April to September. On account of the altitude there are wide variations in temperature between day and night (24° during July). But the shelter provided by the eastern cordillera makes the valley climate drier and less harsh than that of the higher valleys, such as those of Cuzco (3390 metres) and the even higher puna grasslands. Thanks to its benign climate, and to the good quality of its land, the valley produces corn, cabbages, beans, barley, and even quite exceptional products for the region, such as white corn and early vegetables and fruit, especially strawberries.

The cordillera: Las Alturas

The eastern cordillera rises above the Sacred Valley to the perpetual snows of Illahuaman. It comprises glaciers dating from the Pleistocene period, amphitheatres, striped and polished rocks and high trough-like valleys with streams running down their sides into trough-like bottoms. On this side, the land is difficult to cultivate because it lies on such a steep incline and also because of night frosts and a lack of irrigation water. In the path of the Amacpunco stream which flows down to Yucay one can harvest a few potatoes, usually made into *chuño* or *moraya* (dehydrated potatoes). Some herds of llamas and alpacas wander on the *ichu* pasture.

The plateau of Maras–Chinchero

There is a strong contrast between these escarpments and snow-capped peaks and the opposing, and highly eroded, side of the Maras–Chinchero plateau (3500 metres). The road to Cuzco skirts some reddish hills, crosses the dry flat fields of the village of Maras and then goes round the lakes which have formed in the hollows. These chalky rocks are less resistant to erosion than the northern side, which explains the difference between them. The difference of altitude and morphology is also reflected in the vegetation. The plateau is very dry, with a subtropical bush, in which one finds mostly *magüey*, small acacias (*molles*) and cactus. Like the north side, this plateau has no trees, and the Yucay valley has a distinctly merry appearance in contrast. Although some good red clay soils found here are suitable for cereal cultivation (wheat and barley above all) and potatoes, these crops are cruelly hampered by the lack of water in the dry season.

The subtropical valleys of La Convención and Lares: the ceja de montaña

Below Yucay and Machu-Picchu the Urubamba river flows on down through the ceja de montaña. This subtropical region is of great economic importance for the inhabitants of the Sacred valley. It is characterized by two zones of different altitude which occur between 500 and 4000 metres: the ceja de montaña has a medium temperature, whereas the *selva* lower down is very hot and rainy. Slopes of 20–80% gradient mark the landscape; the high peaks rise up above narrow ravines and a large portion of the land cannot be cultivated. Nevertheless, some flat surfaces or more gentle slopes are suitable for agriculture on the valley bottom. The main products of the area are tea, coffee, coca, cocoa and tropical fruit. La Convención has become a rich and dynamic area essentially because of these industrial and exportable crops.

3. The economic control of the different levels

At each of these levels human settlement occurs in a different form. We will pay particular attention to the land tenure structure at each level and show how each level's economy complements the others.

Multi-levelled Andean society and market exchange

The nucleus: the valley of Yucay

The valley bottom is cultivated under private property. The great estates, or *haciendas*, contrast with the extreme subdivision of smallholdings, due largely to the unequal distribution of land, and also to the very high population density. The haciendas of family A alone constitute 20.1% of the agricultural land (that is 81.5 hectares) and the archbishopric of Cuzco occupies 5.8%. The peasant lands are extremely fragmented and occupy 61.8% of all cultivated land of the district (that is, 249.7 hectares). This distribution of property, the relations of production which it implies and the cultural oppositions which accompany it are the determinants of a traditional opposition between two social classes: the hacendados and the peasants. In the district as a whole, 430 peasant families own 250 hectares (0.57 hectares per family). The density of population, the intensity of human settlement and the scarcity of arable land, most of which is found on Inca terraces, confer upon the land a unique appearance: the *chacras* (cultivated smallholdings) are dispersed and tiny (average peasant holding: 0.86 hectares, including rented land). Generally, apart from working his own parcel, a peasant leases another piece on a money rent or share-cropping basis; but he does not necessarily choose a piece close to his own holding – rather the contrary. The distribution of the component parts of peasant holdings can be explained in two ways.

In the first place, kinship is of great importance in the formation and distribution of holdings in the area. Some families, together with their clientele, control veritable territories, sometimes assembling their properties and the land they rent in on the same terrace. For example, several members of family B, all of whom live separately in nuclear groups (except certain young couples in the early years of marriage, who are still living with the husband's parents), have adjacent parcels on one of the terraces. Perhaps these family territories are in some sense a reproduction of land once assigned to *ayllus*. Indeed, the ayllu was always associated with a particular family name and within one ayllu there were only a small number of names; this can be seen from the registers of the parish of Yucay, where still in the last century the names of parishioners were recorded along with their ayllu. Furthermore, the members of the family whose holdings are thus concentrated usually live close to one another, or at least in the same moiety (*urayparte* or *wichayparte* – the upper or lower part); and at the beginning of this century, members of one ayllu still lived together in the same quarter within these two moieties. Further research will be necessary to discover the location of land belonging to the former ayllus.

A second explanation has to do with the tendency for families to occupy several plots on different lands suitable for a variety of crops; thus, a family's holding will tend to be dispersed in several places. It is impossible to grow

215

strawberries anywhere but on a terrace; and it is difficult to harvest anything but corn on the heavy, wet riverside land. If a peasant has two *topos* on one terrace, he will probably rent out one topo to his natural or spiritual kinsman, and will in his turn rent in another piece of land from that kinsman in a position some distance from his own parcel. Place names indicate that ever since the sixteenth century, and probably earlier, particular terraces were devoted to particular crops, for example, *sacsapata* and *misk'ampampa* (*sacsa* and *misk'a* are two varieties of corn); these names can be found in sixteenth century documents (Villanueva 1970). Thus the distribution of plots seems to be determined by two factors: on the one hand, the physical concentration of plots belonging to members of the same family appears to be related, in some measure, to the institution of the extended family; on the other hand, the extreme fragmentation of holdings shows that peasants seek to diversify at the same time their crops and their risks by gaining control of plots on different types of land. Combination of these two factors leads to the appearance of 'family domains' where a family assembles lands of differing quality at different altitudes. The principle of spreading risks and growing a diversified range of crops, which lies at the root of vertical control, thus also seems to shape the pattern of valley-bottom cultivation: by indirect operation of the land and relations of reciprocity peasant families build up archipelagoes of 'islands' spread through many fields.

Above Yucay: the community of San Juan

The infertile land of the slopes which overlook the Sacred Valley is utterly different from the lands of Yucay. It is owned by the community of Yucay (the *yucavinos*) and the 40 families of the hamlet of San Juan. Every member of the community has a very low-yielding potato plot. The requisite communal rotation is such that each member of the community returns to his own plot every nine years. In principle there ought to be a periodic redistribution of land, taking into account the needs of each family; in fact this theoretical possession of the rotating parcel is the equivalent of property because every member always returns to the same parcel and, although it cannot be sold, the parcel is passed on from one generation to the next. Thus the community members of San Juan have access only to pasture lands on which they breed a few alpacas and to a few potato plots, whereas the yucavinos also own land in the valley. This economic differentiation implies an unequal relationship, as peasants from higher up come down to work for valley peasants for a very low wage. Of course they also exchange services, but the San Juaninos do not always receive a counterpart for the services they offer, and one cannot therefore really speak of ties of reciprocity.

One might think that the inhabitants of San Juan formed an ayllu like the inhabitants of the different quarters of Yucay, having lost their valley lands at the time of the distribution of ayllu land in private holdings. But there is no trace of this ayllu either in local archives or in oral accounts. It certainly did not exist in the last century, so that the inequality between the peasants from above and those from below appears to date from a much earlier period. Probably the inhabitants of San Juan originally came from the Sacred Valley, and in particular from Yucay. Some of their family names are to be found among the valley peasants. Furthermore, according to the San Juan myth of origin, the story of the patron saint of the hamlet, San Juan Sahagún, was told by an elder of Yucay called Killawaman, later transformed into a mountain (one of the peaks overlooking the valley is, in fact, called Killawaman). One could compare this differentiation with the process described by Murra (1964) for the Lupaqa people, for shepherds and, more generally, for the *mitmaq*. Some members of these communities were responsible for overseeing production at a higher or lower level, where they were sent to live. These colonists, or mitmaq, retained rights in their community of origin, in particular their rights to land. They lived together with colonists from other communities. But gradually, since their pastures and their potato fields were so far away, they lost touch with their ayllu; they lost their rights to the fertile valley lands and the ties of reciprocity which bound them to the nuclear settlement were eroded. We may, therefore, hypothesize that peasants from Yucay, like the mitmaq described by John Murra, were traditionally responsible for the community flocks, and for the cultivation of potatoes. In their case as well, ties of reciprocity with the valley community were broken. Further research is necessary before one can be absolutely certain that the process which has occurred here is the same as that described by Murra. Whatever the history of the matter, it is clear that the economic differentiation has been brought about by the market economy on the basis of a pre-existent inequality which arose independently of market forces.

The sub-tropical valleys of La Convención and Lares

The vertical archipelago continues down to the coffee, cocoa, coca and tea plantations of the ceja de montaña region, with which Yucay is linked by the Cuzco–Quillabamba road. Before the seizure of estates by the peasants in 1964, the valleys were dominated by enormous haciendas. Originally granted by the Spanish Crown to military and civilian officials, these lands were only much later brought into cultivation, and today coffee is an extremely profitable crop. The indigenous Machiguenga people had long since been driven out into the jungle and until the Agrarian Reform of 1964 the hacendado would rent out a plot to peasants from the sierra in exchange for a labour rent performed on the land he directly cultivated. In his turn, this peasant, or *arrendire*, could also rent out a part of his tenancy to a sub-arrendire, or *allegado,* who fulfilled the arrendire's obligations on the hacendado's land. Ever since the seventeenth century peasants have come down from the sierra (especially from the valley of Yucay and from the plateau of Maras–Chinchero) to work on these haciendas. Indeed, the region has been colonized according to a variant of the vertical model. Before the construction of the railway and later the road from Cuzco to Quillabamba, the peasants of Yucay used to take their products by mule to be sold in the valley of La Convención. From time to time they would take their animals down to La Convención laden with the products of their own temperate valley (above all corn and bread) and would bring back coca and cotton which they sold in the region of Yucay and in Cuzco, or which they then exchanged again for other products (tubers) from higher levels. Today only the means of transport have changed, while the objects of exchange themselves remain the same; this is one way in which the peasants of the temperate valley can control the production of the subtropical valleys. But there is a second way in which they can obtain access to these products from the lower levels, which bears a much closer resemblance to the processes described by Murra.

Prior to the Agrarian Reform of 1964, many yucavinos would rent in a piece of land in the valley of La Convención. Frequently they would hire an allegado from higher lands in the Yucay region; down at the tropical level the same ties of dependence between the valley and the mountain which we have described between Yucay and San Juan would be reproduced. A surplus would thus circulate from the community member at the puna level (the allegado) to the peasant from the temperate valley (arrendire) and eventually to the landlord of the tropical valley. Thus a dual dependence developed between the higher and the lower levels.

Today, after the Agrarian Reform of 1964, the peasant of the Sacred Valley controls the subtropical level, according to the same model, with three variations:

(1) Usually he rents a plot from a former arrendire of La Convención who has received lands as a result of the Agrarian Reform of 1964, while at the same time retaining his own plot in the valley of Yucay. Since the cropping cycles vary as between the two valleys (the one being tropical, the other temperate), he can harvest in both places in the same year. People go up and down between one region and the other, and when a landowner is absent from Yucay, he entrusts his lands there to a natural or ritual kinsman. In exchange he will return to Yucay from the lower valley, bringing part of his coca and fruit harvest and will also keep an eye out on his kinsmen's behalf for suitable outlets for their corn and fruit from the Sacred Valley.

(2) Some peasants, formerly arrendires of an estate, have subsequently become the owners of the land which they previously rented, as a result of the Agrarian Reform, and most of them have more or less definitively

218

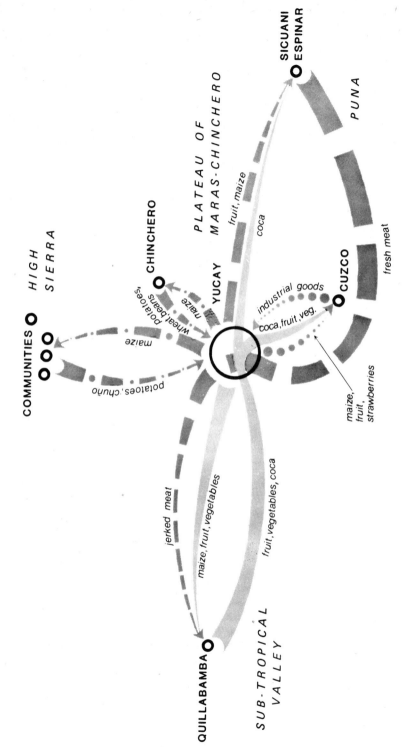

Fig. 8.1. Circuits of exchange based on Yucay

emigrated to La Convención. There they cultivate their parcel themselves, while renting out their plot in Yucay. As a general rule, the smallholder of Yucay will either be a direct cultivator at the upper level and a tenant lower down, or a direct cultivator lower down and a tenant at the upper level. Frequently the head of the family sends his son to the tropical level to take charge of the lands he owns or rents in. Of the 576 children mentioned in a survey of 435 Yucay families, 72 were in the Quillabamba area. Their activities were distributed as follows: 28 farmers, 15 traders, 7 domestic servants, 6 students or schoolchildren, 2 workers, 1 policeman, 5 in diverse trades and 6 without any occupation (according to their parents). This migration between ecological levels would correspond quite closely to Murra's model of colonization.

(3) Finally, a yucavino may frequently go at the time of harvest to work in the valley of La Convención where wages are much higher than in Yucay.

In each of these cases, the cultivators of the subtropical valleys always import labour from a higher level: either from the temperate valley at Yucay, or else from higher regions such as Anta, near the valley of La Convención.

Figure 8.1 sums up these different relations. The same individual may often fall into all three types, since these represent not a unit of cultivation, but a possible type of relationship.

Exchanges between different levels

The peasants of the Sacred valley also have access to the products of higher and lower levels through trade and barter. One must distinguish between traditional subsistence cultivation and commercial cultivation. Subsistence production is stored and consumed, and if there is a surplus it is bartered in small quantities in exchange for products of other ecological levels; these products enable the peasant families to acquire products essential for their diet and which they cannot grow on their own land. Commercial crops are sold in the market after harvest and very rarely consumed; they are grown in order to obtain cash.

For each of these categories the crops differ according to the climatic level. In the temperate valley corn is the traditional subsistence crop, while fruit and vegetables are systematically traded on the market. On the next level up, potatoes play the same role as corn in the valley, and they are exchanged by the peasant women from Maras–Chinchero against products of other levels, while the wool from the flocks of the high plateau is essentially a commercial product. The distinction is not so clear in the case of the subtropical valley of La Convención; here practically all production is traded in the market. However, one can still make a distinction between fruit (avocadoes, papayas, oranges, bananas) and coca, which are sold to the inhabitants of the higher geographical levels of the region and sometimes even exchanged with them, and products such as coffee and tea, which are traded on the market and directly exported to Lima or abroad. The distinction between stored and sold production exists at each level and is all the clearer the less the market economy is developed.

The traditional products of each climatic level are subject to marked variations in the pattern of exchange. The barter of corn from the Sacred Valley against potatoes from the plateau of Maras–Chinchero is the most common instance, taking place at the weekly markets of one or the other level and also at the great annual fairs. Corn is also transported to the sub-tropical valley at the same time as potatoes, against which it has just been exchanged. From this valley coca is brought back and subsequently exchanged in the Yucay region for corn from the Sacred Valley or for products of the higher mountains (potatoes, chuño, beans, quinoa, etc.). The best illustration of the role of these traditional products is found in the pottery trade among inhabitants of the various levels of Yucay. At the great annual regional fairs and, in particular, at the plateau village of Ttiobamba near Maras on 15 August, potters of distant regions such as Tinta and Pucará come to exchange their pottery for traditional products of the region's two levels, corn from the Sacred Valley and tubers from the plateau of Maras–Chinchero. The pottery itself serves as a measure: a container is exchanged for the amount of corn, potatoes or chuño which it can hold. The exact amount is decided partly by the quality of the product, and after prolonged bargaining. The pottery from Tinta consists of vast receptacles 70 cm in height, which are used for making *chicha* (maize beer) and have essential value as a measure: they hold some 18 kilos of corn, that is, one *raki*. The raki of corn obtained in exchange for this article of pottery is poured into a long hand-woven woollen sack which also serves as a measure. The bag contains five raki when full and the height reached by each raki is marked by a line on the bag. Thus the potters have a suitable measure adapted for the products of each ecological level and which is independent of any monetary value: a raki of corn is much more expensive than a raki of potatoes. The value of the pottery is thus not an absolute quantity, but is fixed in relationship to the product of the climatic level where it is sold.

Commercial products are usually sold in Cuzco. Almost the entire production of fruit and vegetables from the valley of Yucay is transported to the town, where it sells well. Strawberries, in particular, are never consumed in Yucay. But an excessively systematic distinction between traditional barter exchange and trade proper would be somewhat artificial. Firstly, both barter and sales for money are often to be observed in the circuit of one single product; thus the peasant women of Yucay gradually dispose of their stock of corn by exchanging it for potatoes from the plateau which they then store and subsequently sell for money in Cuzco or in the subtropical valley. Secondly, there are important regional trading networks which do not go through Cuzco, and which are traditionally conducted quite efficiently by barter. The ancient meat trade between the high plateau regions (Espinar, Canas, Canchis) conducted by the peasants of Yucay is one example. They take their corn to these pasturing areas and bring back fresh llama or alpaca meat. Usually the animals are bought, but they can also be exchanged for corn from the Sacred Valley. The meat is salted and dried in the sun; it is then exported. The trader, aided by a few workers, treats the meat in the courtyard of his house and hires a truck to take it to Quillabamba, the principal town of the subtropical valley of La Convención. For their part, the Indians of the high plateaux bring their llamas down to Yucay laden with chuño, wool and textiles, which, after many weeks of travel, they exchange for corn.

Although today the traditional trading circuits and the commercial circuits coincide, it remains the case that at each level traditional and commercial production represent two different economic systems whose limits are increasingly difficult to define, but which correspond, as far as the peasants are concerned, to two distinct ways of life.

4. Social relationships between the inhabitants of different levels

We have seen how relationships of production and distribution create ties between peasants producing at different ecological levels, and that traditional ties of reciprocity are becoming intertwined with, or are being replaced by, capitalist relationships, such as wage labour.

Reciprocal exchanges of labour appear to operate only between people originating from the same ecological level. Thus a yucavino cultivating a piece of land in the subtropical valley of La Convención is helped on his plot in Yucay by his neighbours and his kin in exchange for the services which he renders to them. In contrast there appear to be no ties of reciprocity, and have not been for some time, between the inhabitants of the Sacred valley (Yucay) and those of the mountains which overlook it (San Juan). Similarly the *ayni* system of mutual exchanges of labour, founded on strict reciprocity, only operates among the inhabitants of one ecological level. This institution requires total equality between the amounts of labour exchanged; help in the potato harvest, for example, is not equivalent to help in the corn harvest. Furthermore, the inequalities separating producers at different ecological levels stand in contradiction with the more or less egalitarian relationship implied by the ayni. In contrast, production relations founded on unequal access to land appear to arise rather between people living at different levels. This does not mean, however, that capitalist relationships are completely absent or even rare among inhabitants of the same ecological level.

The peasants of Yucay do not sell their labour in the estates adjacent to their holdings; their maize must be harvested at the same time as that of the hacendado, and, above all, they despise wage labour, devoid as it is of any element of reciprocity. The labour force on the larger farms of Yucay is seasonal, and is provided by the impoverished inhabitants of the plateau of Maras–Chinchero which overlooks the valley. Here the peasants are usually either *colonos* on enormous haciendas or *comuneros*. Some are colonos in second estates belonging to hacendados from the Sacred Valley up on the plateau. The owner of the Hacienda California of Yucay (250 hectares), which produces corn, also owns the Hacienda Huaypo in Maras (100 hectares) where he grows potatoes. In the same way the owner of the Hacienda Huayoccari, the most beautiful estate in the region, also owns an estate on the plateau of Anta where he raises high grade cattle. Under the Agrarian Reform of 1968 these hacendados were expropriated in the 1970s of all their lands on the plateau – which are now worked by co-operatives – and of part of their lands in the valley. They have therefore encountered serious difficulties in replacing the labour which used to come down regularly from the upper floors, but is now fully employed on the co-operatives. Furthermore, the problems faced by the valley co-operatives in their relations with the plateau floor illustrate the inadequacy of any agrarian transformation which takes no account of the 'vertical ideal'. The Agrarian Reform Law prohibits possession of land in several different places. The old haciendas, made up of islands spread out in the valley and on the plateau, have been dismembered and the separate co-operatives located on different levels, where once there was only one estate, suffer from frequent and often bloody conflicts.

The hacendados, therefore, also have access to the products of different levels. The season of heaviest labour requirements for potatoes and wheat (June and July) is not the same as that for corn in the Sacred Valley (April and May), and these owners can therefore use the colonos from 'above' as wage earners down 'below'; they can even impose this temporary migration on their colonos as a condition for allocating them a plot of land. These temporary wage earners have a very low standard of living and are much less acculturated than the inhabitants of the Sacred Valley. They have few contacts with the yucavinos, who despise their status of wage earners and their *indio* way of life. Thus, each year, 150 workers come down for the harvest to the Hacienda California, and 40 to the Hacienda Vilcanota. They receive board and lodging and are paid 30 soles (less than fifty pence in the 1970s). For their part, as we have seen, the peasants of Yucay prefer to go and work for a wage on the coca, coffee and tea plantations of the valley of La Convención: the dead season in the one place corresponds to the period of intense activity in the other. So the independence of the small-holders of Yucay is only an illusion. If they do not rent out their labour on

Antoinette Fioravanti-Molinié

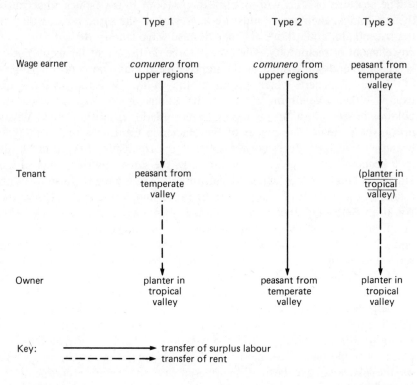

Fig. 8.2. Production relations between inhabitants of different levels in the valley of La Convención

the haciendas, it is not, as one might believe, because they are living in a 'domestic economy'; rather it is because the smallholders in La Convención offer them better wages, as well as the prospect of eventually renting in a piece of land. For their part, the colonos of the plateau of Maras–Chinchero prefer to hire out their labour in the valley of Urubamba, where they can earn money, while the haciendas of their own region offer only access to a plot of land. Thus we observe a pattern of migration from level to level. If we were only to observe relations of production 'horizontally' within each level we would not be able to understand them, for their nature only emerges when we enquire into specific factors of verticality. Here, in the valley of Yucay, the peasant looks for the employer who pays the best wages, and that is not the next-door hacendado. Theoretically, however, he is the hacendado's wage employee. Traditional verticality, once founded upon reciprocity, now carries a distinctive trace of capitalist relations of production, while these are concealed if observation is confined to one single ecological level.

224

Multi-levelled Andean society and market exchange

We shall now try to formalize relations of production between the inhabitants of different ecological levels. In order to do this, we must choose homogeneous criteria for classifying the status of the various producers. We will take elements which define a mode of production, that is, relationships between workers and non-workers, the nature of the surplus, and relations of property (Gutelman 1971). By establishing, with these three criteria, a formula for each status, and by symbolizing with an arrow the relation between them, we can sum up and formalize the production relations analysed above, as figures 8.2 and 8.3 show. Evidently this is only a formalization, which by definition eliminates numerous factors (cultural, religious, etc.) analysed elsewhere. Its object is merely to summarize what has been said. Figure 8.3 has another advantage. It enables us to make comparisons based on precise criteria in time and space. It should be added that many statuses which exist in reality do not appear on the figure, since we have shown only those concerned with vertical relations of control.

These traditional relationships between levels are reinforced by the institutions of *compadrazgo* (co-parenthood). This is not the place to conduct an exhaustive analysis of the phenomenon, but merely to show its place in a multi-levelled economic system. At the time of a child's baptism, or of his first haircut, or of his marriage, the father and the godfather become *compadres* for life. Certain festivals or prayers may give rise to such ties, which are very much sought after, since the social status of an individual is higher the more compadres he has, and above all, the more he is invited by other people to become their compadre. Compadres are obliged to help each other in every possible way and strong social pressures oblige them to do their utmost in this respect. This fundamental relationship commits the entire family, such that the natural kinship system of a community is re-designed by a spiritual kinship relationship. Thus the peasant creates ties of solidarity through his several compadres in a village. But compadres of different levels have different positions with respect to the means of production. Looking for a compadre of a higher status to one's own implies, to some extent, looking for one at a lower geographical level and, indeed, the inhabitants of San Juan have numerous compadres in the Sacred Valley. The compadrazgo relationship obliges them to put themselves at the disposal of these compadres for the harshest work, often providing them with free labour. For their part, the peasants of the Sacred Valley choose their compadres among the powerful personalities of the region, the landlords, and sometimes among the planters of the valley of La Convención. For example, a peasant in Yucay will enable his compadre up in the mountains, who is involved in a court case, to benefit by the power of his other compadre in La Convención. In exchange, the comunero from San Juan will sell his potatoes to the Yucay peasant at an extremely low price while the latter will agree to sell land (which is forbidden by the current Agrarian Reform Law) to the urban

Each criterion of classification is represented by a letter.
1 Participation (t) or non-participation (−t) in the productive process. Each formula containing −t must obviously be complemented by a formula containing t.
2 The different forms of surplus: labour (S_1), rent in kind (S_2), money (S_3). S = no surplus.
3 The three forms of access to land; P_1 = rights to the product of the plot; P_2 = right of *usus*, P_3 = private property; −P = complete separation from private property.
Thus each social status is denoted by three letters standing for the three discriminating criteria.

Example: Share-cropping.
The share-cropper works the land (t) from which he obtains a surplus which is then transferred to the owner (S_2); he does not own the land he works (−P). Thus:

$tS_2 -P$ represents the sharecropper
$-tS_2P_3$ represents the owner of the plot (complementary formula)

The formulae printed one above the other are complementary: where several statuses are superimposed, their respective formulae are written on the same line. Thus, an independent smallholder who is also a share-cropper is written thus:

$$t S_3 P_3 \qquad tS_2 -P$$
$$\qquad\quad -tS_2 P_3$$

proprietor   share-cropper

The figure represents the set of relationships described above:
Arrow a: The comunero from San Juan (1) produces no surplus and has only usufruct rights to his plot, but sells his labour to the Yucay valley smallholder (3)–who could himself be a tenant, share-cropper and wage earner, but these variants have been eliminated for purposes of simplification.
Arrows b and c: The colono from the Maras–Chinchero plateau (2) works for a hacendado in the Yucay valley (4) or on land rented by a yucavino in the valley of La Convención (8).
Arrow d: The smallholder from Yucay can be a wage earner (5) working for a farmer in La Convención (7).
Arrow e: He (the Yucay smallholder) may also rent in land from that same smallholder in La Convención (8).

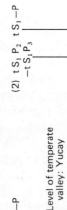

Level of mountain communities: San Juan

(1) $t SP_2$ $t S_1 -P$

Level of temperate valley: Yucay

(3) $t S_3 P_3$ $t S_1 -P$

(4) $-t S_3 P_3$ (hacienda) $t S_1 -P$

(5) $t S_3 P_3$ $t S_1 -P$

(6) $t S_3 P_3$ $t S_3 -P$

Level of the sub-tropical valley of La Convención

(7) $t S_3 P_3$ $t S_1 -P$

(8) $t S_3 P_3$ $t S_3 -P$ $t S_1 -P$

Level of Maras–Chinchero plateau

(2) $t S_1, P_2$ $t S_1 -P$
$-t S_1 P_3$

Fig. 8.3   Formalization of relations between ecological levels

compadre of the farmer in La Convención. At the other extreme, the comunero will sell his entire harvest of potatoes at a low price to the peasant in
Yucay who has persuaded his other compadre to do him a favour. The
dependency which characterizes these relations of compadrazgo reproduces
relations of production; ties of compadrazgo thus not only follow ties of
dependency between different levels, but reinforce and consecrate them.

5. Cultural and symbolic aspects of the vertical economy

Apart from the morphological, economic and sociological relationships
which differentiate between them, cultural differentiation can also be observed among inhabitants of different levels. Furthermore, a hierarchy of cogni-
tive distinctions is manifested in place names, in the description of space, in
mythology, and in the organization of the pantheon. As an example, we
will here make certain observations and put forward hypotheses for future
research.

First of all, the cultural diversity of the populations of these levels must
be emphasized. In the markets, 'Indian' women from the mountain communities, with the flat caps and coloured hand-woven clothes, are clearly
distinguishable from the *cholas* of the valleys, who wear their traditional
'magpie's tail' coat, while the peasants from the Sacred Valley wear a western-
style jacket and trousers, nevertheless keeping a poncho and *ojotas* (sandals
made out of car tyres); the planters of La Convención dress just like any
urban inhabitant. The people from the plateau of Maras–Chinchero and from
the mountain communities only speak Quechua, whereas those from Yucay
are usually bilingual, although older people do not speak Spanish; in Yucay
154 out of 435 heads of family only speak Quechua. The former are illiterate,
whereas a large number of the peasants of Yucay have had primary education
(30.56% of heads of family). Endogamy isolates the ecological levels in their
kinship relations: it would be shameful for a family from Yucay if their
daughter were to marry a comunero from San Juan, whereas the two villages
in the valley bottom, Yucay and Huayllabamba, still exchange women in
marriage. In the mountain communities, traditional marriage, or *sirvinacuy*,
is still customary, whereas in the valley villages Catholic marriages have
become more and more common. The same can be said of traditional
institutions and rituals. Thus, the hierarchical relationships which separate
different geographical levels are replicated by differences in degrees of
acculturation: from the inhabitants of the high puna lands with their
indigenous culture, to the planters of La Convención with their western
culture, passing through this religious syncretism of the peasants of Yucay.

These social and cultural distinctions are described by the terminological
distinction between *indio* and *mestizo*. For the inhabitants of the valleys,
who consider themselves mestizos, the Indian is a person who lives 'at the

top', and whose life is guided by the most barbarous traditions. The inhabitants of Cuzco or Quillabamba consider the mestizos of the valleys of the sierra to be indios: ultimately the term 'Indian' refers to an inhabitant of the level above one's own. True, this terminology becomes increasingly relative the further the market penetrates, and especially with the increase in the number of *cholos*, ex-Indians in the process of proletarianization. Nevertheless, it remains an intensely meaningful terminology for the inhabitants of the different levels and constitutes an important ideological element in the social relationships between them.

The importance of the vertical dimension at the level of human relationships is such that it impregnates all relationships between man and his environment, and this is illustrated by certain observations. The fundamental opposition between quechua and jalga (or puna) underlies any description by peasants of their environment. In describing each one of the levels he will speak of an 'upper' and a 'lower' part; and a distinction is drawn in the valley bottom of Yucay between the plots on the terraces and the plots by the river. This distinction is entirely subjective; for example, the zone exactly half way between Yucay and San Juan will, for the yucavino, be both quechua and puna, but it will be only quechua for the comunero from San Juan (Fonseca 1966).

This fundamental distinction is similarly to be found in the opposition between potatoes and corn. John Murra has shown that this is an extremely ancient opposition, not only between two products, but between two agricultural systems. The cultivation of tubers was characteristic of a subsistence agriculture practised long before the Inca conquest, whereas the cultivation of corn was diffused, and sometimes imposed by the Inca state in its search for the surpluses it required. It is indeed an opposition between two ways of life (Murra 1960). Today one finds this characteristic reappearing in Yucay. There is no doubt that for the inhabitants of the valley the cultivation of corn is more prestigious than that of the potato; the potato never figures in the *despachos* (ritual cures of magical origin), whereas certain ears of corn, chosen according to the direction of their grain, are carefully kept for such rituals; thus, *chicha* is indispensable for magical cures and for *pagos*, the offerings made to the mountain spirits, the *apu*. The maize harvest is always brought to a close by a ceremony, often conducted at an altar; the same is not done for the potato harvest, for which, nevertheless, a fertility offering of corn is made. In short, corn is related to the world of the sacred. However, the potato probably plays a similar role for the inhabitants of the high puna.

Finally, the opposition between high and low is fundamental in the indigenous cosmogony of the valley peasants: the sacred world of the unknown puna, savage and untamed, is opposed to the tamed, irrigated and fertile valley. The mountains are the domain either of evil forces which must be dispelled, or of supernatural powers which must be won over. The ancestors, or *machu* created by *Roal*, inhabit tombs dug in the sides of the mountains. Before the Inca period they used to live in darkness, in a state of barbarism, which led to their destruction by fire; it was the Incas who brought the world the sunlight which destroyed them. Sometimes at night they come out and spread about the ills which only an experienced *curandero* (folk doctor) is capable of curing through the correct rituals. Also in the puna dwell the *condenados*, monsters with tongues of fire who live by eating any peasant who ventures into their domain; their monstrosity is an expiation for the sin of incest which they committed when they were men. A peasant lost in the puna at nightfall may also meet the flying heads and windswept hair of certain women from the community who are endowed with magic powers. The supernatural beings from above are, for the most part, terrifying. But above all, the mountains are the kingdom of the apu, spirits who each occupy one of the peaks which dominate the valley. Their power may be beneficial or maleficent, depending upon the respects paid and on the offerings made to them. As often as possible they must be given a *t'inka*, an offering of coca and cane alcohol, which is sprinkled for them with the fingertips before drinking to their health and invoking their names. The apu have a very strict hierarchy. Some are honoured by the inhabitants of an entire valley, and even an entire region, like Ausangate, who is worshipped in the region of Cuzco. They play a part in magical cures too elaborate to be described here and, more generally, in the daily life of the Indians, for they are invoked as much by workers in the fields as by drinkers at a fiesta. Specific myths are linked to each one of them.

In contrast, the sacred world of the valley is a domesticated and familiar territory. The terraces, it is known, have been passed down by the Inca ancestors and they are opposed, therefore, to the machu of the mountains. The supernatural beings who inhabit the terraces are usually of hispanic origin: the wandering souls of purgatory, teasing and dangerous hobgoblins, the incarnation of the devil as a blond man with blue eyes. There is no myth of origin; the legends of the Sacred Valley record the amorous exploits of a certain marquess or of an Inca princess raped by a Spaniard and saved by an Indian, or they tell of the fate of Inca treasures hidden at the bottom of the lake. The narrators place themselves in 'real' history, in a period of 'culture', in opposition to the Indians of the high mountains who seek an explanation of the real world (of the third age) in a first age, in 'nature', in 'barbarism'.

All the way down the Yucay valley, on the lower escarpments of the mountain, a series of crosses stand above the village and the terraces: Cruz Mocco, Misionero, Yaullimocco, Ccanibamba, Pasión, Calvario and Acco-Acco. On the day of Pentecost, the yucavinos, organized by the quarters in which they live, bring them down to the village to worship them and to carry them in procession. Placed at the frontier of valley land and puna, they mark the division between two spaces and two times: on the one hand, the fearful world of the puna, the sacred universe of origin, the time of pre-hispanic divinities, now confined to the recesses of terrorized memory, and on the other hand, the domesticated quechua valley, the time of the colonial and Christian god. (It is significant, in this respect, that the supernatural beings of the mountain, like the condenado, have committed the sin of incest.) Thus the valley is protected from the phantasms of the past by crosses which may have replaced other, more ancient signs. Are the limits between these two spaces and these historical times quite so precise? On each side of Yucay village, two swamps, *Huachac* and *Soq'os Pujyu* ('baleful spring') are uncultivable; the divinities which dwell in these places are the same as those of the puna, particularly the various forms taken by *soq'a*, an extremely dangerous being, whose punishments are unforgiving. These two areas reproduce, in a sense, ecological and religious features of the puna: the land there, too, is uncultivated and unirrigated. No peasant would dare to go there alone. Furthermore, up in the mountains we do find an island of 'culture'; the hamlet of San Juan. Its myth of origin recalls all its ties with the valley: a peasant from the valley brought the image of a saint from the Yucay church to the midst of the pagan gods of the mountains and founded the hamlet. Thus, each of the two fundamental spaces penetrates the other, and the crosses ward off the threat of disorder which, in a fundamentally vertical universe, this interpenetration represents: disorder at once of space and of time, since the two universes also evoke two historical periods – those preceding and following Spanish colonization – characterized by two completely different conceptions of the order of the world.

It can now be better understood to what extent the categories of high and low and, more generally, verticality are fundamental for Andean man. A multi-levelled ecology implies a specific type of evolution of economic and social relations and underlies a vision of space in which one can even detect mental categories. Does not the classic division to be found in Cuzco, and in most Andean villages, between *hurin* and *Hanan* ('high' and 'low') correspond to this systematic division of space, and the categories it generates?

Note

The author wishes to thank David Lehmann for translating this paper, which appeared originally in a very slightly different form in *Etudes Rurales*, 57, 1975.

Glossary

This list is intended to provide a reader's guide to the most important technical and/or Quechua and Aymara terms used in the book. It does not claim to be either exhaustive or definitive. Many words which are used only once, and whose meaning is explained in the text, are not included here.

abigeo	Cattle thief
agregado	Person who joins an *ayllu* and acquires rights and obligations related to land tenure, but whose tenure is less secure than that of persons who are members by inheritance
aguardiente	Cane or grape alcohol
ahijado/a	Adopted son/daughter; also 'godchild'
alcalde	*Comunidad* office; also 'mayor'
allegado	Sub-tenant renting land from *arrendire* and paying for it, usually in labour
anticrético/ anticresis	A loan in anticresis is akin to pawning. A person lends a sum of money to another in return for usufruct of land or other wealth, until the borrower has returned the original sum. In effect usufruct is in lieu of interest. These contracts are fixed term
aqllakuna	Unmarried women chosen to serve the Inca, for whom they spun and wove cloth
arrendire	Term with same meaning as *colono*, used specifically in the valley of La Convención, Peru
arroba	Unit of weight of agricultural produce (25 lb)
ayllu	In the Inca system, the smallest land-holding unit. Subsequently, an endogamous land-holding unit with some corporate control over individual households' access to land
ayni	The *ayni* principle is as follows: I request or receive a specific service from my kinsman or neighbour, on the understanding that on a subsequent, exactly similar occasion, I will render him exactly the same service
barbecho	Ploughed land ready for sowing
carga	One-half quintal, or one llama-load
caudillo	Political chieftain in command of a private army
ceja de montaña/ ceja de selva	Literally the 'eyebrow' of the forest. An upper-montane belt situated between the tropical forest and the maize-growing

231

Glossary

	temperate lands, just above the cocoa- and coffee-growing levels (Troll 1968)
chancaca	Brown sugar cake; the form in which sugar was generally consumed in the sierra during the mid nineteenth century
ch'arki	Dried, or jerked, meat
chicha/chicha de jora	Maize beer
cholo	Person of Indian descent but, by virtue of cultural adaptation and economic position, above the mass of *indio* peasants in social status
chuño, *or* ch'uñu, *or* moraya	Dehydrated potato; the potato is dried in the sun and then stored (refrigerated) in the ground for long periods
chuqhu/chuqu	Collective work carried out to celebrate a festive occasion, with coca and *chicha* provided by the beneficiary, among the Bolivian Laymi
colono	A peasant obliged to render free labour service, and occasionally to pay a sum of money, against the usufruct of a plot on the *hacienda*
compadrazgo/ compadre	Strictly, ritual co-parenthood; the relationship between a father and his child's godfather, or a mother and her child's godmother. However, the terms *compadre* and *comadre* seem frequently to be used with reference to close friends. A child may have several godparents
comunero	Member of a *comunidad*
comunidad	Peru only. Peasant community in which land is formally vested, and in which membership is determined either by descent or by entry with the approval of the leadership. Nowadays the *comunidad* is not necessarily, or even usually, endogamous. See also Bradby, ch. 4, n.2
corregidor	The lowest-level colonial official appointed by the Crown: judge in the first instance, tribute-collector and president of the local council (*cabildo*), if any. There were seventy *corregidores* in Upper and Lower Peru. The Laymi of Northern Potosí today have an elected official known also as *corregidor*
corregimiento	District of which a *corregidor* was in charge
criollo	Colonial term referring to Europeans/whites born in the colonies
cumbi	Fine cloth woven for the Inca
curandero	Practitioner of indigenous medicine
doctrina	Area of activity of a missionary
enganche/ enganchador	System of labour contracting, whereby workers are hired to work away from their communities of origin, and paid an advance to cover transport and perhaps food, the advance being deducted from final payment of their wages. An *enganchador* is an intermediary working on behalf of an employer in searching for seasonal workers on the *enganche* system
faena	Collective work occasion, organized usually by community leaders with the participation of all *comuneros*

Glossary

fanega	Measure of dry weight (c. 100 litres or 2.75 bushels); *also* area of land which can be sown with a *fanega* of seed
feudatario	As *colono*
forastero	A fiscal category referring, in the colonial period, to outsiders who, by living on lands allocated to *indios*, acquired certain rights and obligations
fundo	Estate or farm
gamonales	Landlords whose treatment of the local population verges on petty tyranny
Guardia Civil	The civil police
hacienda/ hacendado	Large landed property: the *hacendado* is its owner
Hermandad	'Brotherhood', a religious organization to which men and women could belong; more of an abstinence league than a secret society
ichu	*Stepa ichu*: typical vegetal formation of the *puna*
indigenista	'Pro-indigenous', describing a political movement that grew up early this century in Peru with the aim of restoring an idealized 'primitive communism' to the native Andean people
Intendencias	Administrative departments set up in Peru in 1786
jilanqu	Elected head of the smallest administrative unit – the *cabildo* – among the Laymi people
kantu runa	Quechua term meaning literally 'men on the margin' and referring to persons in receipt of usufructuary rights to someone else's land but with no security of tenure and some service obligations to the owner and/or his *comunidad*
kuraka	Indigenous political chief, whose intermediary position between *ayllu* and state under the Inca subsisted in the colonial period, and, in Northern Potosí, subsists today
Laymi	System of collective decisions concerning rotation of land use in communities of the southern sierra of Peru
likina	Temperate valleys: ecological tier in Northern Potosí, Bolivia
magüey	Agave plant
manta	Term used to describe high-altitude cultivable land subject to lengthy fallow periods and communally controlled rotation. Refers to level 2 in Platt, figure 2.2
mayordomo	Official *comunidad* sponsor of a fiesta
mestizos	People of mixed Indian and white descent
minifundio	Projective term referring to a smallholding, implying low productivity of labour and land
minka/mink'a/ minga	In Peru and Bolivia this refers (a) to a work-party performing a service for an individual, such as building or roofing his house. The beneficiary provides coca, cigarettes and (alcoholic) refreshment, and it is presumed that over a period of time all the members of the party will perform similar services for each other in the same group. However, the term is (b) also, and perhaps more usually, used to mean simply wage labour. See also Harris, ch. 3 n23. In Ecuador a *minga* (c) is a work-party, organized to build or repair infrastructural resources such as roads or schools or health centres, in collaboration with governmental agencies which promise to supply the necessary capital.

Glossary

	In Ecuador (d) the term can also mean any kind of rotating communal labour obligation
mita	Under the Inca and Spanish empires, compulsory labour service to the state, i.e. labour tribute. In the colonial period the work was performed for private individuals to whom the state ceded the right
mitmaq/mitimaes	Colonists sent out to settle other lands from their community of origin by the Inca, but who retained their rights to land in that community, *or* settlers shifted from one region of the Inca empire to another, to work for the state
molle	Small acacia trees
montaña	See *ceja de montaña*
mullu	Shell found in large quantities off the coast of Ecuador and, since pre-hispanic times, worked up into rounded pieces which could be strung into necklaces and used for counting
oca	Native Andean tuber (*Oxalis tuberosa*)
originario	Person recognized as having land rights in virtue of his/her descent from a person appearing in the first registrations of the sixteenth century (see Platt, ch.2)
patrón	Employer, landlord
personero	Elected leader of a community under the pre-1969 structure
puna	Treeless grasslands at 3500–4500 feet with extreme diurnal temperature variations and little annual variation. Suitable for pasture of camelid animals and sheep and for the refrigeration of potatoes. It can be divided into moist *puna*, thorn-and-succulent *puna* and desert *puna*, all three of which stretch throughout the Central Andes, from northern Peru to the Atacama desert
quechua	Temperate lands, suitable for maize-growing
quinoa	High-protein native Andean grain (grown only at high altitudes)
reducción	Settlement of a dispersed population into a compact village by the Spanish after the reforms of the viceroy Toledo in 1572
repartimiento	Distribution of goods to the Indian population by the Spanish during the later colonial period, which goods the Indians were then obliged to pay for with their own products, or with money obtained by the sale of their products, often against their will
ron de quemar	Cooking alcohol
SAIS	Sociedad Agraria de Interés Social. Large-scale agricultural production co-operative created under the Peruvian Agrarian Reform between 1968 and 1975
Segunda mayor	Highest authority (one for each moiety) among the Laymi people of Northern Potosí
soles antiguos	'Old *soles*', a system of prices in terms of pre-inflationary amounts of the *sol*, the unit of currency in modern Peru
sub-arrendire	See *allegado*
suni	Upper ecological tier of the Northern Potosí region, Bolivia. In Peru, the cold ecological tier lying between the temperate *quechua* and the treeless *puna*
tanda	Alternating task group, *or* length of alternating work-periods performed by alternating groups

Glossary

tasa	Land tax, also the land on which tax has been paid. Refers to levels 3 to 7 in Platt, figure 2.2
topo	Measure of land
verdelojo	Blue-green coloured cooking alcohol used as a substitute for cane alcohol in present-day festivities in certain parts of the Andes
yanakuna	Under the Incas, section of the population uprooted from their *ayllu* of origin, usually in order to be herdsmen to dominant lords
yanapaña	Aymara term meaning 'to help'

References

Alberti, G. and Mayer, E. 1974. *Reciprocidad e intercambio en los Andes peruanos.* Lima: Instituto de Estudios Peruanos

Albó, Xavier, 1975. La paradoja aymara: solidaridad y faccionalismo. *Cuaderno de Investigación CIPCA,* no. 8. La Paz

1976. La Reforma Agraria en Bolivia. In *Reformas agrarias en América Latina.* Colección Proceso, no. 10. Buenos Aires

Alfaro, Julio and Oré, Teresa. 1974. *El desarrollo del capitalismo en La Convención y los nuevos movimientos de campesinos con tierra, 1963–1973.* Universidad Católica de Lima: Programa de Ciencias Sociales

Aramayo, José Avelino. 1861. *Libre extracción de pastos.* Sucre

Archetti, Eduardo and Stölen, Kristi Ann. 1975. *Explotación familiar y acumulación de capital en el campo argentino.* Buenos Aires: Siglo XXI

Banaji, J. 1977. Modes of production in a materialist conception of history. *Capital and class,* no. 3: 1–44

Barnadas, Josep. 1973. *Charcas: orígenes históricos de una sociedad colonial.* La Paz

Bartra, Roger, 1974. *Estructura agraria y clases sociales en México.* México: Era

Bloch, M.R. 1975/6. Salz in der Geschichte des Geldes. *Mitteilungen der List Gesellschaft,* no. 12/13

Bonilla, Heraclio. 1974. *Guano y burguesía en el Perú.* Lima: Instituto de Estudios Peruanos

1978. Notas en torno a la historia económica y social de Bolivia, 1821–1879. *Histórica* (Lima), II, no. 2

1980. Peru y Bolivia de la Independencia a la guerra con Chile. Ms. Cambridge

Bukharin, N. 1972. *Imperialism and the accumulation of capital,* ed. K. Tarbuck. London: Allen Lane: The Penguin Press

Burchard, R.E. 1974. Coca y trueque de alimentos. In Alberti and Mayer (1974)

Caballero, José-Maria. 1980. *Agricultura, reforma agraria y pobreza campesina.* Lima: Instituto de Estudios Peruanos

Cañete y Dominguez, Pedro. 1952 (1787). *Guía de la provincia de Potosí.* Potosí

Carrera, Nicolás Iñigo. 1980. Genesis, formación y desarrollo de las clases en una zona de pequeños productores: el territorio algodonero argentino. Cuaderno del CICSO, *Serie Estudios* (Buenos Aires), no. 41

Carter, William E. 1965. *Aymara communities and the Bolivian Agrarian Reform.* Gainesville: University of Florida Press

1967. *Comunidades Aymaras y Reforma Agraria en Bolivia.* Mexico. Translation of Carter (1965)

Celestino, Olinda. 1972. *Migración y cambio estructural: la comunidad de Lampián.* Lima: Instituto de Estudios Peruanos

236

References

Clark, R. J. 1968. Land reform and peasant market participation on the north highlands of Bolivia. Interamerican Committee for Agricultural Development (CIDA), Washington DC, *Research Paper* no. 3 (March)

Custred, C. 1974. Llameros y comercio interregional. In Alberti and Mayer (1974)

Dalence, José M. 1975 (1848). *Bosquejo estadístico de Bolivia.* La Paz

Dalton, George. 1961. Economic theory and primitive society. *American Anthropologist*, LXIII: 1–25

Delgado, Oscar. 1967. *Reforma agraria y desarrollo rural en el área del altiplano norte de Bolivia: estudio de caso en el cantón Ancoraimes en las riberas del Lago Titicaca.* Madison, Wisconsin: Interamerican Committee for Agricultural Development (CIDA)

Deustua, José. 1978. Acceso a recursos en Yanque-Collaguas, 1591: una experiencia estadística. In *Etnohistoria y antropología andina.* Lima

Dow, J. 1977. Religion in the organization of a peasant economy. In *Peasant livelihood. Studies in economic anthropology and cultural ecology*, ed. R. Halperin and J. Dow. New York: St Martin's Press

Erasmus, C. 1956. Culture, structure and process: the occurrence and disappearance of reciprocal farm labour. *Southwestern Journal of Anthropology*, XII: 444–69

Espinoza, S., W. 1969. 'El memorial de Charcas': crónica inédita de 1582. *Revista de la Universidad Nacional de Educación*, Chosica, Peru

Favre, H. 1965. *La evolución de la situación de las haciendas en la región de Huancavelica, Perú.* Serie Mesas Redondas, no. 1. Lima: Instituto de Estudios Peruanos
1975. Le peuplement et la colonisation agricole de la steppe dans le Pérou central. *Annales de Géographie*, LXXXIV: 415–41

Figueroa, Adolfo. 1974. *Estructura de consumo y distribución de ingresos en Lima Metropolitana.* Lima: Universidad Católica
1976. *El empleo rural en el Perú.* Report to the International Labour Office
1979. La economía de las comunidades campesinas: el caso de la Sierra Sur del Perú. In *Campesinado e indigenismo en América Latina*, ed. E. Valencia. Lima: CELATS

Flores-Galindo, A. 1973. *Los mineros del Cerro de Pasco: un intento de caracterización social.* Lima: Pontificia Universidad Católica, Departamento de Ciencias Sociales
1977. *Arequipa y el sur andino: siglo XVIII.* Lima: Editorial Horizonte

Fonseca, Cesar. 1966. La Comunidad de Cauri y la quebrada de Chaupiwaranga. Universidad de Huánuco, *Cuadernos de Investigación*, no. 1: 22–3
1972. La economía 'vertical' y la economía de mercado en las comunidades alteñas del Perú. In Iñigo Ortiz de Zúñiga, *Visita de la provincia de León de Huánuco en 1562*, vol. II. Huánuco: Universidad Hermilio Valdizán
1973. *Sistemas económicos andinos.* Lima: Biblioteca Andina

Friedmann, Harriet. 1978. Simple commodity production and wage labour in the American Plains. *Journal of Peasant Studies*, VI: 71–100
1980. Household production and the national economy: concepts for the analysis of agrarian formations. *Journal of Peasant Studies*, VII: 158–84

Gandia, E. de. 1939. *Francisco de Alfaro y la condición social de los indios.* Buenos Aires

Garcilaso de la Vega, Inca. 1960 (1609). *Comentarios reales de los Incas.* Biblioteca de Autores Españoles vol. 133. Madrid

Geertz, C. 1963. *Agricultural involution.* Berkeley: University of California Press

Gerstäcker, F. 1862 (reprinted 1973). *Viaje por el Perú.* Lima: Biblioteca Nacional

Giordano, F. 1875 (reprinted 1905). 'Memoria' in Larrabure and Correa, *Colección de leyes, decretos, resoluciones y otros documentos oficiales referentes al Departamento de Loreto.* vol. XI

References

Gluckman, Max. 1943. *Essays on Lozi land and royal property.* Rhodes Livingstone Paper no. 10. Lusaka

Golte, Jurgen. 1976. Redistribución y complementaridad regional en la economía andina del siglo XVII. In *Actes du XLIIe Congrès International des Américanistes,* vol. IV: 65–87, Paris

1980. *La racionalidad de la organización andina.* Lima: Instituto de Estudios Peruanos

Gomez, Walter. 1978. *La minería en el desarrollo económico de Bolivia.* La Paz

Gonzales, Efraín. 1979. *La economia de la familia comunera.* Documento de Trabajo no. 39, CISEPA. Universidad Católica de Lima

Grieshaber, Erwin Peter, 1979. Survival of indian communities in nineteenth-century Bolivia. PhD thesis, University of North Carolina, Chapel Hill

1980. Survival of Indian communities in nineteenth-century Bolivia: a regional comparison. *Journal of Latin American Studies,* XII: 223–69

Gudeman, S. 1978. *The demise of a rural economy.* London: Routledge

Gutelman, Michel. 1971. Description des structures agraires et formalisation des rapports sociaux en agriculture. *Etudes Rurales,* no. 41: 15–48

Harris, Olivia. 1976. Kinship and the vertical economy. *Actes du XLIIe Congrès International des Américanistes,* vol. IV: 165–77, Paris

1978a. El parentesco y la economía vertical en el ayllu Laymi (Norte de Potosí). *Avances* (La Paz), no. 1

1978b. De l'assymétrie au triangle: transformations symboliques au nord du Potosí. *Annales,* XXXIII: 1108–25

1978c. Complementarity and conflict: an Andean view of women and men. In *Sex and age as principles of social differentiation,* ed. J. La Fontaine. London: Academic Press

Harris, Olivia and Albó, Xavier. 1975. Monteras y guardatojos: campesinos y mineros del norte de Potosí. *Cuadernos de Investigación CIPCA* (La Paz), no. 7

Herndon, W.L. 1853. *Exploration of the valley of the Amazon made under the direction of the Navy Department,* Part 1. Washington DC

Humphreys, S. 1969. History, economics and anthropology: the work of Karl Polanyi. *History and Theory,* VIII: 165–212

Hymer, Stephen and Resnick, Stephen. 1969. A model of an agrarian economy with non-agricultural activities. *American Economic Review,* LIX, no. 4 (September)

Jacobsen, N. 1978. Desarrollo económico y relaciones de clase en el sur andino. *Análisis* (Lima), 5: 67–81

Knapp, G.F. 1924. *The state theory of money.* London: Macmillan and the Royal Economic Society

Kula, Witold, 1974. *Teoría económica del sistema feudal.* Mexico: Siglo XXI (translated into English from the Polish as *Economic theory of the feudal system.* London: New Left Books, 1976)

Larson, Brooke, 1978. Hacendados y campesinos en Cochabamba en el siglo XVIII. *Avances* (La Paz), no. 2

1980. Cambio agrario en una economia colonial: el caso de Cochabamba, 1580–1800. *Estudios Rurales Latinoamericanos,* III, no. 1 (Jan–April)

Leclair, E.E. and Schneider, H.K. 1968. *Anthropology.* New York

Lehmann, David. Forthcoming. Peasantization and proletarianization: recent changes in the rural sectors of Brazil and Mexico. In *Rural poverty and agrarian reform,* ed. S. Jones, P.C. Joshi and M. Murmis. New Delhi: Allied Publishers

Lenin, V.I. n.d. *Imperialism: the highest stage of capitalism.* Moscow: Progress Publishers

Lipton, Michael. 1977. *Why poor people stay poor: urban bias in world development.* London: Temple Smith

238

References

Long, Norman and Roberts, Brian (eds.). 1978. *Peasant cooperation and capitalist expansion in Central Peru.* Austin: University of Texas, Institute of Latin American Studies

Luxemburg, R. 1951. *The accumulation of capital,* London: Routledge and Kegan Paul

Macera, Pablo. 1978. *Mapas coloniales de haciendas cuzqueñas.* Lima.

Macera, P. and Hunt, S. 1977. Peru. In *Latin America: a guide to economic history 1830–1930,* ed. R. Cortes Conde and S. Stein. Los Angeles: University of California Press and American Council of Learned Societies, Joint Committee on Latin American Studies

Marx, Karl. 1867. *Capital,* vol. I (Penguin edition, London, 1976)

Mauss, Marcel. 1951. *The gift.* Glencoe, Ill.: The Free Press

Mayer, Enrique. 1974a. *Reciprocity, self-sufficiency, and market relations in a contemporary community in the Central Andes of Peru.* Cornell University Latin American Studies Program, Dissertation Series, no. 72

1974b. Las reglas del juego de la reciprocidad andina. In Alberti and Mayer (1974)

Mayer, Enrique and Zamallos, César. 1974. Reciprocidad en las relaciones de producción. In Alberti and Mayer (1974)

Meillassoux, Claude. 1975. *Femmes, greniers et capitaux.* Paris: Maspéro

1978. 'The economy' in agricultural self-sustaining societies: a preliminary analysis. In *Relations of production,* ed. D. Seddon. London: Frank Cass

Mitre, Antonio. 1977. Economic and social structure of silver mining in nineteenth-century Bolivia. PhD thesis, Columbia University

1978. La minería boliviana de la plata en el siglo XIX. In *Estudios bolivianos en homenaje a Gunnar Mendoza L.* La Paz

Molina, R. 1980. Economía campesina y migración: la venta estacional de fuerza de trabajo en el contorno rural de los centros mineros del Norte de Potosí (Bolivia). In PREALC. *Economia Campesina y Empleo.* Santiago de Chile, 1981

Molina, Ramiro and Platt, Tristan. 1979. Economía campesina y su articulación con el complejo urbano-minero. In *Estudio socio-económico de los centros mineros y su contorno espacial,* vols. X and XI. La Paz

Molinié, Antoinette. 1980. *Influences urbaines et société rurale au Pérou: le cas de Yucay.* Spanish translation. Lima: Instituto de Estudios Peruanos

Montoya, Rodrigo. 1971. *A propósito del carácter predominantemente capitalista de la economía peruana actual (1960–1970).* Lima

Murra, John. 1956. The economic organization of the Inca state. PhD thesis, University of Chicago. (Published in Spanish translation as *La organización económica del estado inca,* México: Siglo XXI, 1968: Also published as Supplement 1 to *Research in Economic Anthropology.* Greenwich, Connecticut: JAI Press Inc. 1979)

1960. Rite and crop in the Inca state. In *Culture in History,* ed. Stanley Diamond. Translated and republished in Murra (1975)

1964. Rebaños y pastores en la economía del Tawantinsuyu. *Revista Peruana de Cultura,* no. 2. Reprinted in Murra (1975)

1968. An Aymara kingdom in 1567. *Ethnohistory,* XV, no. 2. See also Murra (1970)

1970. Un reino aymara en 1567. Revised version of Murra (1968), published in Murra (1975)

1972a. El control vertical de un máximo de pisos ecológicos en la economía de las sociedades andinas. In *Visita de la Provincia de León de Huánuco en 1562,* ed. Iñigo Ortiz de Zúñiga, Vol. II. Huánuco: Universidad Nacional Hermilio Valdizán. Reprinted in Murra (1975)

239

References

1972b. La Visita de los Chupachu como fuente etnológica. In Iñigo Ortiz de Zúñiga, *Visita* (see Murra 1972a). Reprinted in Murra (1975)

1975. *Formaciones económicas y políticas del mundo andino*. Lima: Instituto de Estudios Peruanos

1978a. La correspondencia entre un 'capitán de la mita' y su apoderado en Potosí. *Historia y Cultura* (La Paz), no. 3: 45–58

1978b. Los límites y las limitaciones del 'archipiélago vertical' en los Andes. *Avances* (La Paz), no. 1

1978c. La guerre et les rébellions dans l'expansion de l'Etat inka, *Annales*, XXXIII: 927–35

Murra, John and Wachtel, Nathan. 1978. Présentation. *Annales*, XXXIII: 889–94

Neale, W. 1957. Reciprocity and redistribution in the Indian village: sequence to some notable discussions. In Polanyi, Arensberg and Pearson (1957)

O'Phelan, Scarlett. 1978. El sur andino a fines del siglo XVIII: cacique o corregidor. *Allpanchis Phuturinqa* (Cuzco), XI/XII: 17–32

Orlove, B. 1977. *Alpacas, sheep and men*. New York and London: Academic Press

Ortiz, Sutti. 1972. *Uncertainties in peasant economy, a Colombian case*. London School of Economics Monographs in Social Anthropology, no. 46. London: The Athlone Press

Pease, F. 1974. Un movimiento mesiánico en Lircay, Huancavelica (1811). *Revista del Museo Nacional* (Lima), XL

Pentland, Joseph B. 1975 (1826). *Informe sobre Bolivia*. Potosí

Perú, Ministerio de Gobierno. Dirección General Estadística. 1878. *Resumen del censo general de habitantes del Perú en 1876*. Lima: Imprenta del Estado

Platt, Tristan. 1978a. Acerca del sistema tributario pre-toledano en el Alto Perú. *Avances* (La Paz), no. 1

1978b. Mapas coloniales de Chayanta: dos visiones conflictivos de un solo paisaje. In *Estudios bolivianos en homenaje a Gunnar Mendoza L*. La Paz

1978c. Symétries en miroir: le concept de *yanantin* chez les Macha de Bolivie. *Annales*, XXXIII: 1081–107

In preparation. *El estado boliviano y el ayllu andino*.

Polanyi, Karl. 1957. The economy as instituted process. In Polanyi, Arensberg and Pearson (1957)

1966. *Dahomey and the slave trade*. AES Monograph no. 42. University of Washington Press

Polanyi, K., Arensberg, C. and Pearson, H. 1957. *Trade and market in the early empires*. New York: The Free Press

Ponce, Gabriel. 1978. En torno a la naturaleza del estado oligárquico. *Avances* (La Paz), no. 2

Preston, David. 1974. Land tenure and agricultural development in the central altiplano, Bolivia. In *Spatial aspects of development*, ed. B. Hoyle. London: John Wiley

Pryor, F. 1977. *The origins of the economy. A comparative study of distribution in primitive and peasant economies*. New York and London: Academic Press

Pulgar Vidal, Javier. n.d. *Geografía del Perú*. Lima: Editorial Universo

Raimondi, A. 1855 (reprinted 1897). Itinerario de los viajes de Raimondi en el Perú en 1855. *Boletín de la Sociedad Geográfica de Lima*, VII, no. 123: 1–120

Rivera, Silvia. 1978a. El *Mallku* y la sociedad colonial en el siglo XVII: el caso de Jesús de Machaca. *Avances* (La Paz), no. 1

1978b. La expansión del latifundio en el altiplano boliviano. Elementos para la caracterización de una oligarquía regional. *Avances* (La Paz), no. 2

References

Rivera, Silvia and Platt, Tristan. 1978. El impacto colonial sobre un pueblo Pakaxa: la crisis del cacicazgo en Caquingora (Urinsaya) durante el siglo XVI. *Avances* (La Paz), no 1

Roberts, B. and Samaniego, C. 1978. The evolution of pastoral villages and the significance of Agrarian Reform in the highlands of Central Peru. In Long and Roberts (1978)

Rodriguez, Gustavo. 1978. Acumulación originaria, capitalismo y agricultura pre-capitalista en Bolivia (1870–1885). *Avances* (La Paz), no. 2

Sahlins, Marshal. 1965. On the sociology of primitive exchange. In *The relevance of models for social anthropology*, ed. M. Banton. ASA Monograph, no. 1. London: Tavistock

1972. *Stone age economics*, Chicago: Aldine Publishing Co.

Salomon, Frank. 1978. Systèmes politiques aux marches de l'empire. *Annales*, XXXIII: 967–89

1980. *Los señores étnicos de Quito en la época de los Incas*. Otavalo (Ecuador): Instituto Otavaleño de Antropología

Samaniego, C. 1974. Location, social differentiation and peasant movements in the central Sierra of Peru. PhD thesis, University of Manchester

1978. Peasant movements at the turn of the century and the rise of the independent farmer. In Long and Roberts (1978)

Sánchez, Rodrigo. 1977. Economy, ideology and political struggle in the Andean highlands. PhD thesis, University of Sussex.

Sánchez-Albornóz, Nicolás. 1978. *Indios y Tributos en el Alto Perú*. Lima: Instituto de Estudios Peruanos

Sempat Assadourian, Carlos. 1978. La producción de la mercancía dinero en la formación del mercado interno colonial. *Economía* (Lima), I, no. 2 (August)

Shanin, T. 1973–4. The nature and logic of the peasant economy. *Journal of Peasant Studies*, I: 63–80 and 186–206.

Smith, Gavin A. 1975. The social bases of peasant political activity: the case of the Huasicanchinos of Central Peru. PhD thesis, University of Sussex.

Spalding, Karen. 1973. Kurakas and commerce: a chapter in the evolution of Andean society. *Hispanic American Historical Review*, LIII: 581–99. Translated in Spalding (1974)

1974. *De Indio a Campesino*, Lima: Instituto de Estudios Peruanos

Thomas, Brooke. 1972. Human adaptation to a high Andean energy flow system. PhD thesis, Pennsylvania State University

1976. Energy flow at high altitude. In *Man in the Andes*, ed. P. Baker and M. Little, Stroudsberg, Pennsylvania: Hutchinson and Ross

Troll, Carl. 1968. The Cordilleras of the tropical Americas. Aspects of climatic, phyto-geographical and agrarian ecology. In *Geo-ecology of the mountainous regions of the tropical Americas*, ed. Carl Troll. Colloquium Geographicum, no. 9. University of Bonn: Geographical Institute (Proceedings of a UNESCO Symposium held in Mexico in 1966)

Urbain, J.-D. 1980. Le système quechua de l'échange: développements métaphoriques et adaptation d'un 'vocabulaire de base'. *L'Homme*, XX: 71–90

Urioste Arana, Jaime. 1978 (1639). *Noticias políticas de Indias del Licenciado Pedro Ramirez de Aguila*. Sucre

Urioste, F. de C., Miguel. 1977. *La economía del campesino altiplánico en 1976*. La Paz: Universidad Católica

Valle, M. 1876. *Cartas escritas de los departamentos de Junín, Huánuco y las montañas de Chanchamayo*. Lima: Imprenta El Nacional

References

Vergopoulos, Kostas. 1978. Capitalism and peasant productivity. *Journal of Peasant Studies*, V: 446–65

Villanueva, Horacio. 1970. Transcription of: Genealogía de la Casa, ascendencia y descendencia de Don Diego Sairitupac Mancocapac Yupanqui Ynga: Testimonio dado por Benito de la Peña, escribano de esta ciudad Cuzco, en 22 de abril, 1522. *Revista del Archivo Histórico del Cuzco*, no. 13

Wachtel, Nathan. 1974. La réciprocité et l'état inca: de Karl Polanyi à John Murra. *Annales*, XXIX: 1346–57

1978. Hommes d'eau: le problème uru (XVIe-XVIIe siècles). *Annales*, XXXIII: 1127–59

1981. Les *mitimas* de la Vallée de Cochabamba – la politique de colonisation de Huayna Capac. *Journal de la Société des Américanistes*, LXVII: 297–324

Weber, Max. 1965. *The theory of social and economic organization*. London: Collier-Macmillan

Webster, Stephen. 1971. Una comunidad indígena en la explotación de múltiples zonas ecológicas. *Wayka* (Cuzco), nos. 4–5

Wennergren, E. and Whitaker, M. 1975. *The status of Bolivian agriculture*. New York: Praeger

Wilson, Fiona. 1978. The dynamics of change in an Andean region: the province of Tarma, Peru, in the nineteenth century. PhD thesis, University of Liverpool

Winder, D. 1978. The impact of the *comunidad* on local development in the Mantaro Valley. In Long and Roberts (1978)

Yepes, E. 1972. *Perú: 1820–1920 – un siglo de desarrollo capitalista*. Lima: Instituto de Estudios Peruanos

Subject Index

accumulation: permanant, primitive, 4, 29, 56, 61; and peasant economy, 2, 143; and vertical control, 112; its impossibility with Inca control of money, 120

barter exchange, 12–14, *116–17*, 221; and ethnic boundaries, 76–9; as proportion of all exchange, 148; contrasted with reciprocity, 152; its circuits and those of money, 221–2

capitalism: its emergence, 10, 25; liberating effects on peasant economy, 7–8; relations of production as a distinct development from relations of exchange, 97–100; relations with pre-capitalism, 201; *see also*, accumulation, peasant economy

circulation: as sphere in which modes of producton meet, 98; mode of as a determinant of the form of social organization, 98

Cochabamba, Bolivia, migration from compared with Northern Potosí, 2, 28–9

compadrazgo (ritual kinship), 11, 74

comunidad, 22–6; and national accounting framework, 4; and national economy, 5; and labour tribute, 20–2; and Agrarian Reform (Peru), 22; and 'modern' cooperation, 25; and social differentiation, 25, *108–10*; and ideology of progress, *106–10*; *see also* verticality and vertical control

differentation of the peasantry: in peasant economies, 6; two Andean patterns, 8; Southern Peru and Northern Potosí compared, 8–9; Carchi, Yucay, Andarapa compared, 13; and *comunidades*, 25; limits imposed by permanent primitive accumulation, 61; in Andarapa, Peru, 166

ecological zones: in Bolivia, *30–5*, 74–5; in Peru, *126–8*; and risk-aversion, 133–4

ethnic economy: defined, 72; and implicit prices in barter, 77; as productive community, 90

ethnicity and ethnic identity, 71–2; and marriage, 75; their multiple and interdependent character, 81; and verticality, 227–8

exchange: in contrast to vertical control, 111–14; meaning of, 114; effect of time on, 115; forms of, *115–19*; relationship between time and impersonality in, 117

haciendas: problems of control in, 195–6; and inheritance, 197; maintenance and demise of vertical control in, 197–207; impotence of in face of immigrant capitalists, 205–7

household: transactions between members of, 14; fission and regroupment in relation to land tenure, 43–7; sex and age structure and bi-zonal cultivation, 50–1; as production unit, 76; peasant family as nuclear family, 130–1

Inca Empire: colonization and forced migration in, 18; strategy of advance, 20

inheritance: and women, 197–9; *see also* land tenure

kinship: as social memory of exchange relations, 113; as legitimizing language for wage-labour, 10, 11; as feature of capitalist productive organization, 12; and sharecropping, 14; and strategies for access to land, 42–6, 74; its role in reducing exclusiveness of access, 82; among Tarma oligarchy, 194; influence on location of parcels, 215–16; *see also compadrazgo*, labour cooperation

labour cooperation, *88–91*; and monetary exchange, 24; its embeddedness, 79–80; and absence of calculation of return, 85; as 'helping', 84–7; with direct return, 87–8; and kinship, genealogical and ritual, 84–8; and fiestas, 86–8; *see also* reciprocity

labour tribute *(mita)*: under Inca, 18; under Spanish Empire, 21; and intermediary

243

Author Index

245

Cambridge Studies in Social Anthropology

EDITOR: JACK GOODY

*Also published in paperback